Gay Marriage and Democracy

Polemics

Stephen Eric Bronner, Series Editor

The books in the Polemics series confront readers with provocative ideas by major figures in the social sciences and humanities on a host of controversial issues and developments. The authors combine a sophisticated argument with a lively and engaging style, making the books interesting to even the most accomplished scholar and appealing to the general reader and student.

Gay Marriage and Democracy

Equality for All

R. Claire Snyder

ROWMAN & LITTLEFIELD PUBLISHERS, INC.
Lanham • Boulder • New York • Toronto • Oxford

ROWMAN & LITTLEFIELD PUBLISHERS, INC.

Published in the United States of America
by Rowman & Littlefield Publishers, Inc.
A wholly owned subsidiary of The Rowman & Littlefield Publishing Group, Inc.
4501 Forbes Boulevard, Suite 200, Lanham, Maryland 20706
www.rowmanlittlefield.com

PO Box 317
Oxford
OX2 9RU, UK

British Library Cataloguing in Publication Information Available

Library of Congress Cataloging-in-Publication Data

Snyder, R. Claire, 1965–
    Gay marriage and democracy : equality for all / R. Claire Snyder.
        p.   cm.—(Polemics)
    Includes bibliographical references and index.
    ISBN 0-7425-2786-7 (cloth : alk. paper)—ISBN 0-7425-2787-5 (pbk. : alk. paper)
    1. Same-sex marriage—United States.   2. Gay rights—United States.
3. Democracy—United States.   4. Homophobia—United States.   I. Title.
II. Polemics (Rowman & Littlefield, Inc.)
HQ1034.U5S58   2005
306.84'8—dc22   2005018300

Printed in the United States of America

♾ ™ The paper used in this publication meets the minimum requirements of American
National Standard for Information Sciences—Permanence of Paper for Printed Library
Materials, ANSI/NISO Z39.48–1992.

For Mikki

Contents

Acknowledgments

With great joy I thank all who have helped bring me to this moment.

My first debt of gratitude goes to Jyl J. Josephson and Cynthia Burack for inviting me to contribute to their edited volume, *Fundamental Differences: Feminists Talk Back to Social Conservatives* (Lanham, MD: Rowman & Little-field, 2003), which inaugurated my research for this project. The piece I wrote for them examined the linkages between antigay and antifeminist politics and has since been reprinted in William F. Grover and Joseph G. Peschek, *Voices of Dissent: Critical Readings in American Politics*, 6th ed. (New York: Longman, 2005).

Preliminary versions of parts of my argument have also been published as "The Christian Right's 'Defense of Marriage': Democratic Rhetoric, Anti-Democratic Politics," *The Public Eye* XVI, no. 3 (Fall 2002): 1–11; and "The Federal Marriage Amendment and the Attack on American Democracy," in *The Logos Reader: Rational Radicalism and the Future of Politics*, eds. Stephen Eric Bronner and Michael J. Thompson (Lexington, KY: University Press of Kentucky, 2005), forthcoming. The latter was originally published in *Logos: A Journal of Modern Society and Culture* 3, no. 4 (Fall 2004), available at www.logosjournal.com/snyder_election.htm.

George Mason University generously supported this research by providing me with study leave during Spring 2003 and Spring 2004. More specifically, I'd like to thank Provost Peter Stearns, Dean Danielle Struppa, and my department chair, Bob Dudley, for allowing me time off from my teaching responsibilities. I also extend a huge debt of gratitude to James J. Mathy for generously funding my second semester of leave time via the Mathy Award for junior faculty. I've also been blessed with wonderful colleagues in the

Department of Public and International Affairs, who provided encouragement and moral support during the preparation of this manuscript.

Previous versions of this work have been presented in a number of venues, including annual meetings of the American Political Science Association and the Southern Political Science Association. I would particularly like to thank Gustavus Adolphus College (and its student group, Queers & Allies), George Mason University (and its student group, the Pride Alliance), Linfield College (and its Department of Political Science), and Congregation Bet Mishpachah for inviting me to do presentations of this work—all of which led to productive discussions that helped me make my argument more effectively.

The following people benefited me greatly by providing substantive comments on my ideas and/or written work: Jyl J. Josephson, Val Lehr, Jill Locke, David Gutterman, Allison Turkel, Leslie Abatiello, Rachel Sexton, Mikki Hall, the Reverend Lee D. Snyder, Anne Snyder, Vincent Lankewish, Becky Salokar, Jason Geiger, Carol Cochran, Rabbi Leila Gal Berner, and Mary Dougherty.

This book would not be in existence today without the assistance and support of the editorial team at Rowman & Littlefield, Laura Gottlieb, Andrew Boney, and Terry Fischer, and the series editor, Stephen Eric Bronner.

To my family goes my final debt of gratitude. Although they will never know it, Zenia, BJ, Tazzie, and Clyde contributed to the completion of this project by buoying my spirits during the months in Rehoboth Beach, Delaware, where I wrote the bulk of the manuscript. As always, I thank my parents, Lee and Anne Snyder, my brother Tim, and his wife Lisa for their unconditional love. And finally, my deepest heartfelt thanks go to my lover and fiancée Mikki Hall for her intellectual insights and for all of the many ways she has inspired and sustained me during the delivery of this manuscript.

CHAPTER ONE

~

What Does Same-Sex Marriage Have to Do with Democracy?

On October 3, 1996, Richard Ramirez, convicted serial killer and professed Satanist, married Doreen Lioy, a freelance magazine editor, in a simple ceremony in San Quentin prison. At the time, Ramirez, commonly known as the "Night Stalker," resided on death row, convicted of committing fourteen murders, five attempted murders, and six rapes. Ramirez met his bride while in prison, when she initiated contact with a letter. They were married three years later.[1] While Ramirez is notorious, inmate marriage is not unusual. Many inmates marry while in prison, and they have a constitutional right to do so.[2] Prisoners marry for love, they marry for companionship, they marry for spiritual reasons, and they marry for the benefits.

In contrast to the "Night Stalker" and his bride, Del Martin (age eighty-three) and Phyllis Lyon (age seventy-nine) have been committed life partners for over fifty years, yet they are not allowed to marry each other because they are both women. Consequently, they get none of the benefits of marriage. So, for example, when one of them dies, her widow will receive no Social Security survivorship benefits. Although they have been together, through thick and thin, for over half a century, they remain strangers in the eyes of the law.

That all changed briefly in 2004. On February 10 of that year, San Francisco mayor Gavin Newsom ordered the county clerk "to provide marriage licenses on a nondiscriminatory basis, without regard to gender or sexual orientation."[3] Calling the ability of lesbian and gay couples to marry a "fundamental right," Newsom reasoned that his pledge to uphold the California state constitution required him to overrule a state law prohibiting same-sex

1

because it violates the constitutional principle of legal equality. As , Martin and Lyon were civilly married in a San Francisco courthouse on February 12, 2004, becoming the first same-sex couple to be legally married in the United States. Five months later, however, the California Supreme Court voided their marriage, ruling that the mayor's decision had violated the principle of "separation of powers."[4]

Do Martin and Lyon have a fundamental right to marry? Is marriage a fundamental right? According to the U.S. Supreme Court it is. In a long series of cases, from *Meyer v. Nebraska* (1923) to *Turner v. Safley* (1987), the Court has consistently viewed marriage as a fundamental, constitutional right. That is why even the "Night Stalker" has the right to marry.[5] Nevertheless, many people insist that same-sex couples should not be accorded an equal right to marry. In fact, some conservatives want to amend the U.S. Constitution to ensure that they are not.

Should the United States allow lesbian and gay couples to marry? This book takes a position that may not at first seem self-evident. By the end of the book, I hope to convince the reader that the fundamental principles of American democracy not only allow, but also *require* the legalization of same-sex marriage. While it may be true at this moment in time that the majority of American citizens oppose allowing lesbians and gays the equal right to marry, it is my position that democracy cannot be reduced to a process of majority rule; it requires a number of other principles as well. Most importantly, by definition democracy requires *equality among citizens* in order to exist. Such equality comes into existence through the rule of law—the doctrine that laws must be applied equally to all citizens. In fact, it is my position that equality is so essential to democracy that if a democratic society passes laws that disenfranchise a group of citizens, it can no longer claim to be democratic. For example, Nazi Germany was not democratic, even though the Nazis were originally elected, and even though they may have had the support of the majority of Germans at the time. Civic equality and the rule of law constitute essential foundational principles of democratic government that cannot be legitimately infringed.

Three Models of Democracy

Civic Republican Democracy

In response to my argument that American democracy requires same-sex marriage, some readers may respond, "but America is not a democracy; it's a republic," as if the term "republic" refers to representative government that stands apart from citizens. While this is a common misconception—based on Madison's redefinition of the term in his argument for constraints on popular sovereignty and democratic participation[6]—that is not what the word "republic" actually meant historically.[7] According to the rich tradition of civic republican political theory,[8] a republic is a sovereign political community of *equal citizens*, who protect liberty and establish justice by governing themselves for the common good under *the rule of law* (legal equality).[9] Civic republican political theorists ground their belief in popular sovereignty on the Roman principle that "what affects all must be decided by all."[10] They prioritize political liberty for both the republic and its citizens, and they understand liberty to mean not being dominated by the arbitrary will of other individuals.[11] They assume equality among citizens, which for them "does not consist solely of equality of civil and political rights; it also affirms the need to ensure all citizens the social, economic, and cultural condition to allow them to live with dignity and self-respect."[12] And they believe that citizens must actively participate in self-government and stand ready to protect the republic from internal and external enemies.[13] Thus, a republic requires an actively engaged citizenry. While it permits representation, it cannot, pace Madison, be reduced to rule by a guardian class of political elites.

Liberal Democracy

In the early years of American history, the civic republican vision of democracy played an important role. Over time, however, the United States has become more of a "liberal democracy." While in common parlance the term "liberalism" generally refers to the traditional agenda of the Democratic Party—as in "tax and spend liberals"—the *political theory* of liberalism actually undergirds much of the political agendas of *both* the Democratic *and* Republican parties in America.[14] Liberal political theory originated in the seventeenth century, with John Locke's social contract theory of limited government and his defense of private property. Its principles overlapped with the economic liberalism of Adam Smith, the father of free market capitalism. Central to both versions of classical liberalism is the idea that naturally free and equal individuals should remain free to pursue their own self-interest, whether political or economic, with minimal interference from government, which should only act to enforce the rules of the game (proceduralism).

Over time, however, political philosophers extended the basic principles of classical liberalism—such as liberty, equality, individual self-determination, and equal opportunity—to produce a vision of government that would take a more active role in securing real opportunities for all by leveling the playing field economically. This eventually developed into a justification for "welfare state liberalism," which the Democratic Party traditionally supported. Many contemporary Republicans continue to embrace the classical liberalism of Locke and Smith (now called neoliberalism) and/or espouse a highly individualistic version of liberalism called libertarianism, which pares government down to the bare minimum.

In any event, despite partisan differences of interpretation and application, all versions of liberalism emphasize equality before the law. That is why, in general, both the Democratic and Republican Parties now support the principle of legal equality—gender-blind, colorblind law. Support for the principle of legal equality should translate into support for equal rights for lesbian and gay citizens, including the right to civil marriage. For some reason, however, it often does not.

The Republican National Committee (RNC) platform clearly states, "Equality of individuals before the law has always been a cornerstone of our party." When it comes to lesbian and gay citizens, however, the party refuses to apply that core principle: While many Republicans "oppose discrimination based on sex, race, age, religion, creed, disability, or national origin," they apparently accept discrimination on the basis of sexual orientation. In fact, the 2004 RNC platform explicitly states, "we do not believe sexual preference should be given special legal protection or standing in law."[15] Here the Party cedes the floor to the Christian Right, which not only opposes legal equality for lesbians and gays in all areas but also hopes to erode gender equality as well. In fact, the gay issue nicely illustrates the major fissure within the Republican Party, between the Christian Right wing that wants the government to legislate morality and the neoliberal/libertarian wing that essentially says, "I don't care what you do, just don't ask me to pay for it."

The Democratic National Committee (DNC) more consistently supports legal equality for all. Its party platform states,

> All of our people should have the opportunity to fulfill all of their potential, and each of us should be as equal in the eyes of the law as we are in the eyes of God. . . . Our commitment to civil rights is ironclad. We will restore vigorous federal enforcement of our civil rights laws for all our people. . . . We will enact the bipartisan legislation barring workplace discrimination based on sexual orientation. We are committed to equal treatment of all service members and believe all patriotic Americans should be allowed to serve our country without discrimination, persecu-

tion, or violence. . . . We support full inclusion of gay and lesbian families in the life of our nation and seek equal responsibilities, benefits, and protections for these families.[16]

When it comes to the right to marry in particular, however, the Democratic Party also stops short of endorsing full equality. The 2004 DNC platform says: "In our country, marriage has been defined at the state level for 200 years, and we believe it should continue to be defined there. We repudiate President Bush's divisive effort to politicize the Constitution by pursuing a 'Federal Marriage Amendment.'"[17] The platform pointedly does not take a stand on gay marriage, but during the 2004 presidential campaign both John Kerry and John Edwards made it clear that they oppose it. That stance contradicts the party's commitment to legal equality and nondiscrimination, and so makes little sense. (In fact, it seems like unprincipled pandering.) From my perspective, the party's official position should be: "While Democrats are personally divided over the issue of gay marriage, the Party supports the right to civil marriage for lesbian and gay couples as a matter of principle."

Deliberative Democracy

Finally, a third model of democracy deserves comment. Inspired by the New England town meetings of old, theories of deliberative democracy imagine the political process as an ongoing conversation among *equal citizens* about contentious political and moral issues. In this vision, citizens decide for themselves how to resolve controversial matters and actively set the normative direction for public policy, although they are not expected to hammer out every technical detail.[18] Those who embrace this vision of democracy generally argue that a well-functioning democracy requires a certain amount of public deliberation for three major reasons. First, a democratic society needs public deliberation in order to ensure political legitimacy. Whether a republic or a liberal democracy, legitimate government requires the consent of the governed, and without public deliberation, we cannot be sure that the government really has the people's informed consent.

Second, supporters argue that deliberation is a practical necessity given the often divided opinion of the American public. In the face of public dissension, they argue, decisions should not simply be imposed. Instead, "when citizens or their representatives disagree morally, they should continue to reason together to reach mutually acceptable decisions."[19] Consider the Vietnam protests, the massive resistance to court-ordered busing, and the never-ending attacks on *Roe v. Wade*. Such examples illustrate that people will not simply accept political decisions with which they disagree when they have no say in the decision-making process. Conversely, people are much more likely to accept—or even suggest—unpleasant political compromises, such as tax increases or compulsory military service, when they participate in making those hard decisions.

Finally, greater levels of public deliberation could improve American democracy, they argue, by educating participants about public affairs,[20] modeling a nonpartisan way of framing issues,[21] and reconnecting citizens to the political process and each other.[22] In coming together to deliberate, people might learn that a large degree of common ground exists on a wide variety of issues, despite what political elites and the corporate-owned media often imply.[23] If more citizens were to get involved, perhaps we would no longer have politicians and political appointees who pursue their own agendas with little regard for the public will or who lie to the public without fear of being held accountable.

While founded on the principle of equality among citizens, the deliberative model of democracy poses a serious challenge to the argument presented in this book because it calls on citizens to deliberate about controversial issues—like gay marriage—and decide for themselves how the issue should be resolved. While I generally favor public deliberation about controversial political issues, I also insist that some principles are so fundamental to democratic society that they cannot be infringed—even with the consent of the vast majority of citizens. Legal equality is one such principle, and the legalization of same-sex marriage follows logically from the principle of legal equality, even if not everyone yet recognizes this fact. In the 1960s, some people probably asked themselves, "I believe in the principle of legal equality, but does that mean the government can force me to let African Americans move into my neighborhood?" The answer is, "yes, it does." Today, some people may be asking themselves, "I believe in legal equality but does that mean the government has to allow two people of the same sex to marry?" Again, I would argue, the answer is, "yes, it does."

In other words, as a democratic theorist, I support an active vision of popular sovereignty with one important caveat: *legal equality and civil rights should not be subject to public deliberation.* So while citizens should have a large role in making decisions about controversial political issues—whether we should wage war on Iraq, what kind of health care system we want, even determining the best way to integrate the schools—they do not get to decide whether African Americans should be slaves, whether women should have the right to vote, or whether lesbian and gay citizens should be treated equally before the law.

Theoretically, deliberation results in decisions that *all* can endorse, and so "solutions" that disenfranchise a group of citizens or discriminate against a minority would not be approved by those adversely affected. In *realpolitik*, however, everyone at a particular town meeting might be vehemently opposed to gay rights or not understand gay marriage as an issue of fundamental rights. And if lesbians and gay men are afraid to "come out" in a homophobic town, this problem is compounded. But some issues are too important to be compromised. Civil rights, legal equality, and human dignity cannot be legitimately revoked by the majority; they exist as inalienable human rights not subject to community approval. A deliberative democracy cannot call these principles into question because these principles form the necessary prerequisites for democratic deliberation itself.[24]

Democratic Progress

While no adequate model of democracy allows the passage of discriminatory laws, our understanding of what counts as discrimination has evolved over time. When the United States was founded, the law treated men and women unequally, denying women the right to vote, rendering a woman's identity legally invisible upon marriage ("coverture"), and subjecting married women to the authority of their husbands in a variety of ways, even allowing husbands to beat their wives with a stick, as long as it was no thicker than a thumb (the proverbial "rule of thumb").[25] While a few visionaries saw this legal inequality as antidemocratic and antirepublican—for example, Abigail Adams pleaded with her husband to "Remember the Ladies" when writing laws for the new republic[26]—most eighteenth-century people accepted gender hierarchy as natural and thus did not see laws reinforcing women's subordination as discriminatory. From today's perspective, however, societies in which the law treats women as subordinates to men—prohibiting them from appearing in public without a male guardian or denying them the right to work outside the home or go to school, for example—exemplify the opposite of democratic. Even if everyone agrees with such strictures, which is unlikely, putting them into law violates the foundational principle of equality for all citizens and thus, by definition, destroys democratic society. While a liberal democracy leaves women free to choose subordination in their relationships, if that fulfills their religious beliefs or personal inclinations, the foundational principle of legal equality prohibits the creation of laws that treat men and women differently.

The idea that two people of the same sex should be allowed to marry may seem shocking to many people. The idea is relatively new to American political discourse, although not to world history—ancient Rome allowed same-sex marriage,[27] and evidence exists that, during medieval times, the Catholic and Eastern Orthodox churches sanctioned same-sex unions.[28] Only in the 1990s, however, as the American courts came to recognize that denying lesbian and gay citizens the right to marry violates the principle of legal equality, did the issue become a central focus for the lesbian/gay rights movement. What twenty years ago seemed unimaginable to most people, now seems imperative for a just and democratic society: Since marriage is a central experience in the lives of most Americans, barring lesbians and gays from access to marriage marginalizes them from the mainstream of American society in a very fundamental way, and that is simply unacceptable in the world's oldest democracy.

The Plan of the Book

This book strives to *persuade* its readers that they should accept the justness of the gay marriage cause—that same-sex marriage cannot be legitimately prohibited by government and that resolution of the controversy should not be left up to public deliberation or to the states. Because America currently exists as a liberal democracy (despite the existence of other democratic traditions), I take primarily a liberal democratic approach to the issue of gay marriage, although my argument is fully compatible with more republican visions of democracy—and with theories of deliberation that protect equality for all and do not reduce democracy to simple majoritarianism.

Central to liberal democracy is the separation of church and state. When discussing the issue of gay marriage, it's vitally important to draw a distinction between marriage as a *religious rite* and marriage as a *civil contract*. In order to clarify the issues at stake in the debate, I begin my discussion in chapter 2, "What Is Marriage?", by disentangling four different aspects of marriage that often get confused in political discussions—the personal bond, the community-recognized relationship (as in common-law marriage), the religious rite, and the civil contract. In chapter 2, a brief history of marriage illustrates each concept and shows that the definition of marriage has changed radically over time; the institution has not remained the same for 5,000 years as many social conservatives claim. The chapter emphasizes that the political fight for gay marriage focuses on access to *civil marriage* only and documents exactly what benefits and responsibilities that legal contract entails.

My argument contends that many lesbian and gay couples are already married, despite the fact that government refuses to legally recognize those marriages: Same-sex couples are already making personal commitments to each other, they are increasingly recognized as married by their communities, and they are entering religiously sanctioned relationships in some religious denominations. Yet those marriages are singled out for special discrimination by the U.S. government and the governments of almost every state in the union. Consequently, same-sex couples do not get access to a wide array of benefits designed to help committed couples take care of each other as they age, as well as any children who depend upon them.

Chapter 3, "The Logic of Liberalism: American Political Theory and the Case for Gay Marriage," lays out the full democratic argument for gay marriage. It argues that America's dominant public philosophy of liberalism entails a commitment to a set of core principles—including legal equality, separation of church and state, individual rights and liberties, and personal autonomy—and that all these principles logically justify and require full equality for lesbians and gay men, including equal access to civil marriage. Drawing on the work of major liberal philosophers, such as John Locke, Immanuel Kant, John Stuart Mill, John Rawls, and some of the American Founders, I argue that the liberal democratic state may not legitimately impose any particular "comprehensive" moral or religious doctrine on its citizens, but instead must leave individuals free to pursue their own vision of the good life by maintaining legal equality and protecting rights and liberties, including freedom of conscience, the right to privacy, and the right to marry. The chapter not only provides an in-depth overview of the political philosophy of liberalism but also examines a number of constitutional law cases.

Despite the strong theoretical case for legalization, same-sex marriage is opposed by three different strands of conservatism. First, claiming that America is a "Christian Nation," religious conservatives want their understanding of moral truth—that marriage can only exist between one man and one woman—to form the basis for law and public policy in America, despite the fact that no consensus exists among religious denominations about the nature of marriage and despite the Constitution's separation of church and state. Chapter 4, "A False Consensus: Christian Right Politics and the Attack on Same-Sex Marriage," documents that important differences exist over the meaning of marriage, not only between conservative and progressive

Christians and their various denominations, but also between Protestants and Catholics, and between Christians, Muslims, and Jews. Yet despite this religious pluralism, the Christian Right wants the U.S. federal government to establish *one particular religious definition of marriage* as the law of the land, in direct violation of the First Amendment. In a liberal democracy, I argue, the separation of church and state precludes the government from sanctioning any *religious aspects* of traditional marriage; authority over those issues rightly belongs to religious organizations. However, the legal contractual aspects of *civil marriage* clearly fall under the sovereignty of our secular government, which may not legitimately deny gay and lesbian citizens full equality before the law.

Second, traditionalists on the Right generally emphasize the importance of maintaining long-standing societal customs, even if they violate universal principles like legal equality. Chapter 5, "Neo-Patriarchy and the Agenda of the Anti-Gay Right," draws connections between the arguments of today's antigay activists and yesterday's opponents of legal equality for African Americans and women. The chapter demonstrates that opposition to same-sex marriage actually forms a central component of the Christian Right's larger, ongoing effort to reverse the progress of feminism and restore the patriarchal family with its traditional gender roles as the dominant and privileged family form in America. While the Christian Right's agenda may sound extreme, in recent years, its neopatriarchal vision has been embraced by an increasing array of conservative constituencies, who justify it not just in religious but also in secular terms. The chapter examines the interconnected arguments advanced by religious and secular conservatives committed to the politics of neopatriarchy. While the details differ slightly from person to person, their arguments have a similar form and often use the same authorities, and they are generally both homophobic and antifeminist. Thus, these arguments undermine the principles of liberal democracy, despite rhetorical assertions to the contrary.

Third, conservative communitarians stress that the principle of popular sovereignty means that the people get to decide whether gay marriage is acceptable, even if this results in continuing inequality. Chapter 6, "Are Lesbian and Gay Americans Actually Citizens? The Homophobic Myopia of Communitarianism," takes on this argument as well as the assertion that American democracy requires the traditional heterosexual family in order to function properly. This "seedbeds of virtue" approach claims, in short, that American democracy requires virtuous citizens, and the virtues are best learned at home from two *heterosexual, married* parents. The chapter provides a critique of the moralistic conception of "virtue" deployed by such theorists from the perspective of political theory. It also reveals that despite frequent assertions about the supremacy of the traditional family in producing democratic citizens, no empirical evidence actually supports such claims. Arguing that democracy needs *civic virtue* defined as *"public-spiritedness,"* I argue that this type of virtue—as well as democratic virtues like tolerance, deliberation, compromise, consensus-building, civility, and reason-giving—cannot be reliably instilled in children by the family, since families vary greatly in both parenting styles and functionality. Instead of hoping children will pick up the necessary civic virtues at home, I suggest that a better strategy might be to purposefully prepare them for citizenship via a revitalized system of public education. This would allow for the protection of civic virtues without the continued marginalization of lesbians, gay men, and their families.

Lesbian and gay Americans are citizens, just like heterosexuals, and must be treated equally before the law. While many people may view the traditional heterosexual family as the most desirable family form, there is no evidence that it does a better job of producing democratic citizens. And even if there were, lesbian and gay citizens would still have the right to form families and raise children, just like anyone else. The government cannot legitimately pass laws discriminating against lesbian and gay citizens—denying them the civil right to marry or treating their relationships differently than those of heterosexuals. While some people may continue to oppose legal equality for lesbians and gays—which is their First Amendment right—it is my argument that they cannot advocate discrimination against a minority group and simultaneously portray themselves as supporters of democracy.

The book concludes with "Marriage Equality and Sexual Freedom: Toward a More Progressive Union," a response to academic critics on the Left, who argue that the push for gay marriage within the LGBT (lesbian/gay/bisexual/transgender) community narrows the political agenda in a conservative way and may actually result in increasing limitations on sexual freedom for the nonmarried. The chapter responds by explaining that the political theory of liberal democracy outlined in this book *both* requires the legalization of same-sex marriage (legal equality) *and* protects the right of consenting adults to engage sexually with other consenting adults without state interference (right to privacy, individual autonomy). In fact, reinforcing the principles of liberal democracy should actually help secure not only legal equality but also the right of individuals to self-determination in personal matters, including family arrangements and sexuality. Moreover, achieving marriage equality does not preclude working toward other more progressive changes in the area of family policy. In any event, the right of lesbian and gay couples to marry should be supported as a matter of principle by all who value democracy, even by those who personally do not want to marry, just as it should be supported by those who personally do not think it is right. The principle of legal equality is too important to violate.

Notes

1. Anthony Bruno, "Satanists Don't Wear Gold (The marriage of Ramirez and Doreen Lioy)," Court TV's Crime Library, www.crimelibrary.com/serial_killers/notori ous/ramirez/terror_1.html?sect = 27 [accessed 13 March 2005].

2. "The right to marry, like many other rights, is subject to substantial restrictions as a result of incarceration. Many important attributes of marriage remain, however, after taking into account the limitations imposed by prison life. First, inmate marriages, like others, are expressions of emotional support and public commitment. These elements are an important and significant aspect of the marital relationship. In addition, many religions recognize marriage as having spiritual significance; for some inmates and their spouses, therefore, the commitment of marriage may be an exercise of religious faith as well as an expression of personal dedication. Third, most inmates eventually will be released by parole or commutation, and therefore most inmate marriages are formed in the expectation that they ultimately will be fully consummated. Finally, marital status often is a precondition to the receipt of government benefits (e.g., Social Security benefits), property rights (e.g., tenancy by the entirety, inheritance rights), and other, less tangible benefits (e.g., legitimation of children born out of wedlock). These incidents of marriage, like the religious and personal aspects of the marriage commitment, are unaffected by the fact of confinement or the pursuit of legitimate corrections goals." *Turner v. Safley*, 482 U.S. 78 (1987), section III, B.

3. His entire instruction is as follows: "Upon taking the Oath of Office, becoming the Mayor of the City and County of San Francisco, I swore to uphold the Constitution of the State of California. Article I, section 7, subdivision (a) of the California Constitution provides that '[a] person may not be . . . denied equal protection of the laws.' The California courts have interpreted the equal protection clause of the California Constitution to apply to lesbians and gay men and have suggested that laws that treat homosexuals differently from heterosexuals are suspect. The California courts have also stated that discrimination against gay men and lesbians is invidious. The California courts have held that gender discrimination is suspect and invidious as well. The Supreme Courts in other states have held that equal protection provisions in their state constitutions prohibit discrimination against gay men and lesbians with respect to the rights and obligations flowing from marriage. It is my belief that these decisions are persuasive and that the California Constitution similarly prohibits such discrimination. Pursuant to my sworn duty to uphold the California Constitution, including specifically its equal protection

clause, I request that you determine what changes should be made to the forms and documents used to apply for and issue marriage licenses in order to provide marriage licenses on a non-discriminatory basis, without regard to gender or sexual orientation." Quote from "SF Mayor Gavin Newsom's Letter to County Clerk Re: Issuing Marriage Licenses," February 10, 2004, http://news.findlaw.com/hdocs/docs/glrts/sfmayor21004ltr.html [accessed 13 March 2005].

4. "Calif. Same-Sex Marriages Voided," CBSNEWS.com, August 12, 2004, www.cbsnews.com/stories/2004/09/19/national/main644266.shtml [accessed 13 March 2005].

5. Evan Gerstmann, *Same-Sex Marriage and the Constitution* (Cambridge: Cambridge University Press, 2004), 67–83.

6. See James Madison, *Federalist* #10.

7. Robert A. Dahl, *On Democracy* (New Haven, CT: Yale University Press, 1998), 16–17.

8. Just to be clear, my use of the term "republican" refers to the political theoretical tradition of republicanism (Machiavelli, Harrington, Rousseau, Jefferson, and others), which is not directly related to the Republican Party in America.

9. Examples of republican political theory include Cicero, *De re publica* and *De officiis*; Niccolò Machiavelli, *Discourses on Livy*; James Harrington, *The Commonwealth of Oceana*; Jean-Jacques Rousseau, *On the Social Contract* and *Government of Poland*; Thomas Paine, *Rights of Man*; and the writings of Thomas Jefferson; among others.

10. Maurizio Viroli, *Republicanism* (New York: Hill & Wang, 2002), 4.

11. Viroli, *Republicanism*, 8.

12. Viroli, *Republicanism*, 66.

13. R. Claire Snyder, *Citizen-Soldiers and Manly Warriors: Military Service and Gender in the Civic Republican Tradition* (Lanham, MD: Rowman & Littlefield Publishers, 1999).

14. Michael J. Sandel, *Democracy's Discontent: America in Search of a Public Philosophy* (Cambridge, MA: Belknap Press of Harvard University Press, 1996).

15. Republican National Committee, "Party Platform," www.rnc.org/About/Party Platform/default.aspx?Section=4 [accessed 5 August 2004].

16. Democratic National Committee, "The Democratic Platform for America: Strong at Home, Respected in the World," www.dems2004.org/site/pp.asp?c=luI2La PYG&b=97933 [accessed 5 August 2004].

17. Democratic National Committee, "Democratic Platform."

18. David Mathews, *Politics for People*, 2nd ed. (Urbana and Chicago: University of Illinois Press, 1999).

19. Amy Gutmann and Dennis Thompson, *Democracy and Disagreement* (Cambridge, MA: Belknap Press of Harvard University Press, 1996), 13.

20. The practice of deliberation has been shown to increase knowledge among participants. Mark Button and Kevin Mattson, "Deliberative Democracy in Practice: Challenges and Prospects for Civic Deliberation," *Polity* 31, no. 4 (1999): 609–37, 620–21.

21. The deliberative forums convened by National Issues Forums and the Study Circles Research Center do this.

22. Social scientific studies have shown a positive correlation between higher levels of knowledge and higher levels of political participation. Michael X. Delli Carpini and Scott Keeter, *What Americans Know about Politics and Why It Matters* (New Haven, CT: Yale University Press, 1996), 6–7.

23. Morris P. Fiorina, *Culture War? The Myth of a Polarized America* (New York: Pearson Longman, 2005).

24. See Seyla Benhabib, "Toward a Deliberative Model of Democratic Legitimacy," in *Democracy and Difference: Contesting the Boundaries of the Political*, ed. Seyla Benhabib (Princeton, NJ: Princeton University Press, 1996).

25. Linda Kerber, *Women of the Republic: Intellect and Ideology in Revolutionary America* (New York: W. W. Norton & Company, 1986).

26. Abigail Adams, "Correspondence with Abigail Adams (1776)," in *American Political Thought*, ed. Kenneth M. Dolbeare (Chatham, NJ: Chatham House Publishers, Inc., 1998), 82.

27. John Boswell, *Christianity, Social Tolerance, and Homosexuality: Gay People in Western Europe from the Beginning of the Christian Era to the Fourteenth Century* (Chicago and London: University of Chicago Press, 1980), 94.

28. John Boswell, *Same-Sex Unions in Premodern Europe* (New York: Random House, 1995).

CHAPTER TWO

~

What Is Marriage?

What is marriage? If the state of Virginia or Massachusetts issues two individuals a marriage license, what does that mean? Are they married? If a priest or a rabbi conducts a wedding of two people before God, are they married? If two people live together as married for five, seven, or fifty years, and the community recognizes them as such, are they married? If two people privately pledge before God or promise each other mutual love, support, and fidelity for the rest of their lives, are they married?

The answer to each of these questions could be in the affirmative, as there are four different components to the institution we call "marriage"—the personal bond, the community-recognized relationship, the religious rite, and the civil contract. Much of the time, a marriage involves all four aspects; other times, it might not. It is possible that a valid marriage might not include a personal bond of love (if the marriage was arranged), community recognition (if the couple is isolationist), a religious rite (if the couple is agnostic or atheist), or civil contract (if a couple never made it official).

When lesbians and gay men struggle *politically* for the right to marry, they are seeking the state-sanctioned civil contract that guarantees a significant set of legal benefits to married couples, ones that help them take care of each other financially (health insurance, tax benefits, retirement planning) and support each other during difficult times (medical decision making, family and bereavement leave, "spousal privilege" in the courtroom), as well as enable them to provide for their children (second-parent adoption, child custody and visitation in cases of divorce, Social Security survivorship benefits). The political struggle for same-sex marriage is not about the religious rite. In the United States, because of the First Amendment, the government cannot order the Catholic Church or the Southern Baptist Convention to conduct religious ceremonies for same-sex couples. Nor is it about community approval: that will be either extended or withheld by the people; it cannot be government mandated. Nor is it about the personal bond that two people who are in love feel for each other; government does not have the power to control that.

The fight for same-sex marriage is the fight against illegitimate discrimination by the government against the marriages of certain members of its citizenry. It is my argument that many lesbian and gay couples are already married, despite the fact that the government refuses to legally recognize those marriages. Same-sex couples are already making personal commitments to each other, they are increasingly recognized as married by their communities, and they are entering religiously sanctioned relationships in some denominations, including the United Church of Christ, some Episcopal congregations, Reform and Reconstructionist Judaism, and the Unitarian Universalist Church. Yet those marriages are singled out as illegitimate by the U.S. government and the governments of almost every state in the union. (At the time of this writing only the state of Massachusetts allows gay marriage.) As a result, same-sex couples do not get access to the benefits available to heterosexual married couples and their families. That type of discrimination is both illegitimate in terms of our fundamental political principles (as will be argued in the next chapter) and patently unfair.

A Short History of Marriage

The four components of marriage become more clearly defined when we look at the history of marriage. Contrary to what some contemporary critics of same-sex marriage maintain, what Americans understand as marriage and family today is not universal, timeless, or even traditional.[1] When Christian Right leader James Dobson says that if gay marriage becomes legal, "the family as it has been known for more than five millennia will crumble, presaging the fall of Western civilization itself," he speaks ahistorically and inaccurately.[2] Marriage and family have not stayed the same for 5,000 years; they have changed markedly over the course of history, and their particulars have always varied from culture to culture.

Even now in American society, when people use the term "marriage," they often mean very different things, some referring to the personal bond or the community-recognized relationship, and others to the religious rite or the civil contract. For example, when Dobson's group, "Focus on the Family," an influential antigay organization, defines marriage as "a sacred union, ordained by God,"[3] it highlights the institution's religious aspects and de-emphasizes its personal, communal, and civil components. Alternately, other people—such as the individual who asked the popular syndicated columnist Miss Manners, "If my same-sex marriage is eventually invalidated by a constitutional amendment or Supreme Court ruling, am I obligated to return all my wedding presents?"—recognize only the civil aspect, implying that only the state can constitute marriage.[4]

Even within the lesbian/gay/bisexual/transgender (LGBT) community, people hold a variety of views on the issue of marriage. When asked by straight friends if they are going to get married, some couples stress the issue of legal inequality by responding, "There is no such thing as gay marriage. I'm not getting 'married' until it means something." While that approach may make an important political and educational point, it also reinforces the idea that only the state has the power to constitute marriage.

Embracing a limited definition of marriage as only the civil contract, leading academic "queer theorist" Michael Warner criticizes the gay marriage movement for empowering the state. For him "marriage is a state-conferred legal partnership status" only. For example, in his response to lesbian writer Barbara Cox's explanation that she and her partner got married in order to proclaim their "incredible love and respect" for each other in a ceremony before "those who participate" in their world, Warner retorts: "of course it turns out that she has not gotten 'married' in the legal sense; she means that she has had a public ceremony." He dismisses her emphasis on the personal and communal components of marriage as simply "naïveté."[5]

When people define marriage as only the religious rite or only the civil contract, they deny the validity of two of the most important components of the historical institution of marriage, the personal bond and the community-recognized relationship. Indeed for most of recorded history, the state did not constitute marriage; individuals and communities did. Warner acknowledges that the "government now plays a much more direct role in marriage than it has for most of Western civilization's history. . . . In the contemporary United States, unlike most times and places in world history, state certification is a constitutive event, not a secondary acknowledgment of a previously established relationship."[6] He criticizes the gay marriage movement for reinforcing the power of the state and its regulatory apparatus.

In the Eyes of the Community: Marriage without the State

In its origin, marriage was formed by families and recognized by communities; neither governmental approval nor the participation of religious elites was necessary for the formation of marriage. For example, a Jewish wedding has never required the presence of a rabbi. Traditionally, a Jewish wedding was considered valid when the community, represented by two witnesses, saw the bride accept a ring from the groom and heard him say the prescribed blessing (still used today in traditional Jewish weddings): "Behold, thou art consecrated unto me by this ring, according to the law of Moses and of Israel."[7] While the bride did not actively participate in the ceremony, her acceptance of the ring constituted her consent.[8]

The fathers of the bride and groom originally presided over the Jewish rite of marriage, which actually has two parts, now combined. The first part is the *Kiddushin*, during which the bride accepts the ring, and the two are considered married. The second part, the *Nissu'in*, marks the beginning of cohabitation. "In earlier times, the first part took place in the house of the bride and was presided over by the bride's father, who pronounced the blessing over the wine (mixed with water). The second part was held in the groom's house and was presided over by the groom's father. It culminated in the wedding feast and its table prayers."[9] The family and community controlled marriage, which was constituted by consent and enacted via cohabitation.

Since the first century C.E., a Jewish wedding has also required a *ketubah* (a marriage contract) "signed by two witnesses who testify that the groom has 'acquired' the bride in the prescribed manner and agreed to support her,"[10] although *ketubot* originated centuries before that.[11] Significantly, while a formal *ketubah* is technically required, Jewish law also maintains that "if witnesses testify that a Jewish couple is living together as husband and wife, a *bet din*, a court of rabbis, would consider the traditional *ketubah* to be in effect."[12] So here we see a marriage being valid when recognized by the community, even when not formally sanctioned by religious law.

For most of recorded history, marriage as an institution upheld male dominance, giving the husband customary and legal power over his wife. In the biblical Hebrew tradition, for example, male family heads arranged marriages for their daughters, and a wife was essentially considered "property" of her husband, whom she had to obey.[13] A man could take more than one wife, as long as he could support them, and the biblical prohibition on adultery restricted the behavior of married women only.[14] Moreover, a husband could divorce his wife by simply handing her a decree of divorce in front of two witnesses and sending her away. The wife, on the other hand, could not get a divorce without her husband's consent.[15]

At the same time, however, the Jewish community also provided some protections for married women. For example, while the *ketubah* was not a mutual agreement, but rather a legally binding document the bride agreed to accept, it improved the condition of women at the time by providing them with "legal status and rights in marriage." It required the husband to provide for his wife's needs and made divorce "costly."[16] If a woman's husband died before she had children, his brother was required to marry and provide for her, a tradition called levirate marriage. If he refused, she had legal recourse.[17]

In ancient Greece, a private agreement between men initiated the marriage process but marriage itself required community recognition; the personal bond between husband and wife mattered little. Fathers and grooms arranged marriages on the basis of economic and political considerations, and reproduction formed the primary purpose of marriage. The bride, usually only fourteen, had absolutely no say in the matter, and "the feelings of the two individuals were not considered in the act of marriage."[18] This approach to marriage made sense to people at the time because the household or *oikos* constituted the main economic unit in society; control of women gave male family heads control over reproduction and consequently inheritance.

In ancient Greece, the marriage process began with *engye* (the pledge), followed by *ekdosis* (the transfer). First, the girl's father (or male guardian) made the pledge, "I hand over this woman to you for the ploughing of legitimate children."[19] The girl's presence during *engye* was not required.[20] Next, the two men settled the dowry, designed to protect the wife in case of divorce. A three-day public ceremony, to which the entire town might be invited, completed the marriage process. Traditionally, the procession from the father's house to the groom's house formed the centerpiece of the ceremony. As the procession began, "the groom grabbed her wrist, while the bride's father delivered her to her husband's control, saying in front of witnesses, 'I give this girl to you for the production of legitimate children.'" The bride was treated as a "symbolic captive," as community members escorted the married couple to the groom's family home.[21]

While marriage began as a transfer between men, it was community recognition over time, however, that actually constituted marriage. That is, "marriage itself was recognized and validated . . . by the communally witnessed rituals and household events which over time established its legitimacy as an Athenian marriage. . . . Marriage thus should be understood as a social process rather than a legal moment."[22] In fact, Athenian marriage did not require a legal procedure. "Despite the unquestioned importance, both practical and ideological, of marriage in Athenian society as the relationship that created and supported the citizen household, there was no formal legal recognition or legal definition of the state of matrimony in classical Athens. Marriage itself was not defined by Athenian law, nor were individual marriages legally certified or registered."[23] The law merely recognized marriages after the fact, when it needed to determine legitimacy, regulate inheritance, and specify who could claim citizenship (available only to the children of two Greek citizens).[24]

In ancient Greece, the state recognized other forms of marriage besides *engye*. For example, if a man died without male heirs but with an unmarried daughter, his closest male relative had the option of marrying the girl and taking control of her property—a form of marriage called *epidikazein*. If he opted not to marry her, the next closest male relative would get the option, and so on. A third type of marriage, *pallake*, existed for girls who did not have a dowry; they were given to men as concubines. However, "a woman could also become a *pallake* if she installed herself without the help of her *oikos* [household], by choosing to cohabitate . . . with a man." Finally, a fourth kind of official relationship existed for *hetairai*, well-educated, sexually free women who were considered "respectable companions" for men. This fourth marriage-type relationship occurred when a *hetaira* formed a monogamous relationship with a man but did not live with him. If they cohabitated, she would become his concubine.[25]

While same-sex marriage did not exist in ancient Athens, "homosexuals joined by 'affection, warmth, and love' were deemed to be suited for 'lifelong relationships.'" In fact, "the ideal union, at least among the cultured elite, was homosexual." The Greeks considered homosexual attraction "natural," "ubiquitous and entirely ordinary." Men were still expected to marry women and produce legitimate offspring, and "marriage was respected as an institution that provided progeny and good housekeeping." However, "it was not expected to fulfill one's longing for a soul mate."[26] In general, men did not look to their wives for companionship and emotional satisfaction.

In Rome and the territories governed by Rome, families controlled marriage and the state considered it mostly a private, personal matter to be dealt with by the people involved. While the state did regulate "the consequences of marriage," in terms of property and children, and prohibited relatives and people of different classes from marrying each other, no state certification or ceremony was necessary for a valid marriage. In contrast to Greece, which disregarded personal feelings, in Rome "the validity of a marriage was based on the desire of both parties to be married," as well as "on the absence of any legal hindrances to marriage, such as prohibitions based on kinship or social status."[27] If the law became involved, "the judge investigated only whether the couple lived together with *affectio maritalis*, 'the intention of being married,' as evidenced by their behavior and words."[28]

While fathers still arranged marriages, the Romans believed that a woman should not be forced into marriage against her will. "Emphasizing consent as the primary determinant of a valid union, Roman authorities spread this notion throughout the empire, and eventually throughout the whole Western world."[29] And while marriage gave a husband legal rights over his wife, either party, not just the man, could terminate the relationship at will.[30] And in fact, divorce was quite common.[31] Neither marriage nor divorce required the approval of governmental or religious officials.

As in Greece, the law in Rome recognized four different types of permanent long-term relationships. A highly class-based society, Rome had different names for the marriages of upper- and lower-class citizens: *confarreatio* for patricians and *coemptio* for plebeians. Patricians often had elaborate wedding ceremonies that combined civil and religious elements,[32] although by the beginning of the Common Era, Roman marriage had become "entirely secular."[33] Because *confarreatio* did not allow for divorce, over time this form of marriage became very rare.[34]

The third, less formal version of legal marriage was called *usus*. If a man cohabitated with a woman *without interruption* and treated her as his wife for one year, they were considered married, and "she became liable to all the restrictions and obligations to which a recognized marriage subjected a woman."[35] Not surprisingly, many women wanted to avoid losing legal rights through marriage and were able to do so by taking three days away from home so that their cohabitation would be interrupted.[36] *Usus* is comparable to what we today call common-law marriage.

Finally, while men and women of different ranks were not allowed to marry, Roman law recognized their relationships as *concubinatus*. Although monogamous and as permanent as marriage, *concubinatus* differed from marriage in that it did not give the man legal power over the woman and her children.[37] Technically, this fourth type of state-recognized relationship was not considered marriage, but it is similar enough to warrant comparison here.

Yet while Roman law prohibited marriage between individuals of different social classes, it allowed same-sex marriage, according to an award-winning study by John Boswell, who served as the A. Whitney Griswold Professor of History at Yale University until his death in 1994. In ancient Rome, he discovered, "many homosexual relationships were permanent and exclusive. Among the lower classes informal unions . . . may have predominated, but marriages between males or between females were legal and familiar among the upper classes. . . . [And] by the time of the early Empire references to gay marriages are commonplace."[38] Moreover, not only were same-sex marriages recognized legally and celebrated publicly, but sometimes they actually helped advance the careers of powerful men.

In response to the revelation that same-sex marriage existed in Rome, some people erroneously believe that the Roman Empire's acceptance of homosexuality contributed to its demise. For example, the president of Focus on the Family suggests this connection in a 2004 fund-raising letter, opining that gay marriage will destroy the American family:

> The apostle Paul described a similar society in Romans 1, which addressed the epidemic of homosexuality that was rampant in the ancient world and especially in Rome at that time. He wrote, "They have become filled with every kind of wickedness, evil, greed and depravity. They are full of envy, murder, strife, deceit and malice. They are gossips, slanderers, God-haters, insolent, arrogant and boastful; they invent ways of doing evil; they disobey their parents; they are senseless, faithless, heartless, ruthless" (v. 29–31, NIV). It appears likely now that the demise of families will accelerate this type of decline dramatically, resulting in a chaotic culture that will be devastating to children.[39]

Academic scholarship on Roman history, however, does not support the contention that homosexuality led to the fall of the Roman Empire.[40] Moreover, while "the common impression [is] that Roman society was characterized by loveless hedonism, moral anarchy, and utter lack of restraints," in reality "most citizens of Roman cities appear to have been as sensitive to issues and feelings of love, fidelity, and familial devotion as people before or after them."[41] Nevertheless, in the end, however, Roman acceptance of homosexuality and same-sex marriage did not survive the triumph of Christianity.[42]

The Origins of Christian Marriage

For hundreds of years, the Christian Church did not try to establish a distinctly Christian institution of marriage. In fact, the Church discouraged marriage, viewing celibacy as the spiritual ideal. Christians who chose to marry generally followed local community customs, and the Church accepted civil marriages as valid.[43] Over time, however, the Church would take control of marriage away from families and communities and intertwine the civil contract with religious rite. This helped the Church consolidate its power and authority in medieval Europe.

Jesus himself said little about marriage and nothing about procreation or child rearing in relation to marriage. Yet he condemned divorce in absolute terms: "What therefore God has joined together, let not man put asunder. . . . Whoever divorces his wife and marries another, commits adultery against her; and if she divorces her husband and marries another, she commits adultery" (Mark 10:9–11).[44] Speculating as to how Jesus would address the question of same-sex marriage, religious scholar Jack Miles argues that "were Jesus to return to Earth" today, he would probably be quite "disappointed . . . to discover that the 'Defense of Marriage Act' has nothing at all to do with the prohibition of divorce but is, instead, a law that prevents the creation of new marriages—namely, gay marriages."[45]

Because Jesus said absolutely nothing about homosexuality, Miles surmises that, were he alive today, "we must assume that he would maintain his silence. Had he wanted to take a position about that matter, he would have done so back in Galilee. Deference to biblical inerrancy was never his way. . . . On the contrary, his zero-tolerance prohibition of divorce was a bold and deliberate revision of the biblically grounded but (in his view) unacceptable Jewish practice of his day."[46] Miles concludes that Jesus would probably advise contemporary conservatives as follows: "'If your people are determined to bring your country into accord with my teaching . . . then let them dissolve all second marriages and write my prohibition of divorce into their Constitution. But if they insist on overruling that prohibition, then let them look to their other prohibitions and consider revising them as well. For how can you say to your brother, "Let me take the [speck] out of your eye," when there is a [log] in your own?'" (Matthew 7:4).[47]

Yet while Jesus said nothing about homosexuality and little about marriage, the Apostle Paul, whose writings form the bulk of the New Testament, did address the issue of marriage, deeming it to be less worthy than a life of celibacy but better than burning with sexual desire and risking sin. (His condemnation of homosexual "passions" will be examined in chapter 4.) In his First Letter to the Corinthians, Paul presents what came to be the "authoritative position on marriage and sex" for Christians:[48]

It is well for a man not to touch a woman. But because of the temptation to immorality, each man should have his own wife and each woman her own husband. The husband should give to his wife her conjugal rights, and likewise the wife to her husband. For the wife does not rule over her own body, but the husband does; likewise the husband does not rule over his own body, but the wife does. Do not refuse one another except perhaps by agreement for a season, that you may devote your-

selves to prayer; but then come together again, lest Satan tempt you through lack
of self-control. I say this by way of concession, not of command. I wish that all
were as I myself am. But each has his own special gift from God, one of one kind
and one of another. (1 Cor. 7:1–7)

This valorization of celibacy, the justification for the Catholic doctrine of
unmarried clergy, hindered the Church from comprehensively addressing the
question of marriage until the twelfth century.

In addition, Paul notably neglects to mention children in his discussion
of marriage, emphasizing instead the conjugal relationship between husband
and wife. He justified marriage "as a solution to the problem of sexual desire
rather than as the means to procreation."[49] This view of marriage directly
contrasted with Jewish and Roman beliefs at the time, which viewed reproduction as the primary purpose of marriage. "Paul's emphasis on the relationship between spouses is reminiscent of his near-contemporary Plutarch, who
also tended to see child-bearing as secondary to the partnership, moral and
sexual, of husband and wife."[50] This original Christian perspective contrasts
with the view of many contemporary Christians who argue that marriage is
designed for bearing and rearing children, not to allow two people to have a
satisfying and committed relationship with each other, and therefore same-
sex couples should not be allowed to legally marry because their unions cannot biologically produce children.

By the fourth century, the fathers of the Western Church began to distinguish Christian marriage from the civil marriage of Rome. For example,
"Augustine emphasized that marriage in the Church was something very different from marriage among the Gentiles (that is, the pagans) or among the
Israelites. He thought that marriage was indissoluble in the Church but
impermanent outside it."[51] In addition, early Christianity also rejected the
distinction drawn in Roman law between marriage and concubinage. At the
Council of Toledo in the year 400, church leaders equated monogamous concubinage with marriage. Writing shortly thereafter, Augustine also articulated this view. He disapproved of the common practice of ambitious young
men, who would take a concubine for a while and then dismiss her to make
a good marriage with a woman of his social class, considering such practices
the moral equivalent of adultery.[52] St. Jerome concurred with this view. "The
consensus of these passages [in early Christian theology] is clear: as long as a
union is monogamous and permanent, its validity under Roman law is unimportant."[53] The Church recognized it as marriage.

Early Christianity rejected the Roman practice of having different types of legal relationships for couples—marriage for some and concubinage for others—because Christian scripture proclaims the spiritual equality of all people. Legal inequality between free people and slaves was invalid because in Christ "there is neither slave nor free," Paul explains, "for you are all one in Christ Jesus" (Gal. 3:28).[54] In the eyes of the Church, committed free-slave relationships were the equivalent of marriage, even if Roman law failed to recognize them as such. But in light of today's debate over the legal status of same-sex marriages, consider the rest of Paul's passage: "There is neither Jew nor Greek, there is neither slave nor free, there is neither male nor female; for you are all one in Christ Jesus" (Gal. 3:28). The Church saw Roman class distinctions in marriage law as invalid. Are contemporary gender distinctions also invalid? If there is no male or female in Christ, then shouldn't the Church allow same-sex marriage?

Marriage as Personal Bond

In American society today, people often understand marriage as a personal relationship between two people. Particularly in the context of American individualism, marriage is often understood as merely an individual choice and personal commitment. Academic "queer theorist" Michael Warner condemns this understanding of marriage as naïve because it fails to consider the ways in which the state controls marriage, determining who can and cannot marry and bestowing benefits upon those who can. Marriage "is a public institution, not a private relation," he insists, although in reality, it is both.[55] Some conservative opponents of gay marriage also oppose the individualistic approach to marriage. For example, according to a spokesman for Focus on the Family–Canada, the debate over same-sex marriage "is not about individual rights. 'Laws and institutions aren't about individual relations. . . . Laws and institutions deal with what is best for all of society.'"[56] Yet marriage— especially Christian marriage—has long been precisely about individual relations.

Contemporary critics on the Left and the Right notwithstanding, historically the personal bond, created by consent, has very often constituted the core of marriage. Jewish marriage occurred when the bride consented to marry by accepting the ring from the groom; Roman marriage arose from two people's desire for and consent to marriage. And when the Christian Church finally turned its full attention to marriage, in the eleventh through early thirteenth centuries, it eventually decided that *individuals constitute marriage through the promises they make to each other*—not families, not communities, not the government, not even the Church itself: "Marriage as a sacrament is fulfilled only through the mutual consent of the contracting parties."[57]

More specifically, in the twelfth century, the influential theologian Gratian argued that marriage occurs through mutual consent as expressed through sexual relations and "marital affection." Driving "the point home, he cited the extreme hypothetical case of the couple who exchanged vows in absolute secrecy. Was their marriage valid? Yes, said Gratian, the two had conferred the sacrament on themselves," as long as they completed the union with coitus and shared "marital affection."[58] In other words, "two people sexually attracted who felt affection for each other could marry in total privacy without the assistance or permission of anyone—family, friends, feudal lord, or holy Church." In fact, according to Gratian, "provided there was 'marital affection,' the concubine relationship amounted to an informal and imperfect but nevertheless valid marriage. As long as a man limited himself to one concubine, Gratian ruled, he should not be refused communion."[59] Clearly, "this was a radical doctrine" that not only took power away from parents but also blurred the distinction between informal marriage and casual sex.

Peter Lombard, another important medieval theologian, whose *Books of Sentences* became "a standard text in theology for centuries," and whose thinking directly influenced St. Thomas Aquinas, modified Gratian's view slightly but ultimately established the consensual theory of marriage as the Christian view. Lombard did not think sexual relations and mutual affection alone were enough to demonstrate consent, and he believed that an unconsummated marriage could still be valid. Consequently, he insisted that a valid marriage requires the bride and groom to pronounce "words of the present," that clearly declare their consent. For him, that alone constitutes marriage; "no ecclesiastical formality, no ritual act was necessary in Peter Lombard's eyes."[60] By the end of the twelfth century, Pope Alexander III officially proclaimed that marriage "required the free-will consent of two people," a view reiterated by St. Thomas Aquinas.[61]

For the Catholic Church, before and after the Reformation, marriage is a sacrament. According to its definition, "the sacraments of the Christian dispensation are not mere signs; they do not merely signify Divine grace, but in virtue of their Divine institution, they cause that grace in the souls of men."[62] The seven Catholic sacraments include baptism, confirmation, penance, Eucharist, marriage, ordination, and extreme unction, and each has its own system of canon law, rules, and procedures. (Protestants recognize only baptism and communion as sacraments.[63]) Marriage, considered the least

important sacrament, differs in a number of ways from the six other sacraments. One difference is that it technically requires no formal ceremony or
clerical participation. In fact, it requires no witnesses at all. In medieval days
the Church decided, "the two parties were themselves 'ministers of the sacrament.' Their consciences instructed them in the taking of the sacrament,
and their own testimony was considered sufficient evidence to validate their
marriages in a case of dispute."[64]

Thus, for the Church marriage was a religious rite constituted by the private promise between a man and a woman, which created an unbreakable
personal bond. And because marriage fell under the jurisdiction of canon
law, not civil law, what the Catholic Church decided about marriage had
the force of law across Western Europe.[65] In practice, the early Christian
Church did recognize marriages conducted in secret as valid and indissoluble,
although it preferred the participation of a priest and the presence of two
witnesses. Indeed, "canon lawyers went so far as to endorse secret marriages,
and church courts upheld them, despite many an irate family."[66] Thus, "from
the twelfth century the validity of clandestine marriages had been recognized
by the Church," which did not refuse to accept such marriages until the
Council of Trent (1545–1563)—after the Protestant Reformation.[67]

Although constituted through the personal promise of bride and groom,
medieval Christian marriage was not the egalitarian, individually customized
vision of marriage many people today embrace. While the Church maintained that a woman could not be forced into marriage against her will, once
married, the Church insisted, she entered into "conjugal society, the terms
of which are set by nature."[68] That is, according to the Church, "the choice
of a partner and especially the contracting or noncontracting of marriage are
subject to the free will of the individuals; but any revocation or essential
altering of the terms is beyond the power of the contracting parties; the
essence of the contractural [sic] sacrament is Divinely regulated."[69] Its primary purposes include the prevention of sexual sin and the conception, nurture, and education of children.[70]

The Christian Church's insistence that women cannot be forced into
marriage against their will played a positive role in advancing the position of
women over time. "The now-sacramental nature of marriage with its stipula-
tion of intention and a court system willing and able to annul marriages
formed without free consent, meant that patriarchal, familial control of marriage was breached, in theory at least. . . . Forced marriages increasingly
became a thing of the past."[71]

Yet even as the pre-Reformation Church dominated Western Europe, not

everyone agreed on the nature of marriage. The Jewish community continued its own view of marriage. This was possible because in most countries,
Jews were forcibly isolated in ghettos, sometimes behind locked gates, where
they were allowed to govern their own communities in accordance with Jewish law, *halakhah*, as interpreted by the rabbis.[72] Judaism holds a positive view
of sexuality, does not valorize celibacy, and actually requires rabbis to
marry.[73] "To simplify, the rabbis believed God had created human being *as
flesh*, creating and intending both sexual pleasure and procreativity right
from B'rashit, right from the beginning." To the rabbis, "the husband's most
unshakable duty—more important, even, than providing food or clothes, in
an era when the husband signed a contract promising to do precisely that—
was *onah*, his wife's sexual pleasure."[74] While unmarried sex was condemned,
"*married* sexual joy was a gift from God—just as eating kosher was good. And
just as kosher food was good no matter how you cooked it, so any married
sex—whatever the act might be—was still kosher, as long as it was not
against the woman's will."[75]

Yet despite these differences, the Jewish community agreed with the
Christian Church that the personal bond of the couple constitutes marriage.
As contemporary writer E. J. Graff puts it, "While the Jewish configuration
changed over the millennia, what remained central is marriage as a private
act: only bride and groom could say the magic words that turned them into
husband and wife. After many centuries the rabbis inserted themselves and
their seven blessings into the ceremony, before the big feast, but even they
knew they were not essential: the pair made the marriage within themselves.
Which is why, in Jewish law, a court could neither 'grant' nor refuse a
divorce."[76] While Maimonides, the twelfth-century rabbinic authority,
"advised the Jews of Egypt that marriages required the supervision of an
ordained rabbi," according to *halakhah* "it is not strictly necessary for a rabbi
to officiate at a wedding for the event to be kosher and binding." The rabbi
"does not 'marry' the bride and groom; they marry each other."[77]

Secularizing Marriage

The idea that the secular state constitutes marriage originated with the Protestants, who wanted to take control of marriage away from the Catholic
Church and give it to the newly emerging secular state. The Protestant Reformation in 1517 introduced a radically different vision of marriage into
Western tradition. Marriage would become "a public and secular institution
that the state had the right to regulate," rather than "a sacrament privately

administered and acknowledged only afterwards."[78] As Graff puts it, "the Protestants ushered in a revolution in the very *definition* of marriage—from announced to pronounced, from privately made to publicly bestowed. . . . Protestants still believed that the moment of marriage was when the two said their vows. But that moment was no longer a mystical sacrament, an idea the Protestants openly ridiculed."[79] While Protestants consider baptism and communion sacraments, they do not recognize marriage as such.

The Protestant definition of marriage grew out of Luther's theology, which espouses the doctrine of two kingdoms: the heavenly kingdom of God and the earthly kingdom of humanity. While the two kingdoms necessarily interact with each other, they must remain distinct. "A Christian is a citizen of both kingdoms at once and invariably comes under the distinctive government of each."[80] According to Luther, earthly authority is divided into three arenas that stand equal before God: the domestic realm of the family, the ecclesiastical realm of the church, and the political realm of the secular state. According to Luther, only the state should hold legal authority.[81]

Marriage fell under the authority of civil magistrates. However, this does not mean that Luther saw marriage as religiously irrelevant. Yet while he understood marriage was "divinely created and spiritually edifying," Luther argued that "all parties could partake of this institution, regardless of their faith," and the laws for marriage formation, maintenance, and dissolution; child custody, care, and control; and family property, inheritance, and commerce should remain under "the jurisdiction of the magistrate, not the cleric; of the civil law, not the canon law."[82] The minister's role vis-à-vis marriage would be restricted to pastoral counseling, overseeing marriage ceremonies, providing a marriage registry to publicize unions, issuing reprimands for misbehavior, and participating in the spiritual upbringing of children. His only political roles would consist of teaching magistrates about God's law and lobbying for reforms if marriage laws violated Divine law.[83]

Thus, Protestants had a very different idea of the role of the family in society than the Catholics did. Not a sacrament, marriage was not seen as part of the hierarchy of church orders but rather as "the founding social estate of the earthly kingdom."[84] The role of the family was to teach and model Christian values, morals, and mores, not only to children, but also to society at large, and to replace monasteries and cloisters as caretakers of the poor, the homeless, and the destitute. Just as important as the church, the family stood alongside it, "as indispensable an agent of social order and communal cohesion as the state should be. It was not simply a creation of the civil law, but a godly creation designed to aid the state in discharging its divine mandate."[85] This vision of the family seems to underlie the political agenda of many evangelical conservatives today, as subsequent chapters will demonstrate.

In Christian Europe, this reconceptualization of marriage led to the reform of marriage laws in Protestant areas. In Germany, for example, Protestant legal reform 1) shifted authority over marriage from Church to state; 2) strongly recommended that clergy marry; 3) abandoned the idea that virginity, celibacy, and monasticism were superior to marriage; 4) denied that marriage is a sacrament and made it easier to marry; 5) resuscitated the role of the community in the marriage process, by requiring the participation of parents, peers, and priests, as well as political officials; 6) made betrothal and putative marriage easier; and 7) "introduced divorce, in the modern sense, on proof of adultery, malicious desertion, and other faults, with a subsequent right to remarriage at least for the innocent party."[86] By the nineteenth century, the Protestant view of marriage, bolstered by the forces of secular state building, came to dominate in the West.[87]

"Self-Marriage": The American Common-Law Tradition

When the Protestants settled in what is now the United States, they brought their views of marriage with them. Because most (but not all) of the Founders came from Protestant backgrounds, they did not question the religiously rooted conception of marriage they wrote into law. Because people often lived in areas where no governmental official was available to perform a wedding, however, the Protestant view of marriage as constituted by government did not fully take root at first. Instead, the tradition of "common-law" marriage developed. This form of marriage, which still exists in most states, comes into being when the community accepts as valid a marriage that has not been formally recognized by the state. Because people in early America were so scattered, judges determined that "if you acted as if you were married, or said that you were married, then you were married—in life and in court."[88] Consequently, early Americans actually broke with the Protestant tradition of marriage by giving the power to create marriages back to communities.

The history of common-law marriage illustrates both the communal and personal components of marriage. Community acceptance of this practice—also known as "self-marriage"—testified to the widespread belief that it is the parties' consent to marry each other that matters most, not the words said by a minister or magistrate.[89] "Neighbors' awareness of the couple's cohabitation and reciprocal economic contributions figured a great deal in establishing that a marriage existed between a man and a woman, but consent was the first essential."[90] In addition, it was the norm to consider a couple married as soon as a pregnancy resulted.[91] In short, as Graff puts it, "early nineteenth-century American marriage . . . was made by the couple themselves, and recognized only afterward by law."[92] By the end of the nineteenth century, however, "for the most part marriage in the United States had also become a public, state-regulated status—bestowed by a central authority, hedged by registries, licenses, fees, and witnesses."[93]

The short history of marriage just recounted helps contest the idea that only the state has the power to constitute marriage. In fact, for most of history, individuals and communities constituted marriage, not political or religious elites. Moreover, religious organizations have maintained their own requirements for religious marriage, which can differ markedly from a civil (or alternative religious) view of marriage. A study of history does not reveal one unchanging definition of marriage accepted by all people.

To those who say lesbian and gay couples should not be allowed to get married, I say they already are. Many lesbian and gay couples are already married because they have formed personal bonds through private promises of fidelity, companionship, and mutual support of each other and because they are increasingly recognized as married within their communities, by friends and neighbors, family and coworkers. Many have also received clerical sanction within their own religious denominations. Yet the marriages of gay men and lesbians are singled out by the government for special discrimination.

The Benefits of Civil Marriage

The argument that lesbian and gay couples are already married in three out of four senses, however, should not be construed to imply that the legal right to civil marriage is unimportant. Government-sanctioned civil marriage entails a significant set of legal benefits that are currently available only to heterosexual married couples. With the recent public discussion of the "marriage tax penalty" in the media—which only penalizes couples in which both partners work outside the home—many people do not have a clear sense of what exactly is at stake in the struggle of lesbians and gay men for access to civil marriage. Thus, the remainder of the chapter provides an overview of some of the key benefits provided by civil marriage.

Marriage entails a huge number of benefits, many of which come from the *federal* government. This is a vitally important point. When the state of Massachusetts legalized same-sex marriage, it ensured lesbian and gay couples equal access to *state benefits only*. Because of the Defense of Marriage Act (DOMA), passed in 1996, same-sex couples legally married in Massachusetts get *no federal benefits*. Vermont provides civil unions, and California, Connecticut, Hawaii, New Jersey, New York, and the District of Columbia, as well as a number of cities, provide domestic partnerships; both arrangements offer lesbian and gay couples some or all of the *state or local* benefits of marriage, but again they provide *none of the federal benefits*. Consequently, couples that enter civil unions in Vermont, domestic partnerships in other states, or even marriage in Massachusetts do not receive the federal benefits that heterosexual married couples automatically receive.

While same-sex couples legally married in Massachusetts are denied federal benefits, at least they have grounds to sue the federal government; DOMA denies benefits only to same-sex couples and so the Court may find it to be discriminatory. Couples that have entered civil unions are in a different position. Because the federal government grants no benefits to civil unions, same-sex couples that are civilly united, rather than married, have no grounds to bring suit.

DOMA may be overturned on another basis as well. Because it also allows states not to recognize same-sex marriages performed in other states, DOMA may very well be found to violate the Constitution's "full faith and credit clause" that requires states to recognize each other's contracts. Because the Supreme Court may overturn DOMA, some social conservatives want to pass a constitutional amendment defining marriage for the entire country, thus taking away the traditional right of the states to define marriage for themselves.

Federal law treats lesbian and gay couples as legal strangers, no matter how long they have been together. The General Accounting Office has identified over 1,000 federal laws for which marital status is a factor and classifies them under the following categories: social security and related programs, housing, and food stamps; veterans' benefits; taxation; federal civilian and military service benefits; employment benefits and related laws; immigration, naturalization, and aliens; Indians; trade, commerce, and intellectual property; financial disclosure and conflict of interest; crimes and family violence; loans, guarantees, and payments in agriculture; federal natural resources and related laws; and miscellaneous laws.[94]

Many of the federal benefits of civil marriage help married partners take care of each other as they age; they are not designed primarily to help them raise children. Social Security, for instance, provides survivorship benefits for widows and widowers. Many elderly people rely exclusively on Social Security, and not having access to this economic benefit grossly disadvantages lesbian and gay elders. The "loss of income can be substantial. For example, surviving partners who are 60 years old will lose an average of $9,780 a year—or approximately $166,000 if they live to the average life expectancy of 77. (Based on Social Security Administration calculations that Social Security survivor benefits averaged $815 per month in 2002.)"[95]

Federal law also discriminates against same-sex couples when it comes to other economic issues. For example, federal law allows a widowed spouse to move her husband's retirement savings into her own account, avoiding heavy taxes, and she automatically inherits joint property without paying estate taxes. Both exemptions protect her from having to sell her home on top of losing her husband. In addition, an elderly married couple has the right to live together in a nursing home, and they cannot be forced to sell their mutual home if one of them incurs high nursing home bills. Marriage also allows access to family-related military or veterans' benefits. Because they cannot legally marry, lesbian and gay couples do not get *any* of these federal benefits, no matter how long they have been together. This puts same-sex couples at a distinct economic disadvantage vis-à-vis heterosexual married couples.

Nor do committed same-sex couples have access to the protections offered under the Family and Medical Leave Act of 1993. FMLA guarantees employees of public agencies or private companies of over fifty employees up to twelve weeks unpaid leave per twelve-month period in cases of illness or to care for a new baby or a sick family member. During leave the employer must continue the employee's health insurance coverage and restore his original or an equivalent job upon return. When the Defense of Marriage Act was passed in 1996, FMLA was revised specifically to exclude same-sex couples. Consequently, if a gay man takes time off from work to care for his seriously ill partner or bond with an adopted baby, his employer could fire him. Similarly, employers could also deny bereavement leave to a lesbian or gay employee who loses a partner.

It's also vitally important to note that many benefits bestowed through marriage cannot be established through individual contracts. It is simply not true, as antigay activist Maggie Gallagher and sociologist Linda Waite, who coauthored *The Case for Marriage*, assert, that "gay couples can, with the help of a knowledgeable attorney, set up almost all the legal rights for their partnership that married couples get automatically at the wedding."[96] While it's true that in most states some protections can be established through individual contracts—although this requires same-sex couples to pay often-hefty legal fees to receive what heterosexual couples get for free upon marriage—lesbian and gay couples simply cannot contract for many of the special privileges the law grants married people because of the special nature of their relationship.

Under DOMA, for example, federal law prohibits the extension of Social Security, tax, and FMLA benefits to same-sex partners. Moreover, if a heterosexual person falls in love with someone from another country, that person can immigrate to the United States and apply for citizenship, even if she's simply a "mail-order bride," while the long-term partners of lesbian and gay citizens receive no special immigration status whatsoever. When necessary, married people are granted "spousal privilege" that prevents them from having to testify against each other in court, and if imprisoned, they are often allowed conjugal visits—not the case for committed same-sex couples. (As mentioned previously, prisoners have the right to marry, even murderers, as long as they are heterosexual.[97])

In any event, the protections that can be achieved through contract law are not secure. For example, in 2004 the Virginia legislature passed House Bill 751—called the Affirmation of Marriage Act for the Commonwealth of Virginia—which states:

> A civil union, partnership contract or other arrangement between persons of the same sex purporting to bestow the privileges or obligations of marriage is prohibited. Any such civil union, partnership contract or other arrangement entered into by persons of the same sex in another state or jurisdiction shall be void in all respects in Virginia and any contractual rights created thereby shall be void and unenforceable.

As one of the most antigay marriage bills in the country, HB 751 aims to invalidate legal arrangements between same-sex partners that give marriage-like authority to each other, including medical and legal powers of attorney, joint wills, and estate documents—possibly even joint bank accounts.[98] Thus, it seeks to impede the right of lesbian and gay individuals to enter into contracts. While some condemn the mean-spiritedness of this action, Concerned Women for America praises the bill "because it bars any form of faux marriage 'rights,' regardless of the name."[99]

While in most states some benefits of marriage can be secured through legal contracts, civil marriage *automatically* bestows such benefits without forcing individuals to spend money on lawyers and otherwise inconveniencing them. For example, a married person automatically inherits his or her partner's property in the absence of a will, preventing the need to distinguish what was his from what was hers. When a gay person dies without a will, a distant relative can lay claim to the couple's shared property. Likewise, without a preexisting medical power of attorney, lesbians and gay men do not have the right to make medical decisions on behalf of their partners, in an emergency or at the end of life. Instead the "next of kin" has legal authority, even if that person is an estranged parent or sibling who has no idea about the wishes of the patient. While such problems can often be eliminated through legal agreements, huge problems can result if the necessary paperwork is not in order—or is unavailable. For example, if a gay couple gets in a car accident while on vacation that puts one of them in the hospital, and they cannot produce the proper paperwork, the uninjured partner might be barred from visiting his injured partner. He could not simply say the magic words, "We're married," and be guaranteed consideration by doctors, nurses, and hospital staff.

Some of the benefits of marriage come not from the government but from the traditional compact between employers and employees. For example, many companies offer health insurance benefits for married spouses and dependent children. With over forty million Americans uninsured and the possibility of universal health care unlikely, access to insurance is a serious issue. A couple could go bankrupt trying to pay for medical treatment for the uninsured partner. When children are involved, access to health insurance becomes even more important. In a lesbian couple, for example, if the biological mother has to work to provide health insurance for herself and her children, then she does not have the option of staying home, supported by her partner, while her children are young. And if medical complications prevent her from working during pregnancy, she might lose her job and health insurance, and the baby's other parent would not be able to do anything to help.

While some employers offer the same benefits to domestic partners as they do married partners, they are not required to do so. While employers are not legally required to provide any employees with health insurance, they are not allowed to discriminate on the basis of gender or race, such as offering marital benefits only to men or only to whites. They can, however, discriminate on the basis of sexual orientation, offering benefits to their heterosexual employees while denying them to their homosexual ones.

If an employer chooses to offer health insurance to domestic partners, two inequities remain. First, the domestic partner benefits—often worth thousands of dollars—are added to the employee's taxable income.[100] This does not happen when a married employee adds a spouse to his or her insurance. Second, when a worker gets laid off, federal COBRA law requires the employer to allow the employee the opportunity to extend his or her health insurance coverage for eighteen months by paying the premium. If the individual is married, the spouse may also continue his or her insurance coverage. The law does not guarantee the same protections for domestic partners, even if they were both on the original policy.[101]

Finally, many benefits of marriage arise "from social custom rather than law." That is to say, "a wife can act as the agent for her husband, signing and cashing his checks, changing his plane reservations, making financial and medical decisions in his name. A husband can do the same in the name of his wife."[102] Married people get access to family discounts at gyms, they can use each other's library cards, and they do not have to pay an extra driver fee when they rent a car. To some, these privileges may seem trivial, but to gay and lesbian couples, not having them is annoying, inconvenient, and patently unfair. What's more, it demonstrates to them over and over that their relationships are not respected as valid.

In addition to helping committed partners take care of each other, civil marriage also provides a large number of benefits and protections for children. While some dismiss same-sex couples' desire for marital benefits because they cannot reproduce biologically with each other, gay and lesbian couples are currently raising an estimated one million children.[103] Despite political rhetoric to the contrary, no evidence exists that such couples cannot rear children as effectively as heterosexuals.[104] In fact, "all major research studies, including a 2001 meta-analysis of two decades of studies on the topic, show that the sexual orientation of a parent is irrelevant to the development of a child's mental health and social development and to the quality of a parent-child relationship."[105]

> Research studies have consistently shown that children raised by gay and lesbian parents do just as well on all conventional measures of child development, such as academic achievement, psychological well-being and social abilities, as children raised by heterosexual parents. That is . . . why the leading child welfare organizations, including the American Academy of Pediatrics, the American Academy of Family Physicians and others, have issued statements that dismiss assertions that only heterosexual couples can be good parents—and declare that the focus should be on providing greater protections for the one million to 9 million children being raised by gay and lesbian parents in the United States today.[106]

Other organizations that support same-sex parenting include the American Anthropological Association, the American Bar Association, the American Psychiatric Association, the American Psychoanalytic Association, the American Psychological Association, the Child Welfare League of America, the National Association of Social Workers, and the North American Council on Adoptable Children.[107]

Despite this support from educated professionals in the field, not all states allow "second-parent adoption"—when a biological parent's same-sex partner adopts the individual's child. Even where available "this alternative is not without obstacles. It can impose a significant financial burden and time delay since the same-sex partner seeking a second-parent adoption must hire an attorney, go through a home study and petition and appear before the court before he or she is awarded legal parent status." Only Connecticut, Illinois, Massachusetts, New Jersey, New York, Vermont, and the District of Columbia have made second-parent adoption available statewide. In twenty other states, access varies by county or by judge. "In the remaining 24 states, research has not revealed any second-parent adoptions, which means it is difficult to predict whether they would be granted there. The result: Whether two parents and their children can have a legal relationship depends upon where they happen to live and what judge they happen to get."[108] Such arbitrariness violates the American principle that states American citizens should have the rule of law not the rule of men.

Lack of access to second-parent adoption means that even though the nonbiological parent assumes parenting responsibilities and the child views that individual as a parent, the law considers the nonbiological parent a stranger—even if the person has been present in the child's life since birth or has taken primary responsibility for childcare. Consequently, the second parent cannot put the child on his or her health insurance, cannot take time off from work if the child gets sick, and cannot give medical consent in an emergency without producing a "power of attorney." While this parent may be providing substantial amounts of emotional and financial support to the child, if he or she were to die before the child turns eighteen, that child would be denied Social Security survivorship benefits. Even worse, if the biological parent dies, the second parent may lose custody to a distant relative, who may because of family discord be a virtual stranger; the child might even end up in foster care or be put up for adoption. Finally, if the couple breaks up, the nonbiological parent has no rights to custody or visitation and in fact his or her relationship to the child could be completely severed, even if the nonbiological parent was the primary caretaker. Legal paperwork designed to protect the rights of the second parent may or may not be respected in family court. As Lambda Legal Defense puts it, "wills, health proxies, co-parent adoptions, co-leases, name changes: There are many legal ways that same-sex couples try to protect each other and their children. Still, desired protections may be unavailable, unsuccessful in court or not always respected by individuals, businesses, or the government."[109]

Because civil marriage entails such a significant set of benefits, it is grossly unfair to deny same-sex couples the same opportunity heterosexual couples have to access those benefits. However, some critics of marriage equality dismiss the attempt to establish equity as simply a "benefits grab" by homosexuals. For example, Maggie Gallagher rejects what she sees as the attempt to portray "civil marriage" as "an individual right to a set of legal goodies." According to her, marriage is coming to be seen as simply as "a way of distributing stuff to anyone who wants to claim it,"[110] even though the demand for same-sex marriage comes from committed couples who simply want the same benefits enjoyed by their heterosexual counterparts, not from random any-ones asking for a hand-out. And while Gallagher rejects "the right [of homosexuals] to have the law recognize their own private vision of marriage,"[111] in reality, lesbian and gay couples simply want the same civil recognition of their relationships that their heterosexual counterparts receive.

In *The Case for Marriage*, Gallagher idealizes marriage, portraying it as a virtual panacea for a host of societal and human shortcomings, yet she wants to bar lesbians and gay men from reaping any of its rewards, whether material or psychological.[112] Since most of the rewards she and her coauthor's research ascribes to marriage seem to come from a married couple's ability to establish trust, pool resources, support each other, and expect their relationship to last forever, it is unclear why same-sex couples would not benefit from the institution as well.[113] In fact, the book even admits as much:

> The state of social-science research, as it now stands, sheds little light on the question: Would gay couples (and their children) reap the same benefits from legal marriage that men and women who marry do? As social scientists, the most we can conclude is, Maybe, maybe not. . . . We suspect, but do not know, that adults in such same-sex couples would reap some, but not all, the benefits of marriage. The benefits afforded same-sex couples by marriage would also depend on the extent to which family, friends, and other social institutions supported these unions.[114]

Yet despite this conclusion, Gallagher publicly opposes and works politically against same-sex marriage, speaking authoritatively yet basing her calls for discrimination on nothing other than her own personal opinion.[115]

As it turns out, however, Gallagher is not simply speaking for herself. In 2005 it was revealed that her activism was secretly underwritten by the Bush Administration, via contracts through the Department of Health and Human Services (HHS) and the Justice Department. When her funding sources were exposed, Gallagher "apologized . . . for failing to reveal her contract to assist HHS while writing about the marriage initiative in articles and columns, one of which referred to Bush's 'genius.'" In her words, "It was a mistake on my part not to have disclosed any government contract. It will not happen again." This exposure of undisclosed funding to Gallagher and others prompted the president to denounce his administration's practice of secretly paying pundits to support his agenda. The Human Rights Campaign (HRC), a bipartisan lesbian/gay rights advocacy group, has "questioned in a letter whether federal law or congressional rules were violated when Gallagher twice testified before the Senate on the amendment without disclosing her federal contracts." In response, some Democrats "introduced legislation . . . that would bar funding of 'covert propaganda' or material that is partisan or intended for 'self-aggrandizement' or 'puffery.'"[116]

Heterosexual marriage advocate Mary Ann Glendon also wants to prevent same-sex couples from having access to the many benefits of civil marriage. She argues that at a time when "the state is cutting back on programs to aid the elderly, the disabled, and children in poor families," it is unfair to "favor special benefits for a group of relatively affluent households, most of which have two earners and are not raising children. What same-sex marriage advocates have tried to present as a civil rights issue is really a bid for special preferences of the type our society gives to married couples for the very good reason that most of them are raising or have raised children."[117] But how is the call to treat same-sex married couples exactly the same as heterosexual married couples a demand for "special preferences"? And since the benefits of marriage do not just help couples provide for their children but also help them take care of each other, how can it be legitimate for the government to withhold protections from same-sex married couples, many of whom do in fact have children?

Following Glendon's logic, should the government extend the benefits of marriage only to heterosexual couples that have children or only to less affluent couples? Not to mention the fact that same-sex couples exist in all socioeconomic levels of society. Glendon is concerned about how much same-sex marriage "would cost the rest of society in terms of taxes and insurance premiums." She notes, "The Canadian government, which is considering same-sex marriage legislation, has just realized that retroactive social-security survivor benefits alone would cost its taxpayers hundreds of millions of dollars." But if lesbians and gays did what many conservatives want them to do and turned heterosexual, then they would presumably receive the marital benefits of heterosexual marriage, thus increasing costs anyway. In any event, the funding for Social Security survivorship benefits is supposed to come from the investment of money taken from the deceased worker's own paycheck; it's not a tax-funded handout. Finally, if cutbacks on programs for the elderly, the disabled, and the children of the poor concern Glendon, the solution is to extend funding to programs that help those groups, not to discriminate against lesbian and gay citizens.

In response to conservative concerns about money, HRC argues that same-sex marriage could actually save taxpayers money because it would help families take care of each other more effectively, thus lessening their need for state or federal government assistance.

> For example, two studies conducted in 2003 by professors at the University of Massachusetts, Amherst, and the University of California, Los Angeles, found that extending domestic partner benefits to same-sex couples in California and New Jersey would save taxpayers millions of dollars a year. Specifically, the studies projected that the California state budget would save an estimated $8.1 to $10.6 million each year by enacting the most comprehensive domestic partner law in the nation. In New Jersey, which passed a new domestic partner law in 2004, the savings were projected to be even higher—more than $61 million each year.[118]

These studies provide a counterweight to the alarmism of social conservatives using economic concerns as a way to scare fiscal conservatives.

Nevertheless, whether the extension of marital benefits to same-sex couples helps or hurts economically is not the key issue. The key issue is basic fairness. If government and private business choose to provide benefits to married couples, it is patently unfair to deny those benefits to lesbian and gay couples. Same-sex couples are just as committed to each other as are heterosexual couples. (Indeed, even with access to the full array of marital benefits nearly half of all heterosexual marriages end in divorce.) While some people may believe that heterosexual marriage is fundamentally different from, if not vastly superior to, same-sex marriage, that is really not a good reason to deny lesbian and gay couples access to benefits designed to help committed couples take care of themselves and their children. It's just not fair. And it flies in the face of many of the principles that underlie American democracy, a philosophical and political argument laid out in the next chapter.

Notes

1. See Stephanie Coontz, *The Way We Never Were: American Families and the Nostalgia Trap* (New York: Basic Books, 2000).

2. James Dobson, "In Defending Marriage—Take the Offensive!" Dr. Dobson's Newsletter, Focus on the Family, April 2004, www.family.org/docstudy/newsletters/A0031315.cfm [accessed 25 March 2004].

3. "Focus on the Family Position Statement on Same-Sex 'Marriage' and Civil Unions," *Citizen Link*, October 4, 2000, www.family.org/cforum/research/papers/a0013151.html [accessed 22 July 2002].

4. Judith Martin, "Miss Manners: Present-Day Dilemma," *Washington Post*, March 24, 2004.

5. Michael Warner, *The Trouble with Normal: Sex, Politics, and the Ethics of Queer Life* (New York: Free Press, 1999), 99.

6. Warner, *Trouble with Normal*, 122–23.

7. Mark Searle and Kenneth W. Stevenson, "Jewish Marriage Rite," *Documents of the Marriage Liturgy* (Collegeville, MN: Liturgical Press, 1992), 27.

8. Anita Diamant, *The New Jewish Wedding* (New York: Summit Books, 1985), 36.

9. Searle and Stevenson, "Jewish Marriage Rite," 25.

10. Diamant, *New Jewish Wedding*, 71.

11. Marilyn Yalom, *A History of the Wife* (New York: HarperCollins Publishers, 2001), 4.

12. Diamant, *New Jewish Wedding*, 72.

13. Yalom, *History of the Wife*, 4.

14. Yalom, *History of the Wife*, 12.

15. Yalom, *History of the Wife*, 6.

16. Diamant, *New Jewish Wedding*, 71–72.

17. Yalom, *History of the Wife*, 6.

18. Mark C. Carlson, "Women of Ancient Greece," http://info-center.ccit.arizona.edu/~ws/ws200/fall97/grp2/part5.htm [accessed 1 April 2004]. See also Yalom, *History of the Wife*, 20.

19. Jennifer Powers, "Ancient Greek Marriage" (master's thesis, Tufts University), 1999, http://ancienthistory.about.com/gi/dynamic/offsite.htm?site=http%3A%2F%2Fwww.pogodesigns.com%2FJP%2Fweddings%2Fgreekwed.html [accessed 24 March 2004].

20. Jana Shopkorn, "'Til Death Do Us Part: Marriage and Funeral Rites in Classical Athens," http://ancienthistory.about.com/gi/dynamic/offsite.htm?site=http%3A%2F%2Fwww.perseus.tufts.edu%2Fclasses%2FJSp.html [accessed 1 April 2004].

21. Powers, "Ancient Greek Marriage."

22. Cynthia Patterson, *The Family in Greek History* (Cambridge, MA, and London: Harvard University Press, 1998), 108–9.

23. Patterson, *Family in Greek History*, 108.

24. Patterson, *Family in Greek History*, 110.

25. Powers, "Ancient Greek Marriage."

26. John Boswell, *Christianity, Social Tolerance, and Homosexuality: Gay People in Western Europe from the Beginning of the Christian Era to the Fourteenth Century* (Chicago: University of Chicago Press, 1980), 49.

27. Judith Evans Grubbs, *Law and Family in Late Antiquity: The Emperor Constantine's Marriage Legislation* (Oxford: Clarendon Press, 1995), 55.

28. Yuval Merin, *Equality for Same-Sex Couples: The Legal Recognition of Gay Partnerships in Europe and the United States* (Chicago and London: University of Chicago Press, 2002), 10.

29. Yalom, *History of the Wife*, 28.

30. Bennie Goldin, *In and Out of Marriage: An Historical Survey* (New York: Vantage Press, 2002), 38.

31. Yalom, *History of the Wife*, 30.

32. Goldin, *In and Out of Marriage*, 44–45.

33. Philip Reynolds, *Marriage in the Western Church: The Christianization of Marriage during the Patristic and Medieval Periods* (Leiden and New York: Brill Academic Publishers, 1994), xviii.

34. Suzanne Dixon, *The Roman Family* (Baltimore and London: Johns Hopkins University Press, 1992), 73.

35. Goldin, *In and Out of Marriage*, 46.

36. Goldin, *In and Out of Marriage*, 46; Dixon, *Roman Family*, 73.

37. Goldin, *In and Out of Marriage*, 46.

38. Boswell, *Christianity, Social Tolerance, and Homosexuality*, 82.

39. Dobson, "In Defending Marriage."

40. Boswell, *Christianity, Social Tolerance, and Homosexuality*, 71.

41. Boswell, *Christianity, Social Tolerance, and Homosexuality*, 87. For a similar argument that contests the idea that Romans were depraved and disregarded marriage, see Dixon, *Roman Family*, 96.

42. For a discussion of the interaction between Roman and Christian views of marriage, see Geoffrey S. Nathan, *The Family in Late Antiquity: The Rise of Christianity and the Endurance of Tradition* (London and New York: Routledge, 2000).

43. Reynolds, *Marriage in the Western Church*, xix.

44. All New Testament quotations in this chapter come from the Revised Standard Version of the Bible.

45. Jack Miles, "What Would Jesus Say about Gay Marriage? Divorce, Not Homosexuality, Was the Deviation That Preoccupied Him," www.beliefnet.com/story/140/story_14050_1.html [accessed 18 June 2004].

46. Miles, "What Would Jesus Say?"

47. Miles, "What Would Jesus Say?"

48. Grubbs, *Law and Family in Late Antiquity*, 67.

49. Reynolds, *Marriage in the Western Church*, xxvii.

50. Grubbs, *Law and Family in Late Antiquity*, 66.

51. Reynolds, *Marriage in the Western Church*, xv.

52. Grubbs, *Law and Family in Late Antiquity*, 311.

53. Grubbs, *Law and Family in Late Antiquity*, 312.

54. Grubbs, *Law and Family in Late Antiquity*, 312.

55. Warner, *Trouble with Normal*, 107.

56. DeNeen L. Brown, "Toronto Family Underwhelmed by Gay Marriage," *Washington Post*, May 3, 2004.

57. "Sacrament of Marriage," *Catholic Encyclopedia*, www.newadvent.org/cathen/09707a.htm [accessed 8 July 2004]. The entry includes a detailed argument as to why bride and groom, not the priest, are ministers of the sacrament.

58. Frances and Joseph Gies, *Marriage and the Family in the Middle Ages* (New York: Harper & Row, 1987), 138.

59. Gies and Gies, *Marriage and the Family in the Middle Ages*, 138.

60. Gies and Gies, *Marriage and the Family in the Middle Ages*, 139.

61. Ranft, *Women and Spiritual Equality*, 153.

62. "Sacraments," *Catholic Encyclopedia*, www.newadvent.org/cathen/13295a.htm#II [accessed 8 July 2004].

63. Linwood Urban, *A Short History of Christian Thought* (New York and Oxford: Oxford University Press, 1995), 255.

64. John Witte, *Law and Protestantism: The Legal Teachings of the Lutheran Reformation* (Cambridge: Cambridge University Press, 2002), 207. See also "Sacrament of Marriage," *Catholic Encyclopedia*, www.newadvent.org/cathen/09707a.htm (accessed 8 July 2004).

65. Merin, *Equality for Same-Sex Couples*, 11.

66. Patricia Ranft, *Women and Spiritual Equality in Christian Tradition* (New York: St. Martin's Press, 1998), 150.

67. See "Mixed Marriage," *Catholic Encyclopedia*, www.newadvent.org/cathen/09698a.htm [accessed 8 July 2004]. For an account of the Church's repeated condemnation of clandestine marriages, which clearly kept occurring, see "Clandestinity (in Canon Law)," *Catholic Encyclopedia*, www.newadvent.org/cathen/04001a.htm [accessed 8 July 2004].

68. Witte, *Law and Protestantism*, 206–7.

69. "Sacrament of Marriage," *Catholic Encyclopedia*, www.newadvent.org/cathen/09707a.htm [accessed 8 July 2004].

70. Witte, *Law and Protestantism*, 204–5.

71. Ranft, *Women and Spiritual Equality*, 150.

72. Goldin, *In and Out of Marriage*, 217–18.

73. Christian theologians hold a variety of views of sexuality. The negative view of sex seems to come from St. Augustine, who "believed that sexual desire was a product of the fall and the procreative act was therefore impure, something Paul himself never explicitly stated, although Augustine certainly believed that he faithfully represented Paul's view." Urban, *Short History of Christian Thought*, 327.

74. E. J. Graff, *What Is Marriage for?* (Boston: Beacon Press, 1999), 69.

75. Graff, *What Is Marriage*, 70.

76. Graff, *What Is Marriage*, 194–95.

77. Diamant, *New Jewish Wedding*, 43–44.

78. Graff, *What Is Marriage*, 203.

79. Graff, *What Is Marriage*, 201.

80. Witte, *Law and Protestantism*, 5.

81. Witte, *Law and Protestantism*, 7.

82. Witte, *Law and Protestantism*, 201.

83. Witte, *Law and Protestantism*, 229–30.

84. Witte, *Law and Protestantism*, 230.

85. Witte, *Law and Protestantism*, 231.

86. Witte, *Law and Protestantism*, 202.

87. Merin, *Equality for Same-Sex Couples*, 12.

88. Graff, *What Is Marriage*, 203–4.

89. Nancy F. Cott, *Public Vows: A History of Marriage and the Nation* (Cambridge, MA: Harvard University Press, 2000), 31.

90. Cott, *Public Vows*, 31.

91. Cott, *Public Vows*, 31.

92. Graff, *What Is Marriage*, 203–4.

93. Graff, *What Is Marriage*, 205.

94. United States General Accounting Office, "GAO/OGC-97-16 Defense of Marriage Act," www.marriageequality.org [accessed 4 March 2004].

95. Human Rights Campaign website, www.hrc.org/Template.cfm?Section = Partners&Template = /ContentManagement/ContentDisplay.cfm&ContentID = 12980 [accessed 22 March 2004].

96. Linda J. Waite and Maggie Gallagher, *The Case for Marriage* (New York: Broadway Books, 2000), 20.

97. *Turner v. Safley* 482 U.S. 78 (1987).

98. Justine Bergman, "Lawmakers Bypass Warner, Approve Civil Union Ban," *Boston Globe*, April 21, 2004, www.boston.com/news/specials/gay_marriage/articles/2004/04/21/lawmakers_bypass_warner_approve_civil_union_ban/ [accessed 30 June 2004].

99. Jeremy Sewall, "Virginia Legislature Passes Ban on Civil Unions," www.cwfa.org/articledisplay.asp?id = 5559&department = CFI&categoryid = family [accessed 30 June 2004].

100. Human Rights Campaign, "An Overview of Federal Rights and Protections Granted to Married Couples," www.hrc.org/Template.cfm?Section = Center&Template = /ContentManagement/ContentDisplay.cfm&ContentID = 16954 [accessed 22 March 2004].

101. Human Rights Campaign, "Overview of Federal Rights."

102. Waite and Gallagher, *Case for Marriage*, 20.

103. Human Rights Campaign, "Federal Rights and Protections."

104. Judith Stacey, *In the Name of the Family: Rethinking Family Values in the Postmodern Age* (Boston: Beacon Press, 1996).

105. See Judith Stacey and Tim Biblarz, "(How) Does the Sexual Orientation of Parents Matter?" *American Sociological Review* (April 2001). Quotation from HRC website, www.hrc.org/Template.cfm?Section = Home&CONTENTID = 16799&TEMPLATE = /ContentManagement/ContentDisplay.cfm [accessed 22 March 2004].

106. Stacey and Biblarz, "(How) Does the Sexual Orientation of Parents Matter?"

107. Stacey and Biblarz, "(How) Does the Sexual Orientation of Parents Matter?"

108. HRC, "The State of the Family: Laws and Legislation Affecting Lesbian, Gay, Bisexual and Transgender Families," 23, www.hrc.org/Template.cfm?Section = LGBT_ Families&Template = /TaggedPage/TaggedPageDisplay.cfm&TPLID = 52&ContentID = 12887 [accessed 22 March 2004].

109. Lambda Legal Defense website, www.lambdalegal.org [accessed 18 March 2004].

110. Maggie Gallagher, "The Road to Polygamy," Town Hall, March 16, 2004, www .townhall.com/columnists/maggiegallagher/mg20040316.shtml [accessed 18 February 2004].

111. Gallagher, "Road to Polygamy."

112. Waite and Gallagher, *Case for Marriage*, 200.

113. Waite and Gallagher, *Case for Marriage*, 23–35, 187, 201, 203.

114. Waite and Gallagher, *Case for Marriage*, 200–201.

115. Gallagher, "Road to Polygamy."

116. Howard Kurtz, "Bush Urges End to Contracts with Commentators," *Washington Post*, January 27, 2005.

117. Mary Ann Glendon, "For Better or for Worse? The Federal Marriage Amendment Would Strike a Blow for Freedom," *Wall Street Journal*, February 25, 2004, www.opinion journal.com/editorial/feature.html?id = 110004735 [accessed 19 March 2004].

118. The website cites "Equal Rights, Fiscal Responsibility: The Impact of A.B. 205 on California's Budget," by M. V. Lee Badgett, Ph.D., IGLSS, Department of Economics, University of Massachusetts, and R. Bradley Sears, J.D., Williams Project, UCLA School of Law, University of California, Los Angeles, May 2003, and "Supporting Families, Saving Funds: A Fiscal Analysis of New Jersey's Domestic Partnership Act," by Badgett and Sears with Suzanne Goldberg, J.D., Rutgers School of Law–Newark, December 2003. HRC website, www.hrc.org/Template.cfm?Section = Center&CONTENTID = 16814& TEMPLATE = /ContentManagement/ContentDisplay.cfm [accessed 22 March 2004].

~

CHAPTER THREE

The Logic of Liberalism: American Political Theory and the Case for Gay Marriage

We hold these truths to be self-evident, that all men are created equal, that they are endowed by their Creator with certain unalienable rights, among these are Life, Liberty and the pursuit of Happiness. That to secure these rights, Governments are instituted among Men, deriving their just powers from the consent of the governed.

—Declaration of Independence (1776)

The freedom to marry has long been recognized as one of the vital personal rights essential to the orderly pursuit of happiness . . . one of the "basic civil rights of man" . . . and cannot be infringed by the State.

—*Loving v. Virginia* (1967)

As I have only indicated up till now, the core thesis of this book is that the fundamental principles that underlie American democracy not only allow but also *require* the extension of the right of civil marriage to lesbian and gay couples. This chapter lays out my argument step by step. Here I argue that America's dominant public philosophy of liberalism, which entails a commitment to a set of core principles—including legal equality, separation of church and state, individual rights and liberties, and personal autonomy—logically justifies and requires full equality for lesbians and gay men, including the right to marry. While common parlance generally conflates the term "liberalism" with the traditional agenda of the American Left—as in "tax

47

and spend liberals"—the *political theory* of liberalism (originating with Locke and developed by Kant, Mill, and Rawls) actually undergirds the political agendas of both the Democratic and Republican parties in America, although each emphasizes different aspects of the tradition and interprets the basic principles in different ways.[1] For example, liberal Democrats emphasize equal rights and civil liberties, while neoliberal and libertarian Republicans stress individualism and limited government. All recognize the importance of equality before the law.

While liberalism is not the only political tradition in America,[2] since the 1960s the fundamental principles of liberalism have become so well accepted that they are nearly hegemonic (for better or for worse),[3] even if many Americans do not understand themselves as embracing a coherent philo-sophical tradition. Both the philosophical development of liberal principles in Supreme Court rulings, which affect society at large,[4] and the amplifica-tion of individualism and self-expression through consumer capitalism have contributed to this trend. This chapter focuses on the ways in which the basic principles that constitute the liberal tradition in America all support the right of civil marriage for lesbian and gay couples.

Moral Disagreement and the Origins of Liberal Political Theory

Liberalism originated in the seventeenth century in response to the religious conflict that developed in the wake of the Protestant Reformation. "When an authoritative, salvationist, and expansionist religion like medieval Chris-tianity divides, this inevitably means the appearance within the same society of a rival authoritative and salvationist religion . . . Luther and Calvin were as dogmatic and intolerant as the Roman Church had been."[5] The Catholic/Protestant rivalry yielded a series of bloody religious wars throughout Europe. The resulting "cruelties . . . had the effect of turning many Christians away from the public policies of the churches to a morality that saw toleration as an expression of Christian charity." Others "became skeptics who put cruelty and fanaticism at the very head of the human vices. In either case the indi-vidual, whether the bearer of a sacred conscience or the potential victim of cruelty, is to be protected against the incursions of public oppression."[6] Reli-gious toleration and freedom of conscience eventually emerged out of this milieu.

Beginning first with Thomas Hobbes in 1651 and taking on its liberal form with John Locke in 1688, social contract theorists broke with classical and Christian political philosophers who believed that government should strive to create the "good life" within society—to promote human excellence or to serve God's will. In the wake of moral pluralism and the conflict it generated, political philosophers began to argue that the government should not be in the business of imposing one particular vision of the good life on society but instead should ensure the right of individuals to pursue their own visions of the good life as they see fit.[7] Religious liberty and the separation of church and state developed as part of this new *modern political theory*.

In essence, social contract theory argues that *human beings create government to serve their purposes*. This tradition provides an alternative to the ideal of the Christian state that dominated during the medieval period. Rejecting the contention that government is instituted by God, headed by His anointed leader, and designed to implement His will on earth, social contract theory insists that governments are created through the consent of the governed and that political leaders are authorized by the people to govern in the interests of all citizens. Several versions of social contract theory exist, and John Locke articulated the version that forms the basis for the political theory of liberalism.

Legitimate Government and the Rule of Law

The principle of equality before the law constitutes one of the most fundamental principles of liberal political theory. When Thomas Jefferson and his colleagues declared, "We hold these truths to be self-evident, that all men are created equal," they were not denying that significant differences exist among people. Instead they were insisting that despite differences of wealth, talent, and religious belief, all citizens should be treated equally when they stand before the law. While significant numbers of people have always been treated unequally despite liberal ideals, the *principle* of equality has functioned as one of the bases for progressive change over time—from universal white male suffrage to abolition to feminism to the civil rights movement. And today we face a new struggle: legal equality for lesbians and gay men, including the right to civil marriage.

In making the revolutionary claim that all men are created equal, the American founders drew upon the work of John Locke, whose *Second Treatise of Government* provided philosophical justification for the Glorious Revolution in England in 1688 that established the right of the people to constitutional government. In Lockean social contract theory, human beings create government in order to protect "life, liberty, and estate," which he summarizes with the term "property."[8] It is important to note that while Locke emphasizes governmental protection of property, with this term he includes not only material property ("estate"), but also life, liberty, and the property each has "in his own *Person*."[9] Because human beings instituted government for the sole purpose of protecting "life, liberty, and estate," government cannot infringe on those goods without becoming illegitimate. And when government oversteps the bounds of legitimacy, the people have the right to petition for a redress of grievances and, as a last resort, to wage revolution. Thus, liberalism in its origins, as in its subsequent developments, presents a theory of *limited government* designed to protect the liberty of individuals from the infringement of both the government and other individuals.

In Locke's theory, the formation of the social contract occurs with the establishment of the rule of law, which is implemented to better protect the life, liberty, and estate of individuals. As a philosophical concept, the *rule of law* means that all are held accountable to the same impartial laws, rather than subject to the arbitrary rule of human beings; there must be one set of laws that apply to all people, no matter who they are. For Locke, the rule of law is so important that it actually marks the transition from the state of nature to civil society.[10] Once government is established, the Commonwealth comes to act as an "Umpire" that governs "by settled standing Rules, indifferent, and the same to all Parties."[11] In other words, the legislature is "to govern by *promulgated establish'd Laws*, not to be varied in particular Cases, but to have one Rule for Rich and Poor, for the Favourite at Court, and the Country Man at Plough."[12] All must be treated equally before the law. Consequently, even though the majority rules, the concept of legal equality prohibits the majority from imposing laws that discriminate against unpopular minority groups.

German philosopher Immanuel Kant further developed the concept of the rule of law in his writings at the end of the eighteenth century. If government should not seek to impose a particular vision of the good life on its citizens but rather should leave individuals free to pursue their own religious or moral worldviews, as modern political theory contends, then society must be governed in accordance with man-made laws rather than divine law because different religious denominations have very different ideas about what God has prohibited. For example, traditional (*halachic*) Judaism would prohibit the consumption of pork and shellfish, the Catholic Church would prohibit divorce, and some Protestant denominations would prohibit dancing. At its core, liberalism seeks to prevent destructive conflict over moral issues upon which people do not agree.

Kant provides the philosophical explanation for how human beings can determine universal moral laws that apply to all, without an appeal to scripture. Human beings can determine universal moral law through the use of reason, the capacity that differentiates human beings from other creatures.[13] That is, the capacity for "practical reason" makes it possible for men to construct universal moral laws in accordance with the *categorical imperative*, which states "act only on the maxim through which you can at the same time will that it should become a universal law," one that applies equally to all.[14] With this line of argument, Kant essentially secularizes the Golden Rule of Christianity—"Do unto others as you would have them do unto you"—a principle articulated in different words by most major religions. This means, for example, it is not moral to have one set of rules for others and another for yourself—such as, everyone else has to pay their taxes but I do not—or to create laws that only apply to some—such as, heterosexuals can engage in sodomy but homosexuals cannot.

Kant's emphasis on human-authored law further develops the liberal emphasis on *consent*, one of the foundational principles of democratic self-government. Just as Locke argued that legitimate government has the consent of the governed, Kant insists that a human being "is subject only to laws which are made by himself and yet are universal," defined as impartial and equally binding on all.[15] Universal laws are those every individual would consent to. Would gays and lesbians consent to laws designed precisely to discriminate against them?

Today, legal equality remains a fundamental principle of democracy that can be used for progressive change. In the nineteenth century, Abraham Lincoln recognized the radical principle of legal equality when he ridiculed the Supreme Court's proclamation in the *Dred Scott* case that the Founders "referred to the white race alone, and not to the African, when they declared all men to have been created equal."[16] Perhaps, Lincoln mockingly suggested, the Declaration should be rephrased as "We hold these truths to be self-evident that all British subjects who were on this continent eighty-one years ago, were created equal to all British subjects born and *then* residing in Great Britain."[17] Subsequently, during the civil rights movement, Martin Luther King, Jr., argued that "an unjust law is a code that a majority inflicts on a minority that is not binding on itself." A just law, in contrast, "is a code that a majority compels a minority to follow that it is willing to follow itself."[18] While it did not come easily, legal discrimination against African Americans was finally overturned during the 1960s through an appeal to the American *ideal* of legal equality. Today we face a new question: Shouldn't gay and lesbian couples be treated equally before the law when it comes to the right to marry?

Limited Government and the Protection of Civil Rights and Liberties

The American conception of civil rights and liberties grew directly out of the liberal tradition; both protect the sovereignty of the individual over his or her own life. Contemporary political scientists Theodore Lowi and Benjamin Ginsberg distinguish between "civil liberties" and "civil rights" as follows. Civil liberties are "*protections of citizens from improper government action*," while civil rights are "obligations imposed on government to take a *positive (or affirmative) action to protect citizens from the illegal actions of other private citizens and other government agencies*." In American constitutional law, issues of civil liberty generally "arise under the 'due process of law' clause" in the Fourteenth Amendment, which states that "No state shall make or enforce any law which shall abridge the privileges or immunities of citizens of the United States; nor shall any state deprive any person of life, liberty, or property, without due process of law," whereas civil rights issues arise from the "civil rights clause" of the same amendment, which states that "No State shall make or enforce any law which shall . . . deny to any person within its jurisdiction the equal protection of the laws."[19] Thus, for our purposes, the struggle for same-sex marriage is a civil rights issue because the government is being asked to protect the right of lesbian and gay citizens to marry whomever they choose, whereas the right to privacy is a civil liberties issue because it protects citizens from the interference of government in their most personal decisions. Both constitute important principles in the struggle of gays and lesbians for full equality.

Lockean liberalism had a profound influence on the development of civil rights and liberties in the United States: Individuals create government in order to protect the rights and liberties to which they are naturally entitled. In the *Second Treatise* Locke argues that individuals are naturally free and equal, that is to say, no one is born into a class or caste that is considered subordinate by nature. Consequently, all people should have the same basic rights and liberties and have them protected by the rule of law. In fact, that is the sole purpose of legitimate government. Although it took a while for the implications of this belief to be implemented in practice—and in some areas they still have yet to be fully realized—over time the liberal belief in human freedom and equality led to the overthrow of monarchy and aristocracy, the illegalization of slavery, the formal enfranchisement of women, and civil rights for African Americans and other minorities.

This emphasis on rights and liberties illustrates liberalism's fundamental respect for the *human dignity* of the individual. As the contemporary political philosopher Martha Nussbaum summarizes, what "distinguish[es] liberalism from other political traditions is its insistence on the separateness of one life from another, and the equal importance of each life, seen on its own terms rather than as part of a larger organic or corporate whole."[20] Kant provides an excellent example of this emphasis on human dignity. That is to say, for Kant "the dignity of man consists precisely in his capacity to make universal law, although only on condition of being himself also subject to the law he makes."[21] That is to say, "rational beings all stand under the *law* that each of them should treat himself and all others, *never merely as a means*, but always *at the same time as an end in himself.*"[22] The dignity of the individual human being cannot be violated even in order to advance the interests of the majority.

Drawing on liberal political theory, the American founders created a limited government that would protect rights and liberties. The Declaration of Independence proclaimed that individuals are "endowed by their Creator with certain unalienable rights, among these are Life, Liberty and the pursuit of Happiness" and "that to secure these rights, Governments are instituted among Men, deriving their just powers from the consent of the governed." In other words, as articulated in Locke's *Second Treatise*, our founding philosophy insists that the primary reason for the establishment of government in the first place is to protect the rights of equal individuals.

The First Amendment to the Constitution prevents the Congress from infringing on freedom of speech, freedom of press, freedom of assembly, or freedom of religion. It prohibits Congress from making any laws establishing religion, thus implementing a separation of church and state. The Fourth Amendment protects "the right of the People to be secure in their persons, houses, papers, and effects," a preliminary version of the right to privacy. While some critics of liberalism emphasize that the Bill of Rights at its inception actually protected states' rights rather than individual rights,[23] the fact is that many state constitutions also had bills of rights that protected individuals from the infringement of their rights and liberties by state governments. Of course, the details of these bills varied, as different communities applied liberal principles in different ways. As Jefferson explains, however, "a bill of rights is what the people are entitled to *against every government* on earth, general or particular, and what *no just government* should refuse, or rest on inferences"[24]—whether federal or state. In any event, after the addition of the Fourteenth Amendment to the Constitution in 1868, the Bill of Rights came to protect the rights and liberties of individuals from state as well as national government, although it took some time before individual rights became the "trumps" we know them as today—a process beginning in the 1890s and culminating in a series of Court decisions in the latter half of the twentieth century.[25]

John Stuart Mill further developed the philosophical defense of individual rights and liberties during the mid-nineteenth century. His work clearly articulates the basic liberal contention that people should be free to do and say whatever they want, as long as they are not harming others: "The sole end for which mankind are warranted, individually or collectively, in interfering with the liberty of action of any of their number, is self-protection. That the only purpose for which power can be rightfully exercised over any member of a civilized community, against his will, is to prevent harm to others."[26] This means that the majority may not legitimately use democratic government to take away the rights of a minority, even, Mill stresses, for "their own good." He explains further in this famous passage:

> His own good, whether physical or moral, is not a sufficient warrant. He cannot rightfully be compelled to do or forbear because it will be better for him to do so, because it will make him happier, because, in the opinions of others, to do so would be wise, or even right. These are good reasons for remonstrating with him, or reasoning with him, or persuading him, or entreating him, but not for compelling him, or visiting him with any evil in case he do otherwise. To justify that, the conduct from which it is desired to deter him, must be calculated to produce evil to someone else. The only part of the conduct of any one, for which he is amenable to society, is that which concerns others. In the part which merely concerns himself, his independence is, of right, absolute. Over himself, over his own body and mind, the individual is sovereign.[27]

What constitutes "harm" is open to interpretation, and the "harm principle" has been manipulated to justify coercive social policies. Nevertheless, the key point here is that the right of the individual to self-determination in matters concerning him or herself is absolutely fundamental to the political philosophy of liberalism that underlies American democracy.

The State of Fairness: Political Liberalism in a Pluralistic Society

Individual liberty constitutes the core of liberal political theory and its vision of legitimate government as that which maintains fair treatment for all. As the twentieth-century political theorist Judith Shklar summarizes: "Liberalism has only one overriding aim: to secure the political conditions that are necessary for the exercise of personal freedom. Every adult should be able to make as many effective decisions without fear or favor about as many aspects of her or his life as is compatible with like freedom of every other adult."[28] Liberalism does not seek to provide directives to people about how to live their personal lives, besides requiring behaviors like toleration, nonviolence, and social cooperation with others.

Originally designed to minimize conflict between religious sects, political liberalism remains an effective political philosophy for a truly pluralistic society because it protects the freedom of individual citizens to embrace a variety of religious, philosophical, and moral doctrines rather than attempting to impose one vision on everybody. Consequently, Jews, Christians, and Muslims remain free to live their own lives in accordance with their own particular understandings of divine will without interference from the government, as long as they do not harm others. At the same time, however, no group is permitted to impose its own particular moral worldview on other people in society. While the downside of this is that no religious group gets to live in a society where civil law accords exactly with its understanding of divine law—stores can remain open on the Sabbath and adulterers will not be stoned to death—the benefit is that no group can be forced to follow religious strictures that conflict with its own view—no one will be forced to attend Sunday church services or prohibited from getting remarried because the Catholic Church does not recognize divorce.

In advancing this vision of government, political liberalism distinguishes between the "comprehensive" religious, philosophical, and moral belief systems that individuals use to guide them as they make important decisions in their own lives and the political principles that protect the freedom of citizens to live as they choose as long as they do not harm others. The influential twentieth-century political philosopher John Rawls explains that a "comprehensive doctrine" or belief system "includes conceptions of what is of value in human life, and ideals of personal character, as well as ideals of friendship and of familial and associational relationships, and much else that is to inform our conduct, and in the limit to our life as a whole."[29] While comprehensive doctrines are often grounded in scripture or the teachings of religious leaders, some people derive their most fundamental beliefs from philosophy, cultural traditions, family customs, or even personal intuition. In a free society, people remain free to live in accordance with their own consciences, as long as they do not interfere with the same right of others. In short, as Shklar puts it, "liberalism refers to a political doctrine, not a philosophy of life such as has traditionally been provided by various forms of revealed religion and other comprehensive *Weltanschauungen*" (worldviews).[30]

Political liberalism recognizes that in a free society, people will inevitably hold different views when it comes to substantive moral issues, and sometimes these differing views will be incompatible. As Rawls explains, "a modern democracy is characterized not simply by pluralism of comprehensive religious, philosophical, and moral doctrines but by a pluralism of *incompatible yet reasonable* comprehensive doctrines."[31] For example, Christians believe that Jesus is the Messiah, but Jews and Muslims do not. These views are incompatible yet both are reasonable positions to hold. In a pluralistic society, people are going to disagree about such issues. "Political liberalism assumes that, for political purposes, a plurality of reasonable yet incompatible comprehensive doctrines is the normal result of the exercise of human reason within the framework of the free institutions of a constitutional democratic regime."[32] And it seeks to prevent the destructive conflict that sometimes results from such plurality by protecting the rights of all.

In making this argument, Rawls places himself firmly within the liberal tradition that underlies the American founding. That is to say, in Federalist Paper #10 James Madison recognizes the inevitability of moral and ideological disagreement and oppositional interests in a free society—what he calls "faction." Discussing possible solutions to that potential problem, Madison argues that there are two ways of preventing the emergence of faction: "the one, by destroying the liberty which is essential to its existence; the other, by giving to every citizen the same opinions, the same passions, and the same interests." He condemns both strategies: "It could never be more truly said than of the first remedy that it was worse than the disease. Liberty is to faction what air is to fire, an aliment without which it instantly expires. But it could not be a less folly to abolish liberty, which is essential to political life, because it nourishes faction than it would be to wish the annihilation of air, which is essential to animal life, because it imparts to fire its destructive agency."[33] Madison's famous solution to factious disagreement is the proliferation of factions, so that no one can gain the power to subordinate others.

Thus, while political liberalism protects moral pluralism within civil society, it strongly prohibits any particular group from using democratic institutions to impose its own "comprehensive doctrine" as law or public policy. Government must remain "neutral" in the sense "that the state is not to do anything intended to favor or promote any particular comprehensive doctrine rather than another, or to give greater assistance to those who pursue it."[34] This does not mean that the government must remain completely neutral toward all values. That would be impossible. As Rawls explains, it is acceptable for government to "encourage the cooperative virtues of political life," such as reasonableness, a sense of fairness, and willingness to compromise with others.[35] However, reasonable governmental efforts designed "to strengthen the forms of thought and feeling that sustain fair social cooperation between its citizens regarded as free and equal"—such as teaching tolerance or illegalizing discrimination—do not equate with becoming "a perfectionist state of the kind found in Plato or Aristotle" or establishing "a particular religion as in the Catholic or Protestant states of the early modern period."[36] What I am calling the *state of fairness* seeks only to establish and maintain a fair procedural framework within which free and equal individuals can pursue their own "comprehensive doctrines," whatever they may be.

Liberty, Privacy and the Case of *Lawrence v. Texas*

The right to privacy developed directly out of liberalism's basic commitment to civil liberties[37] and individual self-determination: people should be free to order their private lives as they see fit without interference from others, including the government. While the Constitution does not explicitly mention the "right to privacy," the concept exists implicitly in the political theory of liberalism that underlies the American constitution. Indeed, how could individual liberty meaningfully exist without such a right? The obvious connection between these two concepts within the liberal tradition led the Supreme Court to explicitly affirm the right to privacy in a series of cases, beginning with *Griswold v. Connecticut* (1963), which overturned a Connecticut law making "it a crime for any person to use any drug or article to prevent conception."[38]

In the *Griswold* case, the Court reasoned that a right to privacy exists as the logical extension of explicitly stated constitutional rights. Citing a number of previous decisions, the Court ruled that "the foregoing cases suggest that specific guarantees in the Bill of Rights have penumbras, formed by emanations from those guarantees that help give them life and substance." That is to say,

> various guarantees create zones of privacy. The right of association contained in the penumbra of the First Amendment is one, as we have seen. The Third Amendment in its prohibition against the quartering of soldiers "in any house" in time of peace without the consent of the owner is another facet of that privacy. The

Fourth Amendment explicitly affirms the "right of the people to be secure in their persons, houses, papers, and effects, against unreasonable searches and seizures." The Fifth Amendment in its Self-Incrimination Clause enables the citizen to create a zone of privacy which government may not force him to surrender to his detriment. The Ninth Amendment provides: "The enumeration in the Constitution, of certain rights, shall not be construed to deny or disparage others retained by the people."

It was in the *Griswold* case that the Court famously asked, "Would we allow the police to search the sacred precincts of marital bedrooms for telltale signs of the use of contraceptives? The very idea is repulsive to the notions of privacy surrounding the marriage relationship."[39] Thus, in the American constitutional tradition, *Griswold* gave the first explicit recognition to the right to privacy that is implicit in the liberal concept of civil liberties laid out in the Bill of Rights.

While *Griswold* protects the privacy rights of married people in particular, *Eisenstadt v. Baird* (1972) generalized the right to privacy of individuals, when it overturned a law prohibiting the distribution of contraceptives to single people. In addition, this case also illustrates the liberal vision of the state of fairness—that individuals should be free to live their lives as they choose—which the Court directly relates to the interconnected concepts of individual liberty and the right to privacy. That is to say, in *Eisenstadt* the Supreme Court ruled that "the protection of morals through the deterrence of fornication" was not a legitimate function of the law and that the limitation on contraception violates the "fundamental human rights" established in *Griswold*. "The goals of deterring premarital sex and regulating the distribution of potentially harmful articles cannot reasonably be regarded as legislative aims."[40] Clearly illustrating the blossoming of liberal political theory within American constitutional law, *Eisenstadt* ensures that "the right to privacy would now protect the freedom to engage in certain activities without governmental restriction."[41]

Subsequently, *Roe v. Wade* (1973) solidified the right to privacy. The Court ruled that "this right of privacy, whether it be founded in the Fourteenth Amendment's concept of personal liberty and restrictions upon state action, as we feel it is, or, as the District Court determined, in the Ninth Amendment's reservation of rights to the people, is broad enough to encompass a woman's decision whether or not to terminate her pregnancy." Only the woman herself can assess the impact of an unwanted or dangerous pregnancy on her and her family. "The detriment that the State would impose upon the pregnant woman by denying this choice altogether is apparent."[42] However, the Court also recognized certain restrictions on the personal right to privacy: "a State may properly assert important interests in safeguarding health, in maintaining medical standards, and in protecting potential life. At some point in pregnancy, these respective interests become sufficiently compelling to sustain regulation of the factors that govern the abortion decision. The privacy right involved, therefore, cannot be said to be absolute." Thus, "the right of personal privacy includes the abortion decision, but . . . this right is not unqualified, and must be considered against important state interests in regulation."[43]

In *Planned Parenthood of Southeastern Pa. v. Casey* (1992), the Supreme Court both reaffirms the right to privacy and clearly articulates the modern liberal ideas of liberty, human dignity, and moral autonomy with respect to private personal matters like marriage, family relationships, contraception, procreation, child rearing, and education.

> These matters, involving the most intimate and personal choices a person may make in a lifetime, choices central to personal dignity and autonomy, are central to the liberty protected by the Fourteenth Amendment. At the heart of liberty is the right to define one's own concept of existence, of meaning, of the universe, and of the mystery of human life. Beliefs about these matters could not define the attributes of personhood were they formed under compulsion of the State.[44]

The right to privacy reiterated in *Casey* derives directly from the liberal concept of civil liberties: "it is a promise of the Constitution that there is a realm of personal liberty which the government may not enter."[45] A totalitarian government seeks to control the private life and beliefs of its citizens; the government of a free society does not.

As the arguments in this series of Supreme Court decisions demonstrates, the Court did not simply invent the right to privacy, as many conservatives often assert. To the contrary, the philosophical underpinnings of privacy can be seen throughout the liberal tradition. For example, Locke argues that each person has the right "to dispose, and order, as he lists, his Person, Actions, Possessions, and his whole Property, within the Allowance of those Laws under which he is; and therein not to be subject to the arbitrary Will of another, but freely follow his own."[46] Since no one has "Arbitrary Power over the Life, Liberty, or Possession of another," people cannot cede such power to the commonwealth once it is formed. In other words, government exists to protect the liberty and equality of individuals, not to impinge upon them.[47] Indeed, individuals established the rule of law "not to abolish or restrain, but *to preserve and enlarge Freedom.*"[48]

Despite the obvious connection between privacy and liberty in the philosophy that underlies the U.S. Constitution, many conservatives (strict constructionists) insist that no right to privacy exists because the Constitution does not state it explicitly. For example, Robert Bork asserts that "radical individualism is the only explanation for the Supreme Court's creation, out of thin air, of a general and undefined right to privacy."[49] While many on the Right clearly support the principle of limited government, often they oppose its logical corollary, the right to privacy. Perhaps this opposition is political, rather than principled, because privacy has been the basis for both a woman's right to control her own body and the sexual liberation of individuals from traditional mores, trends vigorously opposed by social conservatives, as will be discussed more fully in subsequent chapters.

Conservative opponents of legal equality for lesbians and gay men often try to reframe the issue by claiming there is no "right to sodomy" in the Constitution. For example, Justice Scalia makes this argument in his dissent in *Lawrence v. Texas* (2003), which overruled a Texas law criminalizing homosexual (but not heterosexual) sodomy:

> Our opinions applying the doctrine known as "substantive due process" hold that the Due Process Clause prohibits States from infringing *fundamental* liberty interests, unless the infringement is narrowly tailored to serve a compelling state interest. . . . We have held repeatedly, in cases the Court today does not overrule, that *only* fundamental rights qualify for this so-called "heightened scrutiny" protection—that is, rights which are "'deeply rooted in this Nation's history and tradition.'" . . . *Bowers* concluded that a right to engage in homosexual sodomy was not "'deeply rooted in this Nation's history and tradition.'"[50]

Of course, the so-called right to engage in homosexual sodomy is not "deeply rooted in this Nation's history and tradition" or explicitly mentioned in the Constitution—nor is there an enumerated right to heterosexual intercourse, even within marriage. However, what is "deeply rooted" in American tradition, as in the liberal tradition as a whole, is liberty and the right of individuals to govern their own private lives in accordance with their own consciences without interference from the government.

Rejecting Scalia's argument, the majority opinion in *Lawrence v. Texas* recognizes the interconnection between liberty and privacy inherent in the liberal tradition:

The *Bowers* Court's initial substantive statement—"The issue presented is whether the Federal Constitution confers a fundamental right upon homosexuals to engage in sodomy . . ."—discloses the Court's failure to appreciate the extent of the liberty at stake. To say that the issue in *Bowers* was simply the right to engage in certain sexual conduct demeans the claim the individual put forward, just as it would demean a married couple were it said that marriage is just about the right to have sexual intercourse. Although the laws involved in *Bowers* and here purport to do not more than prohibit a particular sexual act, their penalties and purposes have more far-reaching consequences, touching upon the most private human conduct, sexual behavior, and in the most private of places, the home. They seek to control a personal relationship that, whether or not entitled to formal recognition in the law, is within the liberty of persons to choose without being punished as criminals. The liberty protected by the Constitution allows homosexual persons the right to choose to enter upon relationships in the confines of their homes and their own private lives and still retain their dignity as free persons.[51]

In addition, the Court explicitly rejects the fabricated claim advanced in *Bowers v. Hardwick* that the American legal tradition has long prohibited homosexuality:

There is no longstanding history in this country of laws directed at homosexual conduct as a distinct matter. Early American sodomy laws were not directed at homosexuals as such but instead sought to prohibit non-procreative sexual activity more generally, whether between men and women or men and men. Moreover, early sodomy laws seem not to have been enforced against consenting adults acting in private. . . . The longstanding criminal prohibition of homosexual sodomy upon which *Bowers* placed such reliance is as consistent with a general condemnation of nonprocreative sex as it is with an established tradition of prosecuting acts because of their homosexual character.

In fact, "it was not until the 1970s"—during a period of right-wing backlash against the gay rights movement, which began with the Stonewall uprising in 1969—"that any State singled out same-sex relations for criminal prosecution, and only nine States have done so."[52]

The Supreme Court in both its majority and concurring opinions recognizes the fundamental principle of legal equality. In her concurring opinion, Justice Sandra Day O'Connor makes the argument for overturning antihomosexual laws on the basis of legal equality:

The statute at issue here makes sodomy a crime only if a person "engages in deviate sexual intercourse with another individual of the same sex." . . . Sodomy between opposite-sex partners, however, is not a crime in Texas. That is, Texas treats the same conduct differently based solely on the participants. Those harmed by this law are people who have a same-sex sexual orientation and thus are more likely to engage in behavior prohibited by §21.06. The Texas statute makes homosexuals unequal in the eyes of the law by making particular conduct—and only that conduct—subject to criminal sanction.[53]

In short, she continues, "the State cannot single out one identifiable class of citizens for punishment that does not apply to everyone else, with moral disapproval as the only asserted state interest for the law."[54] American society no longer condemns nonprocreative sex between heterosexuals—and any outmoded laws that remain on the books will now probably be overturned because of *Lawrence v. Texas*—and the principle of legal equality precludes singling out gays and lesbians for special discrimination.

In its majority opinion, however, the Court does not overrule Texas antisodomy laws primarily on the basis of legal equality. That would leave open the possibility that laws prohibiting consensual sodomy for everybody would be permitted, and the Court apparently wants to be clear that what consenting adults do in private is nobody's business but their own. Thus, the *Lawrence v. Texas* case clearly articulates the idea of the state of fairness, theorized by Rawls and other liberal theorists. While the Court admits that "for centuries there have been powerful voices to condemn homosexual conduct as immoral," it insists that its "obligation is to define the liberty of all, not to mandate its own moral code."[55] The Court clearly condemns the illiberal decision in *Bowers v. Hardwick*, rejecting Chief Justice Burger's contention that "Condemnation of those [homosexual] practices is firmly rooted in Judeo-Christian moral and ethical standards."[56] While that may be true, a liberal state cannot legitimately make laws on the basis of such a "comprehensive" doctrine. Consequently, the Court ruled antihomosexual sodomy laws unconstitutional on the bases of equal liberty, legal equality, individual autonomy, human dignity, and the right to privacy—the logical application of the liberal philosophical principles upon which American democracy is founded.

Justice Scalia rejects modern liberal principles in his dissenting opinion: "Countless judicial decisions and legislative enactments have relied on the *ancient* proposition that a governing majority's belief that certain sexual behavior is 'immoral and unacceptable' constitutes a rational basis for regulation."[57] Note that the operative word here is "ancient." In the ancient, premodern world, the state did indeed impose a particular view of the good life on its citizens or subjects. However, the modern liberal state does not—or at least does not do so legitimately. Instead, it leaves individuals free to live their own lives in accordance with their own moral belief systems. Scalia is correct in his lament that the decision in *Lawrence v. Texas* "effectively decrees the end of all morals legislation"[58] because laws based on particular comprehensive moral doctrines are illegitimate in a liberal democracy.

Just as the liberal state cannot legitimately interfere with the liberty of consenting adults to make their own decisions about intimate matters, it cannot legitimately violate the principle of legal equality by denying gay and lesbian citizens the right to civil marriage. Scalia sees the connection and insists that O'Connor's contention that the Texas law is invalid because it advances no legitimate state interest but is simply designed to express moral disapproval of homosexuality "leaves on pretty shaky grounds state laws limiting marriage to opposite-sex couples. JUSTICE O'CONNOR seeks to preserve them by the conclusory statement that 'preserving the traditional institution of marriage' is a legitimate state interest. . . . But 'preserving the traditional institution of marriage' is just a kinder way of describing the State's *moral disapproval* of same-sex couples."[59] And here Scalia is absolutely correct: The liberal state cannot legitimately deny gays and lesbians the right to civil marriage on the basis of moral disapproval.

Marriage: A Civil and Human Right

Marriage has long been recognized as a "fundamental right" in the United States, and consequently this makes the struggle for gay marriage a civil rights issue. As Evan Gerstmann explains, "the Court has long held that the Constitution protects numerous 'fundamental rights' that are not explicitly mentioned therein; sometimes they are called 'unenumerated' rights. These rights have been elevated to a par with those rights enumerated in the Bill of Rights, including freedom of speech, assembly, and religion."[60] Fundamental rights, "deemed vital to a legally equal society," cannot legitimately be denied.[61]

Marriage was established as a fundamental right in the United States through a long series of Supreme Court cases. The concept of "fundamental rights" did not develop until the end of the nineteenth century. Before that time, marriage was considered a common-law right, rather than a constitutional right.[62] The Court first established a constitutional right to marry in *Meyer v. Nebraska* (1923). There the Court argued that liberty "without doubt" includes "not merely freedom from bodily restraint but also the right of the individual to contract, to engage in any of the common occupations of life, to acquire useful knowledge, *to marry*, establish a home and bring up children, to worship God according to the dictates of his own conscience, and generally to enjoy those privileges long recognized as common law as essential to the orderly pursuit of happiness by free men."[63] Then, in *Skinner v. Oklahoma* (1942), the Court called marriage "one of the basic civil rights of man."[64] Remarkably, neither the *Meyer* nor the *Skinner* case dealt directly with marriage. Thus, Gerstmann comments, "the justices went out of their way to assert that marriage is one of the fundamental rights of humankind."[65] Or perhaps they were simply stating a belief that was generally accepted within American culture at that time.

The idea of marriage as a fundamental right received additional support in a series of cases that actually dealt with marriage laws. Most famously, in *Loving v. Virginia* (1967), the case that overturned a Virginia ban on interracial marriage, the Court reiterated that "the freedom to marry has long been recognized as one of the vital personal rights essential to the orderly pursuit of happiness . . . one of the 'basic civil rights of man' . . . and cannot be infringed by the State."[66] This understanding was reaffirmed in *Zabloki v. Redhail* (1978): "The leading decision of this Court on the right to marry is *Loving v. Virginia* (1967). . . . Although *Loving* arose in the context of racial discrimination, prior and subsequent decisions of this Court confirm that the right to marry is of fundamental importance for all individuals."[67] Finally, the fundamental right to marry was definitively established in *Turner v. Safley* (1987), which established the right of prisoners to marry. "If the Court had any doubt at all about whether the right to marry is a fundamental constitutional right, *Turner* presented it with abundant opportunity to express that doubt. Yet neither the Court nor the government expressed such doubt." Consequently, "after Turner it will be of little value to try to contest that 'the decision to marry is a fundamental right.'"[68] Consequently, Gerstmann concludes, "*the Constitution guarantees every person the right to marry the person of his or her choice*" (as long as they are adults, of course)—even gay men and lesbians.[69]

Furthermore, marriage is considered a universal human right as well. That is to say, the "Universal Declaration of Human Rights" issued by the United Nations over fifty years ago recognizes the right to marry as fundamental to individual liberty and human dignity: "Men and women of full age, without any limitation due to race, nationality or religion, have the right to marry and to found a family. They are entitled to equal rights as to marriage, during marriage and at its dissolution" (Article 16).[70] The document as a whole articulates the basic tenets of liberalism that underlie the concept of individual rights, both civil and human. For example, Article 1 states that "all human beings are born free and equal in dignity and rights. They are endowed with reason and conscience and should act towards one another in a spirit of brotherhood." Article 7 emphasizes legal equality: "All are equal before the law and are entitled without any discrimination to equal protection of the law. All are entitled to equal protection against any discrimination in violation of this Declaration and against any incitement to such discrimination." Article 12 articulates a right to privacy: "No one shall be subjected to arbitrary interference with his privacy, family, home or correspondence, nor to attacks upon his honour and reputation. Everyone has the right to the protection of the law against such interference or attacks."

The LGBT Civil Rights Movement and the Importance of the Courts

While most people may not be fluent in the history of political thought, they would very likely recognize the discussion of liberalism offered here as the articulation of the fundamental principles that underlie American democracy and culture. All of the principles of liberal political theory not only justify but also require the legal recognition of gay marriage—legal equality, individual rights and liberties (including freedom of conscience, the right to privacy, and the right to marry), personal autonomy, human dignity, and the modern state of fairness. This is not to say that all people value philosophical consistency. There are times when people allow personal religious beliefs, political expediency, material interests, or customary prejudices to interfere with the logical extension of liberal principles within the political realm. For example, the Founders knew that slavery stood in direct contradiction to the revolutionary doctrine of the "rights of man," yet because of political expediency, economic interests, and racial prejudice, they allowed the institution to continue.

The civil rights movement of African Americans in the 1950s and 1960s exemplifies the ways in which the egalitarian ideals of liberalism can be utilized to eliminate illiberal practices. Although African Americans had been organizing for years, the Supreme Court decision in *Brown v. Board of Education* (1954) galvanized the movement for legal equality, overturning the concept of "separate but equal" and revealing as illegitimate the existence of two different sets of laws, one for whites and one for blacks.[71]

By 1965, public opinion largely supported the African American civil rights struggle. In the wake of the passage of the Civil Rights Act of 1964, a spring 1965 Gallup poll "showed that 52 percent of Americans identified civil rights as the 'most important problem' confronting the nation, and an astonishing 75 percent of respondents favored federal voting rights legislation.'"[72] When President Johnson signed the Voting Rights Act of 1965 into law, the prospect of full equality for African Americans looked bright.[73]

Yet progress does not usually unfold in a straightforward path. Despite the compelling logic of philosophical liberalism, the American Right actively opposed the civil rights movement. The white supremacist contingent of the Old Right had long fought against racial equality, using intimidation and violence to oppress black people and espousing an explicitly racist ideology. With the general public increasingly uncomfortable with explicit racism, however, right-wing leaders decided to develop a more marketable message, "mainstreaming the ideological positions of the Old Right and developing winnable policies" that "highlighted a protest theme" against a wide range of cultural changes inaugurated by the new social movements of the 1960s.[74] So, for example, political rhetoric would incite fear of ghetto riots and crime, rather than explicitly espouse black inferiority.

Fifty years later, despite this ideological contestation of the 1960s, most Americans, even the most conservative, look back upon the civil rights movement as one of the great success stories of American democracy precisely because it appealed to the fundamental principles upon which America was founded: legal equality, individual rights, and human dignity. White supremacists still exist, of course, but at this point they are arguably marginal to American politics—although some, like Timothy McVeigh, who was executed for the Oklahoma City terrorist attack, may still pose a danger. Indeed, there is no guarantee that the "logic of liberalism" will continue to move forward or that its gains will remain in place once accomplished. As University of Pennsylvania political theorist Rogers Smith argues, the progress of liberalizing forces is generally "serpentine" rather than steady.[75]

In 2005, at the time of this writing, American society stands in the midst of the LGBT civil rights movement. Principled court decisions have made the legalization of gay marriage possible for the first time in American history, and this has galvanized activists on both sides of the issue.[76] While American public opinion remains divided, the courts have repeatedly ruled in favor of legal equality. As expected, these decisions have created a backlash from conservatives opposed to gay marriage, resulting in legislative efforts to prevent or reverse the extension of legal equality to lesbians and gay men.

The Hawaiian Supreme Court put gay marriage on the national radar during the 1990s. In 1993, the court ruled in *Baehr v. Lewin* that denying same-sex couples access to marriage constitutes sex discrimination, which the equal rights amendment to the state's constitution renders suspect.[77] The fact that a male can marry a female but a female cannot marry a female violates the principle of gender equality. This ruling was the first in the nation to question the exclusion of lesbians and gay men from civil marriage. The court did not immediately order the legalization of same-sex marriage, however, but instead returned the case to the lower court to determine whether a compelling state interest exists to justify continued sex discrimination. On December 16, 1996, the lower court found no compelling reason to justify discrimination. Conservatives objected, of course, and a compromise was reached in the legislature. "Under the compromise, the legislature placed on the November 1998 ballot a proposal to amend the state constitution 'to clarify that the legislature has the power to reserve marriage to opposite-sex couples,' and to enact a new statute extending 'certain rights and benefits . . . to couples composed of two individuals who are legally prohibited from marrying under state law (same-sex couples and blood relatives).' "[78] In the end, the *Baehr* decision was voided but many rights were granted to same-sex couples under the Reciprocal Beneficiaries Act.

The next major court decision came on December 20, 1999, when the Vermont Supreme Court ruled, in *Baker v. State*, that because the state constitution is committed to the principles of inclusion and social equality, same-sex couples may not be excluded from access to civil marriage and denied its benefits.[79] The marriage exclusion constitutes unconstitutional discrimination. That said, however, the court allowed the possibility that the legislature could create an alternative way to accord same-sex couples the benefits of civil marriage. Vermont Governor Howard Dean "immediately proposed creating a new domestic partnership institution for same-sex couples, with all the same benefits and duties of marriage but without the traditional name."[80] After a lot of political wrangling, the governor signed the Civil Unions law on April 26, 2000.

Finally, in 2003, the state of Massachusetts became the first (and so far only) state in the union to legalize same-sex marriage. In *Goodridge et al. v. Dept. of Public Health* the Massachusetts Supreme Court reasoned as follows:

> Marriage is a vital social institution. The exclusive commitment of two individuals to each other nurtures love and mutual support; it brings stability to our society. For those who choose to marry, and for their children, marriage provides an abun-

dance of legal, financial, and social benefits. In return it imposes weighty legal, financial, and social obligations. The question before us is whether, consistent with the Massachusetts Constitution, the Commonwealth may deny the protections, benefits, and obligations conferred by civil marriage to two individuals of the same sex who wish to marry. We conclude that it may not. The Massachusetts Constitution affirms the dignity and equality of all individuals. It forbids the creation of second-class citizens. In reaching our conclusion we have given full deference to the arguments made by the Commonwealth. But it has failed to identify any constitutionally adequate reason for denying civil marriage to same-sex couples.[81]

The court notes that Americans remain divided over the issue of same-sex marriage, and that there are "strong religious, moral, and ethical convictions" on both sides of the issue. "Neither view," however, "answers the question before us. Our concern is with the Massachusetts Constitution as a charter of governance for every person properly within its reach." Quoting *Lawrence*, they conclude, "Our obligation is to define the liberty of all, not to mandate our own moral code." Consequently, they find that the exclusion of same-sex couples from civil marriage to be "incompatible with the constitutional principles of respect for individual autonomy and equality under law." On May 17, 2004, more than 1,000 lesbian and gay couples were legally married in the state of Massachusetts. Same-sex marriage will remain legal there until at least 2006 because that is the earliest time that conservatives could get an antimarriage amendment on the state ballot.

In the face of these principled court rulings, conservatives have mobilized against legal equality. In reaction to the Hawaii decision, Congress passed the Defense of Marriage Act (DOMA) in 1996, which says that if a state legalizes gay marriage, other states do not have to recognize it and that such marriages will not accrue any federal benefits. This law may be found to violate the U.S. Constitution, which states, "Full faith and credit shall be given in each state to the public acts, records, and judicial proceedings of every other state" (Article IV, section 1). That is one reason why conservatives want to pass the Federal Marriage Amendment (discussed in the next chapter). Thirty-eight states have passed DOMA legislation, but these acts may be found unconstitutional by state Supreme Courts. That is why many states are amending their constitutions to prohibit same-sex marriage; eleven states passed such amendments in the November 2004 election.

Nevertheless, at the time of this writing, lower court judges in Washington, California, and New York have ruled that prohibitions against gay marriage are unconstitutional violations of legal equality. In all three cases, the judges' decisions have been stayed until the cases can be reviewed by their states' supreme courts. Because prohibitions against same-sex marriage so obviously violate the fundamental democratic principle of legal equality, it is expected that it will be legalized in all three states.

While many conservatives attribute these court decisions to "activist judges," we can see from the political theoretical material covered in this chapter that the courts are simply applying fundamental American political principles in a consistent way. Even though a majority of Americans may not approve of same-sex marriage, that is not a legitimate reason to continue infringing on lesbian/gay civil rights. The entire purpose of civil rights is that everyone gets them even if the majority does *not* approve, particularly when they don't approve. Public opinion did not support the decision of the Supreme Court that legalized interracial marriage in 1967. A 1958 Gallup poll showed that only 4 percent of the public favored interracial marriage.[82] Even in 1965, "at the crest of the civil-rights revolution, a Gallup poll found that 72 per cent of Southern whites and 42 per cent of Northern whites still wanted to ban interracial marriage."[83] Today, however, 90 percent oppose "laws against marriages between blacks and whites."[84] It is the job of the U.S. Supreme Court to rule on principle, and sometimes court rulings contribute to changes in public opinion over time.

Conclusion

Same-sex marriage is an idea whose time has come. The philosophical principles of liberalism not only allow but also *require* the legalization of same-sex marriage. In a liberal democracy the law must treat all individuals equally, regardless of race, gender, or sexual orientation. The state must protect the civil rights of all, including the right to marry, and refrain from interfering with an individual's personal liberty or invading that individual's privacy. The government may not legitimately pass laws that impose a particular moral doctrine on individuals without their consent but instead must leave people free to pursue their own visions of the good life without interference. So while President George W. Bush may sincerely believe that heterosexual-only marriage is a "sacred covenant,"[85] and Senate Majority Leader Bill Frist may personally consider it "a sacrament,"[86] they are not free to use their governmental authority to put their own comprehensive religious doctrines into civil law or amend the U.S. Constitution to impose their personal beliefs on America's morally pluralistic society. Similarly, ordinary citizens who disapprove of homosexuality are also entitled to their opinions; however, they do not have the right to interfere with the liberty of others. Legal discrimination against an unpopular minority is simply unacceptable.

Notes

1. Michael J. Sandel, *Democracy's Discontent: America in Search of a Public Philosophy* (Cambridge, MA: Belknap Press of Harvard University Press, 1996), 4–5.

2. Rogers Smith, "Beyond Tocqueville, Myrdal, and Hartz: The Multiple Traditions in America," *American Political Science Review* 87, no. 3 (September 1993): 549–66, 550.

3. Sandel, *Democracy's Discontent*, 3–24.

4. Sandel, *Democracy's Discontent*.

5. John Rawls, *Political Liberalism* (New York: Columbia University Press, 1996), xxv.

6. Judith H. Shklar, "Liberalism of Fear," in *Political Thought & Political Thinkers*, ed. Stanley Hoffmann (Chicago: University of Chicago Press, 1998), 5.

7. John Rawls, *Political Liberalism*, xxvi; Michael Sandel, *Democracy's Discontent*, 7; and Peter Berkowitz, *Virtue and the Making of Modern Liberalism* (Princeton, NJ: Princeton University Press, 1999), 4.

8. John Locke, *Second Treatise of Government*, in *Two Treatises of Government*, ed. Peter Laslett (Cambridge: Cambridge University Press, 1998), 323.

9. Locke, *Second Treatise*, 287.

10. Locke, *Second Treatise*, 324.

11. Locke, *Second Treatise*, 324.

12. Locke, *Second Treatise*, 363.

13. Immanuel Kant, *Groundwork of the Metaphysic of Morals*, trans. H. J. Paton (New York: Harper & Row, Publishers, 1956), 119.

14. Kant, *Metaphysic of Morals*, 88.

15. Kant, *Metaphysic of Morals*, 100.

16. Abraham Lincoln, "Speech on the Dred Scott Decision (1857)," in *American Political Thought*, ed. Kenneth M. Dolbeare (Chatham, NJ: Chatham House Publishers, Inc., 1998), 223.

17. Lincoln, "Dred Scott," 224.

18. Martin Luther King, Jr., "Letter from the Birmingham City Jail (16 April 1963)," in *American Political Thought*, 485.

19. Theodore Lowi and Benjamin Ginsberg, *American Government: Freedom and Power*, 2nd ed. (New York: W. W. Norton & Company, 1992), 110–11.

20. Martha Nussbaum, *Sex and Social Justice* (New York & Oxford: Oxford University Press, 1999), 10.

21. Kant, *Metaphysic of Morals*, 107.

22. Kant, *Metaphysic of Morals*, 101.

23. Sandel, *Democracy's Discontent*, 35.

24. Jefferson to Madison, December 20, 1787, in *Jefferson Writings*, ed. Morrill D.

Peterson (New York: Library of America, 1984), 916, emphasis mine. Sandel includes this quote in his discussion but disregards it in making his argument. See *Democracy's Discontent*, 35.

25. See Evan Gerstmann, *Same-Sex Marriage and the Constitution* (Cambridge: Cambridge University Press, 2004), 74, and Sandel, *Democracy's Discontent*.

26. Mill, *On Liberty and Other Essays* (Oxford: Oxford University Press, 1998), 13–14.

27. Mill, *On Liberty*, 13–14.

28. Shklar, "Liberalism of Fear," 3–4.

29. Rawls, *Political Liberalism*, 13.

30. Shklar, "Liberalism of Fear," 3.

31. Rawls, *Political Liberalism*, xviii, emphasis mine. Rawls is careful to note that by "reasonable" he means only those doctrines that accept the validity of democratic constitutionalism. Thus he deliberately excludes doctrines that are "unreasonable," "irrational," or "even mad," such as those of the "Unibomber" or Osama bin Laden.

32. Rawls, *Political Liberalism*, xviii.

33. James Madison, "Federalist #10," in *The Federalist Papers*, ed. Clinton Rossiter (New York: NAL Penguin Inc., 1961), 78.

34. Rawls, *Political Liberalism*, 193.

35. Rawls, *Political Liberalism*, 163.

36. Rawls, *Political Liberalism*, 195.

37. Lowi and Ginsberg, *American Government*, 124.

38. *Griswold v. Connecticut*, 381 U.S. 479 (1965), 1.

39. *Griswold v. Connecticut*, 381 U.S. 479 (1965), 1.

40. *Eisenstadt v. Baird*, 405 U.S. 438 (1972), 1.

41. Sandel, *Democracy's Discontent*, 97.

42. *Roe v. Wade*, 410 U.S. 113 (1973), 153.

43. *Roe v. Wade*, 410 U.S. 113 (1973), 154.

44. *Planned Parenthood of Southeastern Pa. v. Casey*, 505 U.S. 833 (1992). Quotes from *Lawrence v. Texas*.

45. *Planned Parenthood of Southeastern Pa. v. Casey*, 505 U.S. 833 (1992).

46. Locke, *Second Treatise*, 306.

47. Locke, *Second Treatise*, 357.

48. Locke, *Second Treatise*, 306.

49. Robert H. Bork, *Slouching Towards Gomorrah: Modern Liberalism and American Decline* (New York: Regan Books, 1996), 103.

50. *Lawrence*, Scalia, A., dissenting opinion, 8–10.

51. *Lawrence et al. v. Texas*, 539 U.S. 558 (2003), Syllabus, 1–2.

52. *Lawrence et al. v. Texas*, 539 U.S. 558 (2003), 9.

53. *Lawrence*, O'Connor, S., concurring opinion, 3.

54. O'Connor, S., concurring opinion, 6.

55. *Lawrence et al. v. Texas*, 539 U.S. 558 (2003), Syllabus, 2.

56. *Lawrence et al. v. Texas*, 539 U.S. 558 (2003), 11.

57. Scalia, Dissenting opinion, 5, emphasis mine.

58. Scalia, Dissenting opinion, 15.

59. Scalia, Dissenting opinion, 17.

60. Gerstmann, *Same-Sex Marriage*, 69.

61. Gerstmann, *Same-Sex Marriage*, 7.

62. Gerstmann, *Same-Sex Marriage*, 73–74.

63. *Meyer v. State of Nebraska*, 262 U.S. 390 (1923), 1, emphasis mine.

64. *Skinner v. Oklahoma*, 316 U.S. 535 (1942), 541.

65. Gerstmann, *Same-Sex Marriage*, 67.

66. See *Loving v. Virginia*, 388 U.S. 1 (1967).

67. See *Zabloki v. Redhail*, 434 U.S. 374 (1978).

68. Gerstmann, *Same-Sex Marriage*, 83.

69. Gerstmann, *Same-Sex Marriage*, 67.

70. United Nations, "Universal Declaration of Human Rights," www.udhr50.org/UDHR/default.htm (accessed 10 Sept. 2003).

71. *Brown v. Board of Education*, 347 U.S. 483 (1954).

72. Maurice Isserman and Michael Kazin, *America Divided: The Civil War of the 1960s* (Oxford: Oxford University Press, 2000), 138.

73. Isserman and Kazin, *America Divided*, 139.

74. Jean Hardisty, *Mobilizing Resentment: Conservative Resurgence from the John Birch Society to the Promise Keepers* (Boston: Beacon Press, 1999), 38.

75. Smith, "Beyond Tocqueville," 559.

76. See Urvashi Vaid, *Virtual Equality: The Mainstreaming of Gay and Lesbian Liberation* (New York: Anchor Books, 1995).

77. *Baehr v. Lewin*, 852 P.2d 44 (Haw. 1993). For a discussion of the reasoning, see William N. Eskridge, Jr., *Equality Practice: Civil Unions and the Future of Gay Rights* (New York: Routledge, 2002), 18–22.

78. Eskridge, *Equality Practice*.

79. *Baker v. State*, 744 A.2d 864 (Vt. 1999).

80. Eskridge, *Equality Practice*, 56. For a detailed account, see chapter 2.

81. *Goodridge et al. v. Dept. of Public Health* (Ma. 2003), 1.

82. Carolyn Lochhead, "Pivotal day for gay marriage in U.S. nears Massachusetts move to legalize weddings may intensify backlash in other States," *San Francisco Chronicle*, May 2, 2004, www.sfgate.com/cgi-bin/article.cgi?file = /chronicle/archive/2004/05/02/MNGM26EHU81.DTL [accessed 3 May 2004].

83. Steve Sailer, "Is love colorblind?—public opinion about interracial marriage," *National Review*, July 14, 1997, www.findarticles.com/p/articles/mi_m1282/is_n13_v49/ai_19617224 [accessed 1 April 2005].

84. Public Agenda website, www.publicagenda.org/issues/angles_graph.cfm?issue_type = race&id = 203&graph = majpropracedating.jpg [accessed 1 April 2005].

85. Sheryl Gay Stolberg, "Vocal Gay Republicans Upsetting Conservatives," *New York Times*, June 1, 2003.

86. "Frist Backs Constitutional Ban on Gay Marriage," *USA Today*, June 29, 2003, www.usatoday.com/news/washington/2003–06–29-frist-gay-marriage_x.htm [accessed 13 September 2003].

CHAPTER FOUR

~

A False Consensus:
Christian Right Politics and the
Attack on Same-Sex Marriage

For centuries there have been powerful voices to condemn homosexual conduct as immoral, but this Court's obligation is to define the liberty of all,
not to mandate its own moral code.

—Supreme Court, *Lawrence v. Texas* (2003)

Marriage in the United States shall consist only of the union of a man and
a woman. Neither this Constitution, nor the constitution of any State, shall
be construed to require that marriage or the legal incidents thereof be conferred upon any union other than the union of a man and a woman.

—Proposed "Federal Marriage Amendment" to the U.S. Constitution
(2004)

The American Constitution created a secular government that acts to protect the civil rights and liberties of individuals rather than impose a particular vision of the "good life" on its citizens. Freedom of conscience and the
separation of church and state are central to the political philosophy of liberalism. These principles, enshrined in our founding documents, have become
almost universally accepted norms in U.S. society today.[1] Nevertheless, conservative religious organizations are currently mobilizing their supporters
across the country to undermine these basic principles, appealing to popular
prejudice against an unpopular minority.[2] Because of their personal religious
beliefs, they seek to deny lesbians and gay men legal equality and the right

to civil marriage. While conservative Americans are free to practice their religious beliefs and live their personal lives however they choose, neither federal nor state government in the United States can legitimately generate public policy supporting a particular religious worldview. Nor can it let the beliefs of some—even a majority—violate the civil rights of other individuals in society or deny equality before the law to certain groups of citizens.

Is America a "Christian Nation"?

Despite the First Amendment's prohibition against the establishment of religion by government, the Christian Right and its supporters have recently come to insist that America is really a "Christian nation." Christian Right organizations often assert that this country was founded on Christianity and that democracy itself grows out of the Christian religion. For example, the Family Research Council (FRC) proclaims that "The American system of law and justice was founded on the Judeo-Christian ethic."[3] Because it shares this belief, Concerned Women for America (CWA) seeks "to protect and promote Biblical values among all citizens—first through prayer, then education, and finally by influencing our society—thereby reversing the decline in moral values in our nation."[4] Apparently, the Republican Party accepts this claim. Its 2004 platform reads, "Our country was founded in faith and upon the truth that self-government is rooted in religious conviction."[5]

Another leading Christian Right group, Focus on the Family (FOF), less explicitly espouses a religious vision for American government. Yet its mission statement clearly articulates the specifically Protestant theological vision discussed in chapter 2:

> **We believe** that God has ordained three basic institutions—the church, the family and the government—for the benefit of all humankind. The family exists to propagate the race and to provide a safe and secure haven in which to nurture, teach and love the younger generation. The church exists to minister to individuals and families by sharing the love of God and the message of repentance and salvation through the blood of Jesus Christ. The government exists to maintain cultural equilibrium and to provide a framework for social order.[6]

While this articulation says nothing about mixing church and state, FOF actively works to influence public policy. For example, because one of its "five guiding principles" states, "we believe that the institution of marriage was intended by God to be a permanent, lifelong relationship between a man and a woman," they have taken an active role in lobbying for the passage of the Federal Marriage Amendment and other antigay policies, as have FRC and CWA, among others.

Some conservatives insist that the Judeo-Christian Ten Commandments provide the foundation for American law. For example, Alabama judge Roy Moore, briefly famous for placing a 5,280-pound granite monument of the Ten Commandments in the state courthouse, denies that his action violated the constitutional separation of church and state. "'It is required that this nation acknowledge God's law as its foundation, because both the Constitution and Bill of Rights enshrine those principles,' he says." When the Alabama Supreme Court ruled Moore's action a violation of the "establishment clause" in the First Amendment, it outraged many Christian conservatives.[7]

In reality, however, the Constitution (which includes the Bill of Rights) does not enshrine the Ten Commandments. While criminal laws against murder and theft do correspond to two of the commandments (Deut. 5:17), neither crime is mentioned in the Constitution. Besides, many non-Christian societies prohibit these crimes as well. Furthermore, if we actually examine the Ten Commandments, it is clear that American law does not codify most of the Decalogue—for example, "You shall have no other gods beside Me" and "You shall not make for yourself a sculptured image, any likeness of what is in the heavens above, or on the earth below, or in the waters below the earth. You shall not bow down to them or serve them" (Deut. 5:7–9). With the exception of perjury and other official proceedings, you incur no penalty if you "swear falsely by the name of the Lord your God" (Deut. 5:11) in your everyday life or if you "bear false witness against your neighbor" (Deut. 5:17) via gossip, unless such libel causes demonstrable economic harm. State laws no longer force people to "observe the sabbath day and keep it holy" (Deut. 5:13), tell them to "honor your father and your mother" (Deut. 5:16), or criminalize adultery (Deut. 5:17). Finally, how could a law ever prevent a person from coveting what belongs to his neighbor? Doesn't the success of consumer capitalism depend on the violation of that commandment?

The Judeo-Christian Ten Commandments do not form the foundation for the American legal system. In fact, the First Amendment to the Constitution mandates the separation of church and state: "The Congress shall make no law respecting an establishment of religion, or prohibiting the free exercise thereof." In other words, the government can neither help advance the beliefs of one particular religion nor interfere with the way its citizens practice their various religions. At its inception this separation was considered good for both government and religion. While conservatives are certainly correct in pointing out that originally the Bill of Rights protected states' rights—the right of communities to be free from congressional interference—rather than individual rights as we know them today, leaving the states free to establish religion, in fact only five states actually permitted the establishment of religion.[8] And with the passage of the Fourteenth Amendment in 1868, the First Amendment prohibition applies to the states as well.

Nevertheless, some conservatives still insist "there is no such thing as 'separation of church and state' in America's history."[9] How can they make such a claim? CWA supporter Orin Simmerman argues the point by citing the fact that the early colonists who came to this continent seeking religious freedom were driven by their Christian beliefs. Yet while it might be said, in this sense, that "Biblical principals [sic] gave the ideas that sparked the building of this nation," it is misleading to conclude from this that "the roots of our country are in the Bible."[10] While liberty and equality may arguably be biblical values, they also derive from the Greco-Roman (pagan) tradition that preexisted Christianity. Moreover, while many colonists sought religious freedom, which is why the Founders mandated the separation of church and state, the system of government they established—three branches of government, checks and balances, civil liberties, and elected government—does not derive from the Bible. What biblical passages could support such a claim?

In opposition to what many Christian conservatives repeatedly assert, American democracy did not grow out of Christianity but rather developed as a combination of two political traditions, liberalism and civic republicanism, both of which provide alternatives to a Christian polity. As explained in chapter 3, the liberal tradition emerged to offer a solution to religious war, by presenting a theory of government based on individual liberty and consent that separated church and state, rather than on a religious worldview.

Civic republicanism, the other important political tradition in the early years of the American republic, actually developed in direct opposition to Christianity, inspired by the pre-Christian Roman Republic. You can see this clearly when you read the major republican political theorists.[11] For example, Nicolo Machiavelli favored a rigorous and militarily strong republic and blamed Christianity for making men weak.[12] Jean-Jacques Rousseau goes so far as to label the term "Christian republic" an oxymoron: "These two words are mutually exclusive. Christianity preaches nothing but servitude and dependence. Its spirit is so favorable to tyranny that tyranny always profits from it. True Christians are made to be slaves. They know it and are scarcely moved thereby; this brief life is of too little worth in their view."[13] Thomas

Jefferson's advocacy of secular government and religious freedom is well known,[14] and Thomas Paine's book *Age of Reason* was commonly considered "as full-throated an attack on Christianity as *Common Sense* had been on monarchy."[15] While Protestant Christianity constitutes an important influence on American politics, it did not form the foundation of American democracy.

Finally, Christian conservatives argue that the American Founders believed that democratic political institutions would only work if grounded on religious mores within civil society, emphasizing a comment made by John Adams: "Our Constitution was made only for a moral and religious people. It is wholly inadequate to the government of any other."[16] The Christian Right hopes that once the religious beliefs of the American Founders are established, a theory of constitutional interpretation that privileges "original intent" will authorize the imposition of Christian moral precepts on American society at large.[17] William Bennett supports this project of revisionist historiography with his book *Our Sacred Honor: Words of Advice from the Founders*, which catalogues stories, letters, poems, and speeches that emphasize the religious beliefs that animated many in the founding generation (among other things).[18]

Despite the simplicity of this argument, the relationship between religion and democracy in the American context is a complicated one. Many scholars have demonstrated that Protestant Christianity fed into the emergence of democracy in a number of ways.[19] In the first place, Christianity in general and Protestantism in particular emphasize the idea of equality before God. While this idea has coexisted with all kinds of political inequality, nonetheless the concept of spiritual equality does not in any way contradict the ideal of political equality. Although the concept of civic equality first developed in non-Christian Greece and Rome, the Protestants revived this value via Luther's "priesthood of all believers," although Luther himself did not favor democracy. In the American context, however, spiritual equality dovetailed with the republican ideal of civic equality that came from England via those influenced by the work of James Harrington and others.[20]

Second, Protestantism began as a questioning of church authority, which paved the way for the questioning of other forms of authority—eventually both monarchical and patriarchal.[21] Finally, the Protestant emphasis on literacy provided colonists with a necessary prerequisite for the emergence of democratic self-government. In fact, "reading the Bible was so highly valued that the ability to read was nearly universal among seventeenth-century Puritans, men and women both."[22] In short, while I am not suggesting—and in fact would contest the assertion—that Protestant Christianity is a necessary precondition for democracy, several key concepts central t‿ ᵗʰᵃt religion dovetail nicely with democratic and republican ideals and histⱼrically fed into the emergence of democracy in America.

Nevertheless, despite any "elective affinity" between Protestant Christianity and democracy, the fact remains that the founding generation *intentionally* took the extremely radical step of constructing a secular government, constitutionally required to remain neutral toward religion. As political scientists Isaac Kramnick and R. Laurence Moore rightly stress, "God is nowhere to be found in the Constitution, which also has nothing to say about the social value of Christian belief or about the importance of religion for a moral public life."[23] Indeed the fact that the American Constitution institutionalized a secular state was both revolutionary and controversial.

The American populace has always been religiously pluralistic. Early Americans represented a large number of religious sects, especially after the proliferation of denominations during the early nineteenth century.[24] Nevertheless, because most (but not all) of this pluralism existed under the umbrella of Protestantism, the informal culture that developed in the United States during the eighteenth and early nineteenth centuries was imbued with Protestant values and traditions, even if it may not have been recognized at the time as growing out of a *particular* tradition. During the latter half of the nineteenth century, however, the heterogeneity of American society increased greatly. More specifically, by 1893 an increasing number of immigrants were coming from southern and eastern Europe (Italy, Austria-Hungary, Russia, Poland, Greece, and the Balkans) and from Asia (China and Japan), rather than from northern and western Europe (Great Britain, Ireland, Germany, and Scandinavia), as had been the case during the first part of the nineteenth century.[25] These changes increased the numbers of Jews and Catholics in the American populace, greatly increasing the level of religious pluralism in the country. Changes in immigration laws in the 1960s further expanded the number of different religious traditions practiced within American civil society. Consequently, even if America used to be a "Christian nation," it is not anymore.

The Christian Ideal of Monogamous Marriage

The Founders came from mostly Protestant backgrounds, and despite their establishment of a secular state, sometimes they imported religiously rooted beliefs into law. For example, early Americans legally institutionalized their own Christian vision of monogamous marriage as the law of the land (while also developing common-law marriage as discussed in chapter 2). Because they came from a common religious tradition, they did not question their shared commonsense understanding of marriage and did not understand it as a violation of church/state separation. As Nancy Cott puts it, the taken-for-granted assumption or "common sense of British colonials at the time of the American Revolution was Christian," and "Christian common sense took for granted the rightness of monogamous marriage."[26]

At the time of the Founding, however, the Christian ideal of monogamous marriage was not the norm globally. To the contrary,

> at that time, Christian monogamists composed a minority in the world. The pre-dominance of monogamy was by no means a foregone conclusion. Most of the peoples and cultures around the globe (so recently investigated and colonized by Europeans) held no brief for strict monogamy. The belief systems of Asia, Africa, and Australia, of the Moslems around the Mediterranean, and the natives of North and South America all countenanced polygamy and other complex marriage practices, which British and European travel writings on exotic lands recounted with fascination. Anglo-America itself was set down in the midst of polygamist and often matrilineal and matrilocal cultures. No doubt Christians in Britain, Europe, and America at the time thought monogamy was a superior system, but it had yet to triumph.[27]

Although the Christian Bible does not explicitly define marriage as a monogamous heterosexual dyad or prohibit polygamy, in practice Christians have implemented that form of marriage, which they now accept as the norm. Nevertheless it remains a *distinctively Christian* definition of marriage.

The importation of English common-law assumptions about the privileges and duties of husbands and wives reinforced the Christian definition of marriage, and both traditions "inflected the legal features of marriage in the United States."[28] That is to say, "the legal oneness of husband and wife derived from common law but it matched the Christian doctrine that 'the twain shall be one flesh.' . . . Anywhere on the wide and shifting spectrum of Protestantism in the early republic, from deism to Anglicanism, these basic Christian beliefs about marriage were in place."[29] In other words, the definition of marriage that is taken for granted as natural and timeless today is actually a very particular vision, not at all eternal or universal, although Christians have been quite successful at spreading their views around the world. Now that American society has become more religiously pluralistic, how can specifically Christian moral precepts be legitimately imposed on everyone through civil law?

Christian-Right Theology and the Attack on Religious Freedom[30]

Although the Christian Right claims "same-sex marriage violates freedom of conscience" because "Christians, Jews and Muslims would be forced to endorse behavior that they recognize as contrary to their beliefs,"[31] its organizations are actually trying to impose their own particular religious worldview on everyone in American society in direct violation of the separation of church and state. Despite the use of democratic rhetoric, the opposition of right-wing Christians to gay marriage is contingent upon their religiously grounded definition of marriage as a sacred religious rite. According to the FRC, marriage is "the *work of heaven* and every major religion and culture throughout world history."[32] CWA proclaims marriage "*a covenant established by God* wherein one man and one woman, united for life, are licensed by the state for the purpose of founding and maintaining a family."[33] For FOF, "marriage is *a sacred union, ordained by God* to be a life-long, sexually exclusive relationship between one man and one woman."[34] Phyllis Schlafly credits the Judeo-Christian tradition for advancing the position of women by championing monogamous marriage,[35] although this view of marriage is actually more Christian than Judaic, as we shall soon see. Indeed, because of its particular conservative Christian worldview, the Christian Right has made opposition to same-sex marriage a centerpiece of its political agenda.[36]

The Christian Right's vision of heterosexual-only marriage directly relates to its understanding of gender difference, which it bases on its particular interpretation of the Bible. To justify male dominance, the Christian Right privileges the second version of the creation story in Genesis, in which God created Eve out of Adam's rib to be his "helper" and declared that the man and his wife would become "one flesh" (Gen. 2:18–24), rather than on the first story in which "God created man in His image, in the image of God He created him; *male and female He created them*" (Gen. 1:26–27, emphasis added).[37] Additionally, instead of reading the latter version as establishing gender equality at the origin, or even androgyny, as some religious scholars do, the Christian Right interprets it to mean "God's purpose for man was that there should be two sexes, male and female. Every person is either a 'he' or a 'she.' God did not divide mankind into three or four or five sexes."[38]

(This argument directly contests contemporary gender scholarship on inter-sexuality, which shows that around 4 percent of the population has sexual characteristics of both male and female.[39]) Right-wing Christians bolster their selective reading of the "Old Testament" with a smattering of "New Testament" verses, such as woman is the "weaker vessel" (1 Peter 3:7), "man was not made from woman, but woman from man" (1 Cor. 11:8), "the head of a woman is her husband" (1 Cor. 11:3), "wives be subject to your hus-bands, as to the Lord" (Eph. 5:22), and "the husband is the head of the wife as Christ is the head of the church" (Eph. 5:23).

The Christian Right's selectively literalist interpretation of the Bible not only emphasizes the natural authority of husbands over their wives but also condemns homosexuality as a particularly grave sin. This condemnation relies on just a few passages in the entire Bible. Liberal Christians emphasize that these passages must be read in the overall context of Christianity's mes-sage of love and nonjudgmentalness. Even if homosexuality is a sin, they point out, Jesus said "Judge not, that you be not judged" (Matt. 7:1). The legitimacy of multiple religious interpretations seems to be recognized by Paul, who said, "the spiritual man judges all things, but is himself to be judged by no one. 'For who has known the mind of the Lord so as to instruct him?'" (1 Cor. 1:15–16). This passage implies that a gay or lesbian religious person should not be judged by other human beings, but only by God.

Furthermore, liberal Christians insist that biblical passages that appear to condemn homosexuals must be understood in historical context. For exam-ple, Paul said, "slaves, be obedient to those who are your earthly masters, with fear and trembling, in singleness of heart, as to Christ" (Eph. 6:5). In the nineteenth century, slaveholders used Paul's teaching to justify slavery, but today most people understand slavery as incompatible with the Christian message of human equality. They now argue that Paul was advising slaves on how to behave in a society that allows slavery, not advocating the continua-tion of the practice. People are beginning to view biblical prohibitions on homosexual practices as needing similar contextualization.

The Christian Right believes that scripture clearly prohibits homosexual-ity. First, they interpret God's destruction of Sodom and Gomorrah (Gen. 18:16–19:29) as punishment for homosexuality. According to the Revised Standard Version of the Bible, God sends two angels to Sodom to destroy it for its "very grave" sin (Gen. 18:20), and Lot offers them lodging for the night. But before they lay down to sleep, the entire male population of the town comes to Lot's door, asking "Where are the men who came to you tonight? Bring them out to us, that we may know them" (Gen. 19:5). Lot tries to appease the crowd by offering his daughters instead. The mob refuses, and the angels ultimately destroy the town, as God had already decreed.

Why did God destroy the city? Religious scholars vigorously disagree about the meaning of Genesis 19, debating two major questions. First, what did the men mean when they said they wanted to "know" the visitors? In his award-winning book *Christianity, Social Tolerance, and Homosexuality,* Yale historian John Boswell explains that contrary to popular belief, the term " 'to know' . . . is very rarely used in a sexual sense in the Bible." In fact, "the passage on Sodom is the only place in the Old Testament where it is generally believed to refer to homosexual relations."[40] CWA quotes the New King James Bible, which translates the disputed passage as "Bring them out to us that we may know them carnally."[41] *Etz Hayim,* the authoritative "Torah and Commentary" of Conservative Judaism, translates the phrase as "bring them out to us, that we may be intimate with them" but explains, "this means commit rape (see Judges 19:22)."[42]

Second, regardless of translation, the question remains: Why exactly did God destroy Sodom and Gomorrah? Was it because the townsmen attempted to have homosexual relations with the angels, as the Christian Right insists? Or was it because they attempted to *rape* the angels? Could it have been for general wickedness, an interpretation supported by the fact that God planned to destroy the city well *before* the incident with the angels (Gen. 19:13)? Finally, could God have condemned the town for being inhospitable toward visitors?[43] The dominant contemporary interpretation is the fourth one: the city was destroyed for the sin of inhospitality—considered a "sacred obligation" in ancient times.[44] This is how the story was originally understood and that interpretation has been "increasingly favored" since 1955.[45]

In other words, premodern religious scholars did not understand the Sodom and Gomorrah story to be about homosexuality at all. In fact, Boswell explains, "a purely homosexual interpretation of this story is . . . relatively recent. None of the Old Testament passages which refer to Sodom's wickedness suggests any homosexual offenses, and the rise of homosexual associations can be traced to social trends and literature of a much later period."[46] In fact, Jesus's own comments about the story did not reveal any concern about homosexuality (Matt. 10:14–15; Luke 10:10–12). Boswell believes the refusal of classical scholars "to see the account as a moral about homosexual behavior cannot be lightly disregarded, especially in the face of so little evidence to support a homosexual interpretation."[47] For him the most "obvious" possibility is that the city was destroyed for attempting to rape the angels.[48]

In addition to Genesis 19, the Christian Right also bases its condemnation of homosexuality on the sentences in Leviticus that proclaim "do not lie with a male as one lies with a woman; it is an abhorrence" (Lev. 18:22) and "if a man lies with a male as one lies with a woman, the two of them have done an abhorrent thing; they shall be put to death" (Lev. 20:13), completely ignoring the fact that the Ten Commandments did not include a prohibition on homosexuality.

In any event, if one were to do a literal reading of Leviticus 18:22, the question remains: what does the phrase "do not lie with a male as one lies with a woman" actually mean? Could "the text be trying to tell us not to make love to a male as if he were a female—that is to say, gay love and straight love are indeed different," as Jewish scholar Arthur Waskow argues?[49] Does it prohibit only certain sexual acts, rather than same-sex love relationships,[50] like those of Jonathan and David[51] or Naomi and Ruth?[52] If one wants to be literal, Leviticus 18:22 actually says nothing at all about lesbianism. Finally, from a more interpretive perspective, even if we accept that the verse in question documents that "in biblical times homosexual acts were forbidden," how do we know that this prohibition still applies in today's society? "After all, the Bible also countenanced other things we no longer accept as moral," like slavery, for example.[53]

In its commentary of Leviticus 18:22, the Rabbinical Assembly of Conservative Judaism comments, "Aside from this verse and its parallel in 20:13, the Bible mentions homosexuality only in the context of rape (Gen. 19:5, Judg. 19:22) and apparently with regard to prostitution (Deut. 23:18–19). In its condemnation here, the Torah uses the word *to-eivah*, which appears more than one hundred times in the Bible to describe an object or act as repulsive."[54] Homosexual acts between men were not singled out as particularly offensive to God.

While claiming to offer a literal reading of the Bible when it comes to Leviticus 18:22 and 20:13, the Christian Right completely disregards the wide array of other practices prohibited in Leviticus, such as eating pork or touching a football made of pigskin (Lev. 11:7–8), wearing cotton/poly blends (Lev. 19:19), and trimming the hair on the side of the face (Lev. 19:27).[55] "Ex-gay" Stephen Bennett stresses the use of the term "abomination" in his reading of Leviticus 18:22:[56]

> What does God think about homosexuality? The verse says, "It is an **abomination!**" This means that it is detestable, loathsome, repulsive and heinous. It is one of the strongest words to describe God's hatred of something. It is a stench in God's nostrils like the smell of vomit! It is something that is disgusting, nauseating,

revolting and sickening to God. The reason it is an abomination is that it is so contrary to what God has designed and established for the good of mankind.[57]

What Bennett fails to mention is that the Bible also refers to eating shellfish as an "abomination" (Lev. 11:10).[58]

While the Christian Right makes much of the English term "abomination," the original meaning of the Hebrew word to'evah is disputed by religious scholars.[59] For example, as Rebecca Alpert argues, "according to the second-century commentator Bar Kapparah, [to'evah] means 'to'eh ata ba— you go astray because of it' (see Babylonian Talmud, Nedarim 51b). This play on words has been taken to mean that it is not intrinsically an evil to engage in homosexual acts, but rather that they have negative consequences," which in medieval times might be not reproducing, or abandoning your wife.[60] Boswell concurs that the term meant "ritually unclean for Jews, like eating pork or engaging in intercourse during menstruation," rather than "inherently evil, like rape or theft,"[61] which explains why eating shellfish is also considered an abomination.

The laws in Leviticus—addressing sexual practices, ritual cleanliness, dietary strictures, and male circumcision, among other things—functioned to distinguish the Jews from other peoples, and most Gentile converts to Christianity did not consider them binding.[62] Notably, unlike the Christian Right today, they did not accept Leviticus 18:22 and 20:13 as valid, while disregarding the rest of Mosaic law. As Boswell explains it,

> viewed through the lenses of powerful modern taboos on the subject, the prohibition of homosexual relations may seem to have been of a different order: to those conditioned by social prejudice to regard homosexual behavior as uniquely enormous, the Levitical comments on this subject may seem to be of far greater weight than the proscriptions surrounding them. But the ancient world . . . knew no such hostility to homosexuality. The Old Testament strictures against same-sex behavior would have seemed to most Roman citizens as arbitrary as the prohibition of cutting the beard, and they would have had no reason to assume that it should receive any more attention than the latter.[63]

The early Church decided that non-Jewish converts to Christianity would not be bound by Mosaic law, with four exceptions: Gentiles should "abstain from the pollutions of idols and from unchastity and from what is strangled and from blood" (Acts 15:20). Christians did not prohibit homosexual behavior on the basis of Leviticus 18:22 and 20:13, and Jews were not known for their opposition to homosexuality but for their rituals, dietary laws, and mandatory circumcision.[64]

Finally, the Christian Right also bases its condemnation of lesbian and gay sexuality on three passages in Paul's writings—two words and two sentences total. They cannot base it on what Jesus said because he never even mentioned homosexuality—or even sexuality in general—as discussed in chapter 2. Paul proclaims that the law is given for the "lawless and disobedient," including "the ungodly and sinners, for the unholy and profane, for murderers of fathers and murderers of mothers, for manslayers, immoral persons, sodomites, kidnapers, liars, perjurers, and whatever else is contrary to sound doctrine" (1 Tim. 1:8–10). He also says, "Do not be deceived; neither the immoral, nor idolaters, nor adulterers, nor homosexuals, nor thieves, nor the greedy, nor drunkards, nor revilers, nor robbers will inherit the kingdom of God" (1 Cor. 6:9–10).

Boswell contends that the Greek words translated in the Bible as "sodomites" and "homosexuals" have different meanings when viewed in historical context. The Greek word translated as "sodomite" referred to "male prostitute" until the fourth century, and the Greek word for "homosexual" had a number of meanings, including "unrestrained" and "wanton." What's more, until the twelfth century, the latter referred to masturbation. Boswell notes that we no longer consider those who masturbate barred from heaven, not because the meaning of the Greek word has changed but because of shifts in popular morality.[65]

The book of Romans provides the clearest condemnation of homosexuality—among women as well as men. The King James Version of the Bible reads as follows: "For this cause God gave them up unto vile affections: for even their women did *change the natural use* into that which is against nature: and likewise also the men, *leaving the natural use* of the woman, burned in their lust one toward another" (Romans 1:26–27, emphasis added). While controversy does not exist about the translation of words in this passage, Boswell notes that some religious scholars believe Paul refers to Rome's "orgiastic pagan rites in honor of false gods"—idolatry—an interpretation he finds unconvincing.[66] Boswell sees the passage as condemning not "gay *persons* but only homosexual *acts* committed by heterosexual persons." In addition, his interpretation stresses the *change* from straight to gay sex mentioned in the passage and reads the verses in the context of the larger book of Romans, the "whole point" of which is "to stigmatize persons who have rejected their calling, gotten off the true path they were once on."[67] Boswell also emphasizes that the phrase "against nature" must have meant simply something unexpected or out of the ordinary rather than something particularly sinful. Paul could not have been referring to a violation of natural law because the concept of natural law did not develop until centuries later. Thus, he must have used the term "against nature" as it was generally used in the ancient world, to denote "extraordinary, peculiar."[68]

The point of this overview of biblical interpretation is not to establish any one reading of the Christian Bible as definitive, but rather to complicate the Christian Right's claim that the meaning of scriptural passages is self-evident. Indeed, how can any English translation of the Bible capture the exact meaning of the original text, especially thousands of years later? Although some conservative Christians and orthodox Jews believe that God essentially dictated the content of the Bible, most religious scholars believe that different parts of the Bible were written at different times by different people. Scripture may be the inspired Word of God, but it has been recorded and passed down over the years by human beings. Moreover, the task of religious teachers is generally to make the Word of God understandable to their contemporaries, explaining ideas in a way that takes account of the historical and cultural features of their own age, so that it makes sense to ordinary people. Therefore, it's appropriate for scholars to take historical context into account and consider changes that have occurred over the centuries when they interpret biblical passages.

We inevitably read texts through our own historically shaped lenses and sometimes through our political beliefs as well. In any event, people of good will often disagree about the meaning and implications of biblical passages, and in a liberal democracy they have the religious freedom to do so. What they do not have the freedom to do is to use their own particular interpretations to justify civil laws that discriminate against those they see as violating religious law.

Papal "Considerations" of Same-Sex Marriage

While the Christian Right is certainly entitled to its own interpretation of scripture, not all Christians agree with its understanding of marriage (or homosexuality). For example, Catholics consider marriage a sacrament and Protestants do not. As discussed in the second chapter, this was a major issue during the Protestant Reformation in the early sixteenth century. "The Protestants insisted that marriage was a secular ceremony, and not (as Catholics had finally decided in 1215) a mystical and irreversible sacrament."[69] That is why Protestants allow for divorce, while Catholics do not.

More specifically, while the Catholic Church had propagated "the idea that private vows were the sacrament that created marriage—if you said you were married, married you were"[70]—Protestant reformers were troubled by the chaos this definition of marriage sowed in practice, particularly in relation to patriarchal authority in the family and control over property. For example, how could parents prevent their children from marrying without their permission? "How could you run a family business if some pretender suddenly showed up and insisted he was your daughter's husband and therefore had a lien on your possessions?"[71] Concerned with stability and order, early Protestants "considered their marriage reform to be urgent," and so they gave the power to marry over to the civil governments of the emerging nation-states.[72] Many Americans may not be cognizant of the fact that marriage is a sacrament for Catholics but not for Protestants, who recognize only baptism and communion as sacraments.[73] Indeed, even evangelical Protestant leader James Dobson seems ignorant of this point, since he sometimes refers to marriage as "a sacrament designed by God."[74]

Furthermore, even the Catholic definition of marriage has evolved over time. "Today we have the peculiar impression that Catholicism has always had one vision of marriage, but for every marriage rule eventually imposed on Europe, the Church's own debates were abundant." In fact, "it was not until 1215 that the Church finally decreed marriage a sacrament—the least important one, but a sacrament nonetheless—*and* set up a systematic canon law of marriage, with a system of ecclesiastical courts to enforce it—*and* had a fair amount of people willing to observe those rules."[75] Thus, no consensus exists among Christians about the definition of marriage, despite politically motivated rhetoric to the contrary.

In response to the *Lawrence v. Texas* case (2003) that overturned a Texas law prohibiting homosexual sodomy, discussed in chapter 3, the Catholic Church issued "Considerations Regarding Proposals to Give Legal Recognition to Unions between Homosexual Persons" (2003), which lays out the current Catholic case against homosexual unions and instructs elected officials who are Catholic to follow the doctrines of the Church, rather than liberal principles or the will of their constituents, when making public policy decisions.[76] While the document claims to be "addressed not only to those who believe in Christ, but to all persons committed to promoting and defending the common good of society," it actually makes a number of points with which other denominations and religions do not agree, not to mention agnostics and atheists.

While the Vatican presumably has the authority to speak definitively to

Catholics about moral issues, "Considerations" falsely attempts to present the particular doctrines of the Catholic Church as universal truth. First, the document's assertion that "no ideology can erase from the human spirit the certainty that marriage exists solely between a man and a woman"[77] completely disregards the fact that some religions recognize polygamous marriage, a point discussed more fully below. Indeed, the Christian "Old Testament" documents the polygamy of Judeo-Christian patriarchs. Second, Protestants would not accept the document's assertion that "the marital union of man and woman has been elevated by Christ to the dignity of a sacrament," as explained above and, at greater length, in chapter 2.[78] Third, the document claims that "the natural truth about marriage was confirmed by the Revelation contained in the biblical accounts of creation. . . . Marriage is instituted by the Creator."[79] It also asserts "Sacred Scripture condemns homosexual acts 'as a serious depravity . . . (cf. Rom 1:24–27; 1 Cor 6:10; 1 Tim 1:10)."[80] While the Vatican may see these points as universal truth, it is irrelevant for those who do not accept the Bible as the revealed word of God. In any event, since the dawn of modern political theory, divine revelation has not been a legitimate basis for civil law, as fully explained in chapter 3.

Finally, the Vatican sees reproduction as the central purpose of marriage: "God has willed to give the union of man and woman a special participation in his work of creation. Thus, he blessed the man and the woman with the words 'Be fruitful and multiply' (Gen 1:28). Therefore, in the Creator's plan, sexual complementarity and fruitfulness belong to the very nature of marriage."[81] Moreover, for the Vatican the sole purpose of sexual relations is reproduction: "Sexual relations are human when and insofar as they express and promote the mutual assistance of the sexes in marriage *and are open to the transmission of new life.* . . . Homosexual unions . . . are not able to contribute in a proper way to the procreation and survival of the human race."[82] Thus, since "homosexual acts 'close the sexual act to the gift of life,'" they must be, not just immoral, but *inhuman.*[83]

While no one denies that reproduction has been and continues to be an important purpose for marriage in general, not all religious people would agree that reproduction is the only or even the most important purpose of the marital union. For example, Paul never mentions reproduction in his discussion of Christian marriage (1 Cor. 7:1–7). Moreover, "from its inception Judaism has always recognized two purposes of marriage, both spelled out in the opening pages of Scripture": Marriage is not only for reproduction but also for companionship.[84] Moreover, while Judaism used to allow divorce when a wife did not bear children after ten years of marriage, "childlessness is no longer recognized as grounds for divorce."[85] Furthermore, not all religious people believe that the sole purpose of sex is reproduction. For example, unlike Catholicism, the Protestant faith allows for the use of contraceptives, which also closes the sexual act to "the gift of life." Thus, while the Vatican's "Considerations" may speak to Catholics, one cannot accept the document's assertion that it simply "reiterates a truth that is evident to right reason and recognized as such by all the major cultures of the world."[86]

In addition to these disagreements, controversy also exists over the meaning of the biblical phrase "be fruitful and multiply." For example, in *Christianity Today* biblical studies professor Raymond C. Van Leeuwen takes up this issue, beginning as follows:

> Many Christians correctly oppose the sexual and marital chaos that has infiltrated our churches. But in this struggle against sin and for marriage and family, some Christian traditions take a wrong turn. They argue on the basis of the created order (sometimes called *natural law*) and Scripture that God has actually commanded married people to have children. These Christians, who see this command as absolute, argue against birth control, except for what they consider the natural means of abstinence. They claim Genesis 1:28—"Be fruitful, and multiply, and fill the earth"—as a proof text. Birth control seems to disobey this commandment, which is rooted in God's purpose for creation.[87]

While the author says nothing about same-sex marriage, it would presumably be prohibited for the same reasons.

Van Leeuwen disagrees with that biblical interpretation and line of reasoning: "Much could be said in response, but only one comment is essential: *Genesis 1:28 is not a commandment, but a blessing.* It does not refer to *what humans must do* to please God, but to *what God does* for and through humankind. The text says, "God blessed them, and God said to them, 'Be fruitful and multiply'" (RSV). Fertility is not a command but a blessing that God gives to his creatures, to animals as well as humans (Gen. 1:22). The filling of the Earth is a gift of God's wisdom and shows forth his glory as Creator (Ps. 104:24, 31; Isa. 6:3)." He continues, "God gave this blessing to the human race as a whole. He does not give it to everyone. Some couples are barren, and their earnest prayers for children are not fulfilled. Others, like the apostle Paul, are called to life without marriage."[88]

Alternately, Jewish scholar Rabbi Arthur Waskow accepts "be fruitful and multiply" as a commandment but argues that we have already fulfilled it. The Jewish Publication Society translates the passage as "God blessed them and God said to them: 'Be fertile and increase, fill the earth and master it.'" In

fact, Waskow argues, human beings have not only fulfilled this commandment, we have fulfilled it so well that we now risk violating another of God's
commandments:

> Today the sheer number of humans is putting impossible burdens on our global
> ecosystem and plunging into extinction thousands of the species that God com-
> mands in the story of the Flood that we must not allow to die. Today we need to
> encourage, not forbid, forms of sexuality that avoid biological multiplication. We
> might now read the command as teaching us to be fruitful and expansive emotion-
> ally, intellectually, and spiritually rather than biologically.[89]

Thus, Waskow contests one of the central arguments against gay marriage
and makes an ethical case for such relationships.

Religious Disagreements about Gay Unions

Although almost every state in the union denies same-sex couples the right
to *civil* marriage, some religious denominations and individual clergy currently perform *religious* marriages or some comparable form of union for lesbian and gay couples. Reform and Reconstructionist Judaism, the United
Church of Christ, some Episcopal congregations, the Metropolitan Community Church, and the Unitarian Universalists all conduct religious unions for
same-sex couples. In addition, these denominations also support the right to
civil marriage and other legal protections within the secular political realm.

Nevertheless, because passages exist within both the Jewish Bible and the
Christian New Testament that problematize homosexuality, the question of
same-sex marriage is not an easy one for many religious people. Most denominations of Christianity are currently struggling with the question of same-
sex unions or marriages, as is Conservative Judaism. Some denominations are
moving toward acceptance. For example, after a highly publicized debate
that threatened to split the denomination, the Episcopal Church decided to
allow dioceses the option of blessing same-sex unions, but stopped short of
creating an official liturgy for same-sex commitment ceremonies, as progressive Episcopalians had wanted.[90]

Other denominations continue to stand firm in prohibiting same-sex marriages and commitment ceremonies, while accepting gays and lesbians as
church members and supporting many kinds of legal protections. For example, the United Methodist Church continues to insist, after years of vigorous

dissension among the leadership, that "ceremonies that celebrate homosexual unions shall not be conducted by our ministers and shall not be conducted in our churches." This decision has the force of church law. The church has disciplined several ministers for conscientiously violating this prohibition and actually defrocked one.[91]

At the same time, the existence of such conscientious objection reveals that dissension exists within the Methodist Church over its stance on homosexuality. In March 2004, the Reverend Karen Dammann was tried and acquitted, after admitting to being an active lesbian in a committed relationship. The church charged her with "practices declared by the United Methodist Church to be incompatible to Christian teachings."[92] The prosecution believed the case to be straightforward, since the denomination's "Book of Discipline" forbids the ordination of practicing homosexuals.

The defense, however, questioned the legitimacy of church law, summoning "an array of Methodist theologians and clergy members to raise questions about the consistency and justice of the church's stand." For example, retired bishop Calvin D. McConnell argued that "there is a contradiction between the "Book of Discipline" and the Methodist theology of baptism, which he said holds that, upon baptism, all Christians become ministers of the gospel. 'My understanding is that anybody who is received in baptism has full rights of ministry in any position to which they feel called by God,' McConnell said."[93]

In the end, a thirteen-pastor jury acquitted the Reverend, with not a single juror voting to convict her, although two abstained.[94] They found that the Church had not established that homosexuality was in fact "incompatible with Christian teachings." Despite the statement against ordination in the "Book of Discipline," opinion remains divided and, in fact, Methodist social principles support civil rights and liberties for lesbians and gay men.[95]

Yet while some remain divided, other churches brook no tolerance of homosexuality whatsoever. The Southern Baptist Convention, the largest Protestant denomination in the country, espouses a vision of marriage that is not only exclusively heterosexual but also highly patriarchal:

> Marriage is the uniting of one man and one woman in covenant commitment for a lifetime. . . . A husband . . . has the God-given responsibility to provide for, to protect, and to lead his family. *A wife is to submit herself graciously to the servant leadership of her husband.* . . . She, being in the image of God as is her husband and thus equal to him, has the God-given responsibility to respect her husband and to *serve as his helper* in managing the household and nurturing the next generation.[96]

In addition, the Convention not only prohibits same-sex religious unions within the church, but also actively opposes all civil rights for gays and lesbians within the secular political realm. In fact, homosexuals are not even welcome as active church members, just as the denomination barred African Americans from their churches until the 1960s.[97] The Southern Baptist Convention forms a major sector of the Christian Right.

Non-Christian Views of Marriage: Jews, Muslims, and Mormons

Defining marriage as comprised exclusively of one man and one woman was a Christian innovation. "We take monogamy for granted now as 'traditional' marriage, but at the time it was such an outrageous and radical leveling of society—taking away such key political (let alone personal) options from men in power—that imposing this concept took more strength than the Church had for hundreds upon hundreds of years. One wife, and only one, was an incredible—not-to-be-believed—concept."[98]

Currently, Islam, the fastest-growing religion in the world, continues to allow for polygamy, although it does not require it. The Qur'an states, "If you fear that you shall not be able to deal justly with the orphans, marry women of your choice, two, or three, or four; but if you fear that you shall not be able to deal justly (with them), then (marry) only one" (4:3). Today "polygamy is practiced openly in Jordan, Israel, Syria, Yemen, Iraq and Iran, as well as some of the Muslim nations of North Africa—including Egypt, Sudan, Morocco and Algeria" by men who can afford it, usually in agrarian regions. "Though their numbers are small," according to Israeli anthropologist Joseph Ginat, "not all polygamists are premodern illiterate people. Some are teachers, doctors or other professional men." The practice, however, is declining as societies become urbanized.[99]

While many people know that Islam allows for polygamy, fewer may realize that Judaism also has a long tradition of polygamy, although, for the most part, it is no longer practiced. The tradition of polygamy derives from the fact that many of the patriarchs in the Jewish Bible—all of which is included in Christian scripture as the "Old Testament"—had multiple wives, including Abraham, David, and Solomon. Consequently, "according to biblical and talmudic law, polygamy is permitted."[100] In fact, not until the eleventh century did the rabbis implement a thousand-year ban on polygamy, and even that only applied to the Ashkenazic Jews of Europe, not the Sephardic Jews of the Middle East. Interestingly, the rabbis call their ruling a "ban" rather than an "outright prohibition" because "authorities could not consider [polygamous] marriages invalid since the Bible and the Talmud considered them valid."[101] Moreover, it was pressure from the majority religion of medieval Christianity and fear of pogroms that led to the ban on polygamous marriage in the first place. According to Rabbi Rick Libowitz, the rabbis "outlawed polygamy because it was offensive to the Christians, who could find enough rationales for pogroms."[102]

Interestingly, Sephardic Jews who lived in the Muslim-dominated Middle East "continued to consider plural marriages lawful until 1950, when an act of the Chief Rabbinate of Israel extended the ban on polygamy to them as well."[103] Even so, according to Ginat, "those who already had several wives could bring them [to Israel], but no new polygamous marriages could be formed. In cases where a wife cannot bear children or is mentally ill, however, the rabbis can give a husband the right to marry a second woman without divorcing his first wife." And "despite the legal prohibitions, Israeli Bedouin, who are Muslims, continue to practice polygamy," although without official governmental approval.[104]

Despite the oft-cited Levitical prohibitions on homosexuality, every single Jewish legislator and almost every Jewish religious leader in Massachusetts opposes amending the state constitution to allow only *monogamous* heterosexual marriage.[105] Interestingly, the only Jewish leaders to support an amendment are three orthodox rabbis. This is curious because orthodox Judaism seeks a literal application of *halakhah*, which permits polygamy, as just discussed, although it prohibits homosexuality. These orthodox rabbis joined the Catholic Church in supporting an antigay marriage amendment because "to make it look like the Jews support homosexuality, and all the other religions don't, would be a terrible thing." But of course Jews, like Christians, are divided over questions of homosexuality and marriage. What does unify most Jews, however, is support for the separation of church and state.[106]

The Mormon religion, founded by Joseph Smith in 1823 in the United States, originally embraced "plural marriage" as a central tenet. Interestingly, Smith saw "plural" or "Bible marriage" as a return to the traditions of the Hebrew patriarchs. While the idea met resistance at first, in the face of religious persecution, plural marriage became a way to demonstrate a commitment to Mormonism.[107]

Still influenced by Protestant cultural assumptions, the nineteenth-century American courts did not accept the practice of plural marriage as an expression of religious freedom. Instead, they passed a series of laws not only outlawing plural marriage but also criminalizing "a man's *cohabitation* with more than one woman." Penalties included fines, jail time, and the loss of the right to vote, hold political office, and serve on a jury.[108] It was only under the intense pressure of this "anti-Mormon campaign" that the Church of Jesus Christ of Latter-day Saints officially renounced polygamy in 1890, a precondition for Utah to become a state.[109] A fundamentalist sect that broke with mainstream Mormonism, however, still considers polygamy "an ecclesiastical mandate."[110]

My point here is not to make a case for polygamy but rather to underline the fact that the definition of marriage as "only between one man and one woman" is not accepted by all religions but rather is rooted in the Christian tradition.[111] Consequently, the Federal Marriage Amendment, if passed, would impose one particular, religiously rooted definition of marriage on all the citizens of the United States, whether they are Christian or not. The amendment directly violates the separation of church and state, and so it undermines the principles of liberal democracy upon which the United States was founded.

"Roadmap to Polygamy" as Political Red Herring

Opponents of legal equality for lesbians and gays have increasingly advanced the argument that the legalization of same-sex marriage will clear the way for polygamy. For example, antigay, promarriage advocate Maggie Gallagher makes this argument in response to the arrest of two Unitarian Universalist ministers in New Paltz, New York, for conducting weddings for thirteen same-sex couples who did not have government-issued marriage licenses.[112] Clearly, these ministers exercised their religious freedom by marrying those couples in accordance with the beliefs of their own religion, which allows lesbian and gay marriage—marriage as a religious rite. The arrest of these ministers clearly violates the free exercise clause of the First Amendment, even if "New York has a law making it illegal to marry couples without a valid license."[113]

Upon hearing of their arrest, Rabbi Ayelet S. Cohen called the New York Board of Rabbis to see if she could be charged for officiating at a same-sex Jewish wedding. "'They said that if I signed the Ketubah, I could be charged,' Rabbi Cohen said. 'I am happy to say I did sign it.' Like many New York clergy members who have solemnized same-sex marriages in the past, Rabbi Cohen argued that declaring a church rite effectively illegal breaches the separation of church and state." Consequently, she insists that she will continue to exercise her religious beliefs freely and to fulfill her rabbinical duties, including overseeing the marriages of lesbian and gay couples.[114]

Gallagher, however, had a different reaction. According to her, the ministers did not exercise religious freedom but rather "laid down" the "roadmap to polygamy" in two moves. First, Gallagher argues, the ministers want "to utterly separate the idea of civil marriage from the religious ideas that produced it," and second, they "say that this new creature, 'civil marriage,' is an individual right to a set of legal goodies." Somehow, "from there it is a short hop to polygamy."[115]

Gallagher's argument has multiple problems. First, she fails to recognize the four different components of marriage discussed in chapter 2. Civil marriage is not a "new creature," something the ministers made up. To the contrary, the concept of civil marriage preexisted religious marriage; it has existed at least since ancient Greece and Rome, and sixteenth-century Protestant reformers who wanted to give the newly created secular state authority over the constitution of marriage helped establish it as a norm throughout the West. Second, Gallagher makes it sound like lesbians and gays are trying to turn a sacred institution into a "benefits-grab."[116] In reality, however, it is state and federal law that endows civil marriage with a whole host of benefits, as explained in chapter 2, not the same-sex marriage movement. Third, like many of her contemporaries, Gallagher calls the "idea that it takes a husband and a wife to make a marriage . . . a human universal," which it is not. Fourth, Gallagher insists, "some things really are fundamentals of our civilization. We don't permit states to 'experiment' with communist forms of government. We don't allow judges to redefine what a corporation is."[117] What Gallagher fails to comprehend, however, is that the corporation is a legal construct. It exists because judges decided it exists. It did not spring up from nature, nor is it fundamental to Western civilization.

Finally, in condemning the attempt to separate the religious rite from the civil contract, Gallagher supports the continued inscription of Christian religious beliefs onto American civil law, in direct violation of the separation of church and state. Yet while Gallagher defends her own religious beliefs, she does not want to allow others to exercise theirs:

> Our basic ideas about marriage are rooted in specific religiously inspired ideas. Not just the idea that it takes a husband and a wife to make a marriage (which is a human universal), but also other ideas, such as: Men have an obligation to be sexually faithful to their wives (not a human universal), and you can't marry two

women at the same time. If the first idea is illegitimate because it is rooted in religious ideas, what happens to the other two? . . . After all, if Unitarian ministers in New Paltz have a constitutional right to create legal marriages of any kind they choose, then so do Muslim clergy in Brooklyn.[118]

Of course, the marriages conducted by the Unitarian ministers were not, in fact, "legal." They were simply religiously sanctioned. Yet those ministers were arrested and charged with a crime.

Despite the problems with her argument, however, Gallagher's opinion piece does raise one valid issue: If the American Constitution prohibits the establishment of religion as well as interference with the free exercise thereof, can it legitimately prevent traditional Muslims or orthodox Mormons from entering into plural marriages, as their religions allow? This is a complicated question. Certainly, U.S. law does not permit every religiously sanctioned practice—prohibiting a number of traditions, from animal sacrifice to burning the hands of children who masturbate to stoning a woman to death for adultery—nor should it. Practices that involve inflicting pain and cruelty on living beings without their consent cannot be permitted. But same-sex marriage does not do that. Moreover, the argument for same-sex marriage does not rely exclusively on a religious freedom argument.

Same-sex marriage should be legalized because all the principles of liberal democracy justify it, including not only religious freedom but also legal and gender equality, civil rights, and human dignity. Put differently, the philosophy of liberalism that underlies American democracy justifies both religious liberty and same-sex marriage, as argued in chapter 3. While some might defend polygamy on grounds of religious freedom, the practice arguably violates other liberal principles, such as gender equality and human dignity. While a full discussion of this complicated and controversial issue exceeds the scope of this book, fortunately polygamy is only tangentially related to our topic. Gay men and lesbians do not want polygamy; they simply want access to the same monogamous model of civil marriage enjoyed by heterosexuals. Indeed, even religions that traditionally support plural marriage see no connection between gay marriage and polygamy; both the Mormon Church and the Islamic Society of North America have come out in support of the Federal Marriage Amendment.[119]

Why would treating lesbians and gay men equally before the law lead to the establishment of an entirely different form of marriage?[120] The thorny issue of whether polygamy should be allowed on the basis of religious freedom and personal choice functions to detract attention away from an issue of basic justice, as does the ridiculous suggestion that if the state recognizes gay marriage, it would also have to recognize "marriage between a man and his donkey."[121] (It's strange that many ostensibly religious people have difficulty drawing moral distinctions between human beings and animals!) While state-recognized polygamy may or may not be acceptable on the basis of liberal principles, one thing does seem clear: the state should not *criminalize* Muslims who enter into informal plural marriages with consenting adults without state sanction or *prosecute* the clergy who conduct their weddings that are not licensed by the state. How consenting adults conduct their personal lives is not the legitimate business of government in a liberal democracy.

Conclusion

Despite the lack of consensus among the American people about the nature of marriage and despite the wide array of positions among religious denominations on the question of same-sex religious unions, conservatives have introduced a "Federal Marriage Amendment" to the Constitution: "Marriage in the United States shall consist only of the union of a man and a woman. Neither this Constitution, nor the constitution of any State, shall be construed to require that marriage or the legal incidents thereof be conferred upon any union other than the union of a man and a woman." Clearly this Amendment asks the federal government to establish *one particular religious definition of marriage* as the law of the land, thus violating the separation of church and state.[122]

In a liberal democracy, the separation of church and state precludes the government from sanctioning any *religious aspects* of traditional marriage; authority over those issues rightly belongs to religious organizations. Saying that the government should have nothing to say about the *religious rite of marriage* means it cannot legitimately prosecute clergypeople who conduct same-sex weddings. Nor can it force religious organizations to marry gay or lesbian couples, even if the government allows same-sex civil marriage. Who can get married in a particular denomination must be determined by its leadership and congregation, in accordance with its own policy-making process. At the same time, the legal contractual aspects of *civil marriage* clearly fall under the sovereignty of our secular government, which may not legitimately deny gay and lesbian citizens full equality before the law, including access to the state-sanctioned set of legal entanglements that includes both benefits and responsibilities—even if such equality violates the religious beliefs or moral sensibilities of many Americans. Tradition does not justify continued injustice. If you don't approve of gay marriage, don't marry someone of the same sex.

Notes

1. Michael J. Sandel, *Democracy's Discontent: America in Search of a Public Philosophy* (Cambridge, MA: Belknap Press of Harvard University Press, 1996).

2. See Sean Cahill and Kenneth T. Jones, *Leaving Our Children Behind: Welfare Reform and the Gay, Lesbian, Bisexual, and Transgender Community* (New York: National Gay and Lesbian Task Force, 2001). See particularly sections on marriage, fatherhood, and abstinence initiatives.

3. Family Research Council, "Core Principles," www.frc.org/get.cfm?c = ABOUT _FRC [accessed 2 April 2004].

4. Concerned Women for America, "Mission Statement," www.cwfa.org/about.asp [accessed 2 April 2004].

5. Republican National Committee, "Party Platform," www.rnc.org/About/Party Platform/default.aspx?Section = 4> [accessed July 5, 2004].

6. Focus on the Family, "Our Mission," family.org/welcome/aboutfof/a000 5554.cfm [accessed 2 April 2004].

7. William C. Singleton III, "Ten Commandments Judge Praised and Panned: Roy Moore fulfills a campaign promise with a 5,280-pound granite monument," *Christianity Today,* December 3, 2001, 22, www.christianitytoday.com/ct/2001/015/15.22.html [accessed 2 April 2004].

8. Isaac Kramnick and R. Laurence Moore, *The Godless Constitution: The Case against Religious Correctness* (New York: W. W. Norton & Company, Inc., 1997), 35.

9. Orin Simmerman, "The Pledge of Allegiance in Church," June 4, 2003, www .beverlylahayeinstitute.org/articledisplay.asp?id = 4050&department = BLI&category id = commentary [accessed 2 April 2004].

10. Simmerman, "Pledge of Allegiance."

11. For the full argument, see R. Claire Snyder, "A Strange Drift to the Right: The Civic Historiography of Michael Sandel," *New Political Science: A Journal of Politics and Culture* 25, no. 3 (September 2003): 307–26.

12. See, for example, Nicolo Machiavelli, *Discourses*, II-2, 330–31.

13. Machiavelli, *Discourses*, II-2, 130.

14. See, for example, *Jefferson: Political Writings*, eds. Joyce Appleby and Terence Ball (Cambridge: Cambridge University Press, 1999), 390; and Thomas Jefferson, *Notes on the State of Virginia*, edited by William Peden (Chapel Hill, NC: University of North Carolina Press, 1982), 159–60.

15. Joseph Ellis, *American Sphinx: The Character of Thomas Jefferson* (New York: Vintage Books, 1998), 257.

16. Cited in William Bennett, *Our Sacred Honor: Words of Advice from the Founders* (Nashville, TN: Broadman & Holman, 1997), 3.

17. See for example Robert Bork, *The Tempting of America: The Political Seduction of the Law* (New York: Simon & Schuster, 1990), 6–11.

18. Bennett, *Our Sacred Honor.*

19. For the classic account of how the Protestant Reformation allowed for the emergence of capitalism, which can arguably be understood as having democratic aspects, see Max Weber, *The Protestant Ethic and the Spirit of Capitalism.*

20. J. G. A. Pocock, *The Machiavellian Moment: Florentine Political Thought and the Atlantic Republican Tradition* (Princeton, NJ: Princeton University Press, 1975).

21. For a discussion of how Protestantism laid the groundwork for women's equality, see Glenna Matthews, *The Rise of Public Woman: Woman's Power and Woman's Place in the United States, 1630–1970* (New York and Oxford: Oxford University Press, 1992).

22. Matthews, *Rise of Public Woman,* 25.

23. Kramnick and Moore, *Godless Constitution,* 28.

24. Nathan O. Hatch, *The Democratization of American Christianity* (New Haven, CT: Yale University Press, 1991).

25. John Whiteclay Chambers II, *The Tyranny of Change: America in the Progressive Era 1890–1920,* 2nd ed. (New York: St. Martin's Press, 1992), 11.

26. Nancy F. Cott, *Public Vows: A History of Marriage and the Nation* (Cambridge, MA: Harvard University Press, 2000), 9.

27. Cott, *Public Vows,* 9–10.

28. Cott, *Public Vows,* 6–7.

29. Cott, *Public Vows,* 11.

30. Portions of this section were previously published in "The Christian Right's 'Defense of Marriage': Democratic Rhetoric, Anti-Democratic Politics," *Public Eye,* Fall 2002. *Public Eye* is published by Political Research Associates (PRA), an independent, nonprofit research center that studies antidemocratic, authoritarian, and other oppressive movements, institutions, and trends. PRA is based on progressive values, and is committed to advancing an open, democratic, and pluralistic society. PRA provides accurate, reliable research and analysis to activists, journalists, educators, policy makers, and the public at large.

31. Concerned Women for America, "Top 10 Reasons to Support Marriage," www .cwfa.org/main.asp [accessed 8 April 2004].

32. Fund-raising ad in favor of DOMA, paid for by the Family Research Council, included in FRC information packet, emphasis added.

33. Concerned Women for America, "Lawfully Wedded?", *Family Voice,* April 1996, www.cwfa.org/library/family/1996–04_fv_marriage-gay.shtml [accessed 14 November 2000], emphasis mine.

34. "Focus on the Family Position Statement on Same-Sex 'Marriage' and Civil Unions," *Citizen Link,* October 4, 2000, www.family.org/cforum/research/papers/ a0013151.html [accessed 22 July 2002], emphasis mine.

35. Phyllis Schlafly, *The Power of the Positive Woman* (New York: Crown Publishing Group, 1977).

36. Jean Hardisty, *Mobilizing Resentment: Conservative Resurgence from the John Birch Society to the Promise Keepers* (Boston: Beacon Press, 1999), 98.

37. Unless otherwise noted, all "Old Testament" quotations are taken from *TANAKH: A New Translation of the Holy Scriptures, According to the Traditional Hebrew Text* (Philadelphia: Jewish Publication Society, 1985), currently considered the most accurate translation available. All New Testament quotations come from the Revised Standard Version of the Bible, unless otherwise noted.

38. Stephen Bennett, "Homosexuality and the Bible: What Does God Say?" (Huntington, CT: Stephen Bennett Ministries), 3.

39. For a discussion of intersexuality, see Anne Fausto-Sterling, *Sexing the Body: Gender Politics and the Construction of Sexuality* (New York: Basic Books, 2000).

40. John Boswell, *Christianity, Social Tolerance, and Homosexuality: Gay People in Western Europe from the Beginning of the Christian Era to the Fourteenth Century* (Chicago and London: University of Chicago Press, 1980), 94.

41. Concerned Women for America, "Biblical References on Homosexuality and Marriage," March 11, 2004, www.cwfa.org/articles/5358/CFI/family/index.htm [accessed 2 April 2004].

42. The Rabbinical Assembly, *Etz Hayim: Torah and Commentary* (New York: Jewish Publication Society, 2001), 105.

43. Boswell, *Christianity, Social Tolerance, and Homosexuality*, 93.

44. See, for example, Derrick Sherwin Bailey, *Homosexuality and the Western Christian Tradition* (London, 1955); and John J. McNeill, *The Church and the Homosexual* (New York: Beacon Press, 1993), 42–50.

45. Boswell, *Christianity, Social Tolerance, and Homosexuality*, 94–98, 93.

46. Boswell, *Christianity, Social Tolerance, and Homosexuality*, 93.

47. Boswell, *Christianity, Social Tolerance, and Homosexuality*, 95.

48. Boswell, *Christianity, Social Tolerance, and Homosexuality*, 93.

49. Cited in Rebecca Alpert, "In God's Image: Coming to Terms with Leviticus," in *Twice Blessed: On Being Lesbian or Gay and Jewish*, ed. Christine Balka and Andy Rose (Boston: Beacon Press, 1989), 66–67.

50. Alpert, "God's Image," 66.

51. Faith Rogow, "Speaking the Unspeakable: Gays, Jews, and Historical Inquiry," in *Twice Blessed*, 75.

52. Rebecca Alpert, *Like Bread on the Seder Plate* (New York: Columbia University Press, 1997), 48.

53. Alpert, "God's Image," 67–68.

54. Rabbinical Assembly, *Etz Hayim*, 691.

55. For a very funny letter that inspired this line of argument, see J. Kent Ashcraft, "An Open Letter to Dr. Laura," www-users.cs.york.ac.uk/~susan/joke/laura.htm [accessed 22 July 2002].

56. While the RSV translation uses the term "abomination" in this passage, the JPS translation uses the term "abhorrence."

57. Bennett, "Homosexuality and the Bible," 14–15, emphasis in the original.

58. Both the JPS and the RSV translations use the term "abomination" in reference to shellfish.

59. Alpert, "God's Image," 64–65.

60. Alpert, "God's Image," 65.

61. Boswell, *Christianity, Social Tolerance, and Homosexuality*, 100.

62. Boswell, *Christianity, Social Tolerance, and Homosexuality*, 102.

63. Boswell, *Christianity, Social Tolerance, and Homosexuality*, 102–3.

64. Boswell, *Christianity, Social Tolerance, and Homosexuality*, 104–6.

65. Boswell, *Christianity, Social Tolerance, and Homosexuality*, 107.

66. Boswell, *Christianity, Social Tolerance, and Homosexuality*, 108.

67. Boswell, *Christianity, Social Tolerance, and Homosexuality*, 109.

68. Boswell, *Christianity, Social Tolerance, and Homosexuality*, 114.

69. E. J. Graff, *What Is Marriage For?* (Boston: Beacon Press, 1999), 66.

70. Graff, *What Is Marriage For?*, 202.

71. Graff, *What Is Marriage For?*, 200.

72. Graff, *What Is Marriage For?*, 201.

73. Linwood Urban, *A Short History of Christian Thought* (New York and Oxford: Oxford University Press, 1995), 255.

74. James Dobson, "In Defending Marriage—Take the Offensive!" Dr. Dobson's Newsletter, Focus on the Family, April 2004, www.family.org/docstudy/newsletters/A0031315.cfm [accessed 25 March 2004].

75. Graff, *What Is Marriage For?*, 196.

76. The Vatican, "Considerations Regarding Proposals to Give Legal Recognition to Unions between Homosexual Persons" (2003), 5–6, www.vatican.va/roman_curia/congregations/cfaith/documents/rc_con...cfaith_doc_20030731_homosexual-unions_en.html [accessed 7 August 2003].

77. Vatican, "Considerations," 1.

78. Vatican, "Considerations," 2.

79. Vatican, "Considerations," 1–2.

80. Vatican, "Considerations," 2.

81. Vatican, "Considerations," 1.

82. Vatican, "Considerations," 4, emphasis mine.

83. Vatican, "Considerations," 2.

84. Isaac Klein, *A Guide to Jewish Religious Practice* (New York and Jerusalem: Jewish Theological Seminary of America, 1992), 381.

85. Klein, *Jewish Religious Practice*, 389.

86. Vatican, "Considerations," 1.

87. Raymond C. Van Leeuwen, "'Be Fruitful and Multiply' Is this a command, or a

blessing? *Christianity Today*, November 15, 2001, 1, www.christianitytoday.com/ct/2001/ 014/4.58.html [accessed 19 March 2004].

88. Van Leeuwen, "'Be Fruitful and Multiply,'" 1.

89. Rabbi Arthur Waskow, "The Emerging Torah of Same-Sex Marriage," www.shalomctr.org/index.cfm/action/read/section/sex/article/article519.html [accessed 29 March2004].

90. Alan Cooperman, "Episcopal Vote Allows Blessings of Gay Unions," *Washington Post*, August 7, 2003.

91. United Methodist Church, "Homosexuality," updated 6/01, umns.umc.org/back grounders/homosexuality.html [accessed 13 September 2003].

92. *CNN.com*, "Methodist Church Tries Lesbian Minister," www.cnn.com/2004/ US/West/03/18/lesbian.minister.ap/ [accessed 21 March 2004].

93. Alan Cooperman, "Minister in Homosexuality Trial: Compliance with United Methodist Church Law at Issue," *Washington Post*, March 19, 2004.

94. *CBSNEWS.com*, "Clergy Charged for Same-Sex Weds," www.cbsnews.com/ stories/2004/03/19/national/main607508.shtml [accessed 22 March 2004].

95. *CNN.com*, "Church Tries Lesbian Minister."

96. "The Baptist Faith and Message," www.sbc.net/bfm/bfm2000.asp#xv [accessed 13 October 2003], emphasis added.

97. Phuong Ly, "Minority Pastors Preach Diversity: Clergy of Color Help Expand Horizons of White Churches," *Washington Post*, April 4, 2004.

98. Graff, *What Is Marriage For?*, 170.

99. Peggy Fletcher Stack, "Globally, Polygamy Is Commonplace," *Salt Lake Tribune*, Sunday, September 20, 1998, www.polygamy.com/Other-Globally-Polygamy-Is-Commonplace.htm [accessed 14 August 2003].

100. Klein, *Jewish Religious Practice*, 388.

101. Klein, *Jewish Religious Practice*, 389.

102. Rabbi Leila Gal Berner, personal correspondence, 4 August 2003.

103. Klein, *Jewish Religious Practice*, 389.

104. Stack, "Polygamy Is Commonplace."

105. Nathaniel Popper, "Massachusetts Jews Stand Solidly against Anti-Gay-Vows Initiative," February 20, 2004, www.Forward.com [accessed 21 February 2004].

106. Popper, "Massachusetts Jews."

107. Graff, *What Is Marriage For?*, 172–73. For a study of plural marriage in Mormonism, see Kathryn M. Daynes, *More Wives Than One: Transformation of the Mormon Marriage System, 1840–1910* (Urbana and Chicago: University of Illinois Press, 2001).

108. Graff, *What Is Marriage For?*, 175.

109. For a full discussion of this battle, see Cott, *Public Vows*, chapter 5.

110. Katharine Biele, "On polygamy, a crackdown and a bid for legitimacy," *Christian Science Monitor*, January 30, 2004, www.csmonitor.com/2004/0130/p02s01-ussc.html [accessed 20 March 2004].

111. For a discussion of why polygamy does not follow from same-sex marriage, see Graff, *What Is Marriage For?*, 176–77.

112. *CBSNEWS.com*, "Clergy Charged."

113. Maggie Gallagher, "The Road to Polygamy," Town Hall, March 16, 2004, www .townhall.com/columnists/maggiegallagher/mg20040316.shtml [accessed 2 April 2004].

114. Thomas Crampton, "At a Gay Synagogue, a Rabbi Isn't Fazed by Legalities," *New York Times*, March 21, 2004, newyorktimes.com/2004/03/21/nyregion/21wed.html [accessed 21 March 2004].

115. Gallagher, "Road to Polygamy."

116. Gallagher, "Road to Polygamy."

117. Gallagher, "Road to Polygamy."

118. Gallagher, "Road to Polygamy."

119. Brooke Adams, "LDS backs amendment against gay marriages," *Salt Lake Tribune*, July 8, 2004, 166.70.44.66/2004/Jul/07082004/utah/181881.asp [accessed 8 July 2004].

120. For a discussion of why polygamy does not follow from same-sex marriage, see Graff, *What Is Marriage For?*, 176–77.

121. Dobson, "In Defending Marriage."

122. Didi Herman argues that "anti-gay measures in the United States are, at their heart, orthodox Christian measures. Arguably, when they become legislation, the establishment clause is violated." Herman, *The Antigay Agenda: Orthodox Vision and the Christian Right* (Chicago: Chicago University Press, 1997), 168.

CHAPTER FIVE

Neopatriarchy and the Agenda of the Antigay Right

The state's protracted denial of equal protection cannot be justified simply because such constitutional violation has become traditional.

—Richard Kramer, California Superior Court Judge (2005)[1]

The past has a vote, not a veto.

—Rabbi Mordecai Kaplan

Many Americans feel uncomfortable using the term "marriage" to refer to committed same-sex couples—even many who support legal rights for lesbian and gay couples. Because "marriage" has traditionally been heterosexual, the term "gay marriage" seems like a contradiction in terms. It flies in the face of tradition. Some of these folks would prefer the term "civil union" to describe same-sex relationships, reserving the term "marriage" for heterosexuals. Others oppose any recognition for lesbian and gay couples whatsoever because they believe such relationships are morally wrong and that they go against thousands of years of tradition.

The emphasis on tradition plays an important role in conservative social movements. Because the extension of legal equality to previously excluded groups necessarily challenges tradition, traditionalists generally oppose such changes. While not every traditionalist person opposes the extension of legal equality—indeed in the United States one could argue that progressive change is our tradition—the traditionalist Right as an organized political movement has consistently opposed changing the law to create higher levels of legal and social equality—first for African Americans, then for women, and now for lesbians and gay men. The organized opposition to gay marriage can be seen as the latest attempt of the traditionalist wing of the American Right to prevent the extension of equal rights to previously excluded groups.

The political movement against same-sex marriage is about a lot more than just preserving tradition, however. In fact, many opponents actually support the Christian Right's agenda to *change* current traditions by *reversing* the progress of feminism—to undermine women's equality, reinforce male dominance, and *restore* the patriarchal family as the hegemonic family form in America. This agenda is explicitly espoused by Christian Right activists, even if it is not supported by every evangelical Christian in the country. While the Christian Right's agenda may sound extreme to some, in recent years, its neopatriarchal vision has been embraced by an increasing array of conservative constituencies, who justify it not just in religious but also in secular terms.

This chapter examines a variety of conservative arguments against same-sex marriage and situates them within the context of American political history. Drawing parallels between the civil rights movement, the feminist movement, and the lesbian/gay rights movement, I compare Christian Right opposition to legal equality for lesbians and gay men with New Right opposition to gender equality and Old Right opposition to racial equality. Although contemporary conservatives often try to frame their arguments in democratic terms, I show how their agenda actually undermines the principles of liberal democracy, despite rhetorical assertions to the contrary.

Civil Rights and Right-Wing Backlash

When discussing right-wing ideology, it's important to note that three interrelated ideological strands characterize the post-War Right in America: anti-Communism, libertarian opposition to government, and traditionalism.[2] The Old Right (1945–1964) was staunchly anti-Communist and explicitly racist. Its opposition to the civil rights movement appealed to all three strands of conservatism—protecting the tradition of white supremacy, opposing federal interference in states' rights, and fighting Communism. That is to say, "racial equality had always struck the Southern ruling elite as an insanely radical notion, probably Communist in origin."[3] Right-wing leaders portrayed critics of segregation as "'outside agitators' with Communist proclivities"[4] and "'the Southern Negro as the American group most likely to respond to

[Communism's] revolutionary appeal,'" even though empirical evidence shows that African Americans almost universally rejected communism.[5]

The New Right (1965-present) maintains this three-pronged commitment to anti-Communism, libertarianism, and traditionalism, but distances itself from white supremacists, choosing instead to highlight "a protest theme" against a wide range of cultural changes inaugurated by the new social movements of the 1960s, issues of particular concern to previously politically inactive evangelical Christians.[6] The New Right, particularly its Christian Right core, consolidated its base in opposition to women's equality during the battle over the Equal Rights Amendment during the 1970s, fueled the "culture wars" during the 1980s and 1990s, and currently spearheads the movement against lesbian/gay rights. Whether old or new, the American Right has consistently opposed the extension of legal equality. Indeed, that is partly what defines it as the Right.[7]

The Old Right explicitly supported white supremacy at a time when it was socially acceptable to publicly denigrate African Americans. White supremacist communities and states deliberately and systematically disenfranchised African Americans. Even after the passage of the Fifteenth Amendment to the Constitution in 1870, granting black men the right to vote, southern white communities refused to allow them to exercise that basic right *for nearly a hundred years*—until the passage of the Voting Rights Act of 1965. "The old southern politics was transparently undemocratic and thoroughly racist. 'Southern political institutions,' as V. O. Key, Jr., demonstrated, were deliberately constructed to subordinate 'the Negro population and, externally, to block threatened interferences from the outside with these local arrangements.' By protecting white supremacy, southern Democrats in Congress institutionalized massive racial injustice for generations."[8] Whites maintained dominance through legal segregation, economic power, social custom, and even terrorism, exemplified by lynching and other violence.[9]

Legal segregation directly violates the principles upon which American democracy was founded, and this is true whether you consider the United States a liberal democracy or a republic; no adequate theory of democracy allows its citizens to be treated unequally before the law, as explained in chapter 1. Nevertheless, from the "Progressive Era" until the Civil Rights Act of 1964, the South enforced a system of racial segregation with one set of laws for whites and another set of laws for blacks.

The system of white supremacy included a ban on interracial marriage. Since marriage traditionally functions to create bonds between groups, preventing whites and blacks from marrying helped maintain the racial caste system of the South. "In 1912 an amendment was proposed to the U.S. Constitution that would have banned interracial marriage. The next year Massachusetts passed a law intended to block interracial marriages" by preventing the state from "marrying couples from out of state whose marriages would not be valid in their home states."[10] (Interestingly, Republican Governor Matt Romney resurrected this law in 2004 to prevent out-of-state same-sex couples from marrying in Massachusetts.) State bans on interracial marriage continued until 1967 when the U.S. Supreme Court ruled antimiscegenation laws unconstitutional in *Loving v. Virginia*.

It's important to note here, as argued in chapter 3, that public opinion did not side with the Court at that time. A 1958 Gallup poll showed that only 4 percent of the public favored interracial marriage.[11] Even in 1965, "at the crest of the civil-rights revolution, a Gallup poll found that 72 percent of Southern whites and 42 percent of Northern whites still wanted to ban interracial marriage."[12] Nevertheless, despite its unpopularity, the Court ruled that "the freedom to marry has long been recognized as one of the vital personal rights essential to the orderly pursuit of happiness . . . one of the 'basic civil rights of man' . . . and cannot be infringed by the State."[13]

The landmark Supreme Court decision *Brown v. Topeka Board of Education* (1954) helped galvanize the already burgeoning African American civil rights movement.[14] In that case, the Supreme Court rejected the concept of "separate but equal" and ruled that racially segregated schools deny African Americans equal protection of the laws, guaranteed in the Fourteenth Amendment.[15] A second *Brown* decision a year later ordered desegregation.[16] The Court was able to overrule a long tradition of segregation in the South because the American theory of constitutional government requires that all positive laws—those passed by legislatures—accord with the foundational principles enshrined in the Constitution. Just because a law is passed by a democratically elected legislature does not make the law valid. In *Brown* the Court found that segregation violates the constitutional principle of legal equality and so cannot be allowed in a democratic country, even if a majority of citizens want it.

In his struggle against segregation, Martin Luther King, Jr., called for obedience to constitutional law and disobedience to positive law that contradicts constitutional principles. In justifying his position to those who asked how he could advocate obedience to some laws and not to others, King explained the distinction between just and unjust laws, the essential difference being that just laws apply equally to all. First, King explains, an unjust law degrades human dignity by treating one group as inferior to another: "Any law that uplifts human personality is just. Any law that degrades human personality is unjust. All segregation statutes are unjust because segregation distorts the soul and damages the personality. It gives the segregator a false sense of superiority and the segregated a false sense of inferiority."[17] In other words, unjust laws erode the necessary principles of any democratic society: civic equality and human dignity. Thus, laws that discriminate against the marriages of lesbian and gay citizens and consequently denigrate their relationships are unjust.

Second, King insists that just laws apply equally to all, whereas unjust laws create a double standard: "An unjust law is a code that a majority inflicts on a minority that is not binding on itself. This is difference made legal. On the other hand, a just law is a code that a majority compels a minority to follow that it is willing to follow itself. This is sameness made legal."[18] In other words, laws that discriminate against a minority are unjust.

Third, King argues that a law is unjust if it is applied to a group of people without their consent: "An unjust law is a code inflicted upon a minority which that minority had no part in enacting or creating because," for example, "they did not have the unhampered right to vote."[19] By extension, a law that applies to a particular group, to which that group would never consent, would also be unjust.

Finally, King argues that a law is unjust when it is used to disadvantage particular groups: Sometimes "a law is just on its face but unjust in its application. For instance, I was arrested Friday on a charge of parading without a permit. Now there is nothing wrong with an ordinance which requires a permit for a parade, but when the ordinance is used to preserve segregation and to deny citizens the First Amendment privilege of peaceful assembly and peaceful protest, then it becomes unjust."[20] Thus, the resurrection of a previously defunct law for the sole purpose of discriminating against same-sex couples would be unjust.

Although a dual system of law—with one set of laws for European Americans and one for African Americans—clearly violates the principles of the Constitution, white majority communities refused to recognize the injustice of segregation and tried to maintain their traditional position of privilege in society through political resistance and violence. Right-wing forces vehemently and violently opposed the struggle of African Americans for legal equality. Already prepared in anticipation of the *Brown* decision, the Right in the Deep South immediately began to engage in a large number of legislative maneuvers aimed at getting around the Court's ruling and preventing desegregation. For example, the Georgia legislature made it a felony to spend public money on integrated schools. North Carolina and Florida enacted laws to fire teachers whose views on segregation differed from community standards.[21] In Mississippi voters approved, two-to-one, a legislative proposal to eliminate the public schools altogether if the federal government decided to enforce integration.[22] State legislatures also

> attempted to ban literature issued by the NAACP and other civil rights groups. Several legislatures voted to insert a replica of the old Confederate battle standard into the flags of their states. In 1959 the Alabama legislature even authorized the burning of a children's book. The inflammatory volume, seized from public school libraries, was *The Rabbits' Wedding*; it featured a marriage between a white bunny and a black one.[23]

(Similarly, in the 1990s the antigay Right fought to ban *Heather Has Two Mommies* and *Daddy's Roommate* from public school curricula. Then in 2005 the Bush administration threatened to pull funding from PBS if it broadcasted an episode of "Postcards from Buster" in which a bunny named Buster visits some children in Vermont who have lesbian parents who were civilly united.) And the list goes on.

White citizens also took action against racial equality by mobilizing "one of the largest grassroots organizing campaigns in recent history." The two main organizations of white resistance were the Citizens' Councils and the Ku Klux Klan. The Councils recruited mostly middle- and upper-middle-class businessmen—respectable folks already active in Rotary, Kiwanis, and Lions' clubs—and local politicians, whereas the Klan appealed to urban workers and marginal small business people.[24] Claiming to have a half a million dues-paying members across the South,[25] the Citizens' Councils exerted influence "by virtue of their close ties with powerful southern politicians and their ability to claim to speak for the entire white community"[26]—which in many counties was actually a minority of the population.[27] The Councils played a key role in mobilizing support for reactionary legislative measures and providing support for politicians in what was at the time the one-party Democratic South. Whereas the Councils "mobilized around specific ballot and legislative measures to deprive black people of electoral power and access to public facilities, the Klan was an outright terror squad with little political focus."[28] Together they fought to protect the traditions of white supremacy.

The Republican Party was able to become competitive in the historically Democratic South by capturing the racist vote, attracting southerners who came to reject the Democratic Party when it started backing civil rights legislation under the Kennedy and Johnson administrations.[29] "When the Republican Party nominated Arizona Senator Barry Goldwater—one of the few [non-Southern] senators who had opposed the Civil Rights Act—as their presidential candidate in 1964, the party attracted many racist southern whites but permanently alienated African-American voters."[30] Goldwater claimed that he did not oppose civil rights in principle, but that he considered it unconstitutional for the federal government to overturn the segregationist policies of the states.[31] Civil rights issues should be decided by the states.

While Goldwater may not have been intentionally racist, his libertarian opposition to government intervention and regulation made him appealing to the racist right because that ideology leaves traditional racism undisturbed. Indeed, staunch segregationist Strom Thurmond switched to the Republican Party so that he could support Goldwater. In any event, Goldwater's success at appealing to southerners opposed to legal equality for African Americans led Republican strategists to see "the mobilization of anti-civil rights constituencies as the key to eventually winning and controlling the White House" and its usefulness "in building a larger Republican voter base."[32] Although Goldwater lost by a landslide in 1964, a candidate with essentially the same views, but with a less extremist image, won the White House in 1980.[33] Remarkably, Ronald Reagan "kicked off his 1980 general election campaign by promoting 'states' rights'—[a] southern code word for segregation—in Philadelphia, Miss., scene of the murder of three civil rights workers 16 years before."[34]

Despite their desire to disenfranchise and oppress African American people, white supremacists sometimes used democratic rhetoric to defend their fundamentally antidemocratic agenda. They opposed so-called activist judges who override the will of the people by legislating from the bench. For example, "James J. Kilpatrick of the Richmond *News Leader* sneered at 'that inept fraternity of politicians and professors known as the United States Supreme Court'—they who 'repudiated the Constitution, spit upon the Tenth Amendment, and rewrote the fundamental law of this land to suit their own gauzy concepts of sociology.'"[35] Similarly, a piece of Council literature, authored by Robert Patterson, proclaims:

the fate of this nation may rest in the hands of the Southern white people today. If we white Southerners submit to this unconstitutional judge-made law of nine political appointees, the malignant powers of mongrelization, communism and atheism will surely destroy this Nation from within. Racial intermarriage has already begun in the North and unless stopped will spread to the South.[36]

The document goes on to present an eight-point platform. "The first three planks affirmed the integrity of the Constitution as it was originally drafted and opposed the Supreme Court's 'irresponsible and revolutionary interpretations of this nation's most sacred document of law and justice.'" The pamphlet goes on to argue that state sovereignty and "'the individual rights of the people are in grave danger from organized groups whose aims and purposes are contrary to the American way of life under which this country grew to a position of world leadership.'"[37]

Right-wing populist George Wallace used similar arguments to condemn federal support for the civil rights of African Americans. Denying the legitimacy of constitutional law, Wallace proclaimed, "It is the spirit of power thirst that led . . . President [Kennedy] to launch a full offensive of twenty-five thousand troops against a university . . . of all places . . . in his own country . . . and against his own people, when this nation maintains only six thousand troops in the beleagured city of Berlin." Thus, "let us rise to the call of freedom-loving blood that is in us and send our answer to the tyranny that clanks its chains upon the South. In the name of the greatest people that have ever trod this earth, I draw the line in the dust and toss the gauntlet before the feet of tyranny . . . and I say . . . segregation today . . . segregation tomorrow . . . segregation forever."[38] In his 1968 run as a third-party candidate, Wallace got support from the two main components of the racist right, the Citizens' Councils and the Klan, as well as the conspiracy-minded, anticommunist John Birch Society[39]—in short, the "Old Right." His base included an array of traditionalists, not only white working people who feared competition from African Americans but also white professionals opposed to changes in the racial caste system.

Today's Antigay Right and the Fight against Lesbian/Gay Civil Rights

The 2004 decision by the Massachusetts Supreme Court that the state's constitutional principles require same-sex marriage has led to a flurry of legislative maneuvers across the country meant to stop the march toward legal equality for lesbians and gays. As mentioned above, the Republican governor of Massachusetts has resuscitated a 1913 antimiscegenation law that "voids marriages conducted in Massachusetts for out-of-state same-sex couples if that marriage would not be accepted in their home state."[40] While this law probably shouldn't even be on the books anymore, given its origins, it has not, in recent history, been used to bar heterosexuals from marrying. As Martin Luther King might point out, the law is also unjust because while neutral on its face, it is being used to discriminate against a group of people and deny them their civil rights—in direct violation of the state's Supreme Court ruling.

As with opponents of the African American civil rights movement, antidemocratic opponents of legal equality for gays and lesbians claim that the rights of the people are being violated by the courts. For example, antigay activist and Harvard law professor Mary Ann Glendon vehemently opposes "the flagrant disregard shown by judges and local officials for the rights of citizens to have a say in setting the conditions under which we live, work and raise our children." She is outraged that "four judges in one state took it upon themselves to make the kind of decision that our Constitution says belongs to us, the people, and *to our elected representatives*."[41]

In other words, when judges reason from the constitutional principle of legal equality—an absolutely fundamental principle of any democratic form of government—and decide that the Constitution prohibits discrimination against an unpopular minority and that religion cannot be used to justify legal discrimination, right-wing opponents proclaim that judges are just arbitrarily making things up. Yet in the American system, it is the role of the courts to apply constitutional principles to new situations never imagined by the Founders.

And like opponents of racial equality in past decades, those opposed to same-sex marriage argue in support of states' rights. For example, Glendon, outraged when local officials in San Francisco, California; Multnomah County, Oregon; and New Paltz, New York, issued marriage licenses to same-sex couples despite state law defining marriage as heterosexual—clearly an act of civil disobedience designed to challenge a discriminatory and unjust law—argues that "many Americans—however they feel about same-sex marriage—are rightly alarmed that local officials are *defying state law*."[42]

But if those opposed to same-sex marriage endorse the principle of states' rights, why do so many favor the Federal Marriage Amendment, which would take away from the states their traditional right to determine who can marry? For example, Robert Bork, an outspoken states' rights advocate, came out in favor of the Federal Marriage Amendment, arguing that it will protect the people from the "liberal activist courts [that] are the real problem."[43] Strangely, he is unconcerned that Federal Marriage Amendment will also prohibit state legislatures from making their own decisions about how to deal with the gay marriage issue—a direct violation of the states' rights principle upon which he ostensibly stands.[44]

In other words, many social conservatives, who have long espoused the importance of states' rights, quickly abandon this principle whenever it helps them to advance their antigay agenda. For example, the Christian Right lambasted Dick Cheney for his principled support of state sovereignty and individual liberty, two important conservative political principles, during the 2000 vice presidential debate. More specifically, when Bernard Shaw asked Cheney about same-sex marriage, he responded as follows:

> This is a tough one, Bernie. The fact of the matter is we live in a free society, and freedom means freedom for everybody. We don't get to choose, and shouldn't be able to choose and say, "You get to live free, but you don't." And I think that means that *people should be free to enter into any kind of relationship they want to enter into*. It's really no one else's business in terms of trying to regulate or prohibit behavior in that regard.
>
> The next step, then, of course, is the question you ask of whether or not there ought to be some kind of official sanction, if you will, of the relationship, or if these relationships should be treated the same way a conventional marriage is. That's a tougher problem. That's not a slam dunk. I think the fact of the matter, of course, is that matter is regulated by the states. *I think different states are likely to come to different conclusions, and that's appropriate. I don't think there should necessarily be a federal policy in this area.*

While Cheney clearly reasoned from the Republican Party's traditional commitment to both individual liberty and state sovereignty, Christian Right leaders portray Cheney's principled response as unprincipled. For example, one Christian Right spokesperson argues, "Cheney's answer troubled family advocates, but drew little opposition from Republicans, who were desperate to end Democratic control of the White House and feared exposing Cheney's softness on the homosexual issue." More ludicrously, they claim his answer reveals that the Bush administration is really advancing a prohomosexual agenda.[45] Perhaps George W. Bush attempted to answer that accusation when he finally came out in support of the Federal Marriage Amendment, a controversial position actually opposed by many Republicans.

A New Civil Rights Movement?

The parallels between the civil rights movement and the struggle for lesbian/gay civil rights seem obvious, even though the oppression of African Americans has been more long-standing and more severe. Both African Americans and lesbian/gay people have been denied legal equality, and both have been subjected to discrimination and violence. In both cases, major social movements have been accelerated by principled court rulings that went against societal traditions and popular sensibilities, and both used civil disobedience to protest unjust laws. In both cases the struggle for democracy was met with a right-wing backlash designed to protect the special privileges of the dominant group.

Nevertheless, the antigay Right wants to undermine the justness of lesbian/gay claims to legal equality by denying the similarity between the lesbian/gay civil rights movement and "The Civil Rights Movement" of the 1950s and 1960s. For example, the antigay Traditional Values Coalition "organize[d] a news conference on Capitol Hill of prominent African American preachers who argued that gay marriage is not a civil right."[46] Coming out in opposition to gay marriage, the Reverend Jesse Jackson—usually a progressive—rejects comparisons with the civil rights movement, stating "gays were never called three-fifths human in the Constitution," he said, and "they did not require the Voting Rights Act to have the right to vote."[47] While Jackson makes a valid point, no one is denying the unique oppression suffered by African Americans. However, just because African Americans have been more severely and comprehensively oppressed than lesbians and gays does not render the latter's struggle for equality trivial or invalid.

No matter who makes it, the assertion that gay marriage is not a civil rights issue is simply erroneous. Marriage has long been considered a civil right, as explained in chapter 3; consequently, the struggle of lesbians and gay men for access to marriage is a civil rights issue. Because of its historical importance, the struggle of African Americans for legal equality in the 1950s and 1960s is generally referred to as "The Civil Rights Movement." That does not mean, however, that there can never be another civil rights movement. Nor does calling gay marriage a civil rights issue minimize the atrocities committed against African Americans in this country for hundreds of years.

Antifeminism and the Rise of the New Right

In the wake of Goldwater's defeat and the passage of the Civil Rights Act of 1964 and the Voting Rights Act of 1965, right-wing leaders decided to repackage their agenda to make it more appealing to mainstream America.[48] While the Old Right's discourse included explicit racism, as just discussed, the New Right makes more subtle appeals, linking "opposition to welfare, affirmative action, and street crime all to negative images of African Americans and their struggle for social equality"—for example, Ronald Reagan's fabricated tale of the Cadillac-driving "welfare queen" or the first George Bush's infamous 1988 "Willie Horton" television ad.[49]

Feminism constituted precisely the enemy the New Right needed to consolidate its base. Liberal feminists—who seek to apply the principles of liberal political theory to women—began accelerating their work toward legal equality in 1962, when President Kennedy convened the Presidential Commission on the Status of Women. The commission's finding of widespread gender inequality—including "discrimination in employment, unequal pay, lack of social services such as child care, and continuing legal inequality"—contributed to the passage of the Equal Pay Act of 1963 "that made it illegal to have different rates of pay for women and men who did equal (i.e., the same) work."[50] Before that it was perfectly legal to pay men more than women for doing the same job.

Then in 1964 Congress passed the Civil Rights Act, which prohibits discrimination in employment on the basis of sex as well as race. (Interestingly, the suggestion that sex be included in the act came from an ardent segregationist who erroneously thought it would lead to the defeat of the bill.[51]) The struggle for gender equality before the law continued during the 1960s, culminating in the fight for the ratification of the Equal Rights Amendment (ERA), which simply stated: "Equality of rights under the law shall not be denied or abridged by the United States or any State on account of sex."[52] At first the ERA seemed like a shoo-in. It passed quickly through Congress in 1972 and within a year was ratified by twenty-two of the necessary thirty-five states.

As with the civil rights movement, however, progress toward legal equality stimulated a right-wing backlash from traditionalists. Old Right activist Phyllis Schlafly successfully mobilized many conservative homemakers against equality for women, appealing to traditionalism and fear of change, as well as to states' rights against the federal amendment. Due to their "precarious social position," homemakers turned out to be "a natural resource for groups that wanted to turn back the clock on the sexual, legal, and labor force trends that had undermined the patriarchal basis of the family in the decades before the ERA struggle."[53] The specter of gender equality hastened "the political awakening of evangelicals," who began to feel "threatened about their ability to promote the supremacy of the traditional nuclear family."[54] Antifeminism "provided a link with fundamentalist churches" and focused "the reaction against the changes in child rearing, sexual behavior, divorce, and the use of drugs that had taken place in the 1960s and 1970s."[55] *Roe v. Wade*, the 1973 Supreme Court decision giving women the right to decide for themselves, within the first trimester, whether or not to bear a child, also helped mobilize conservative Christians, including many Catholics.[56] The conservative mobilization against feminism solidified the New Right, including its Christian Right core, during the 1970s and played a "very important" role in its success, the election of Ronald Reagan in 1980, and the rightward shift in U.S. politics.[57]

The women's movement and the lesbian/gay civil rights movement were linked theoretically and through common struggle, and the Right used this connection to its advantage. For example, long before same-sex marriage was on the radar screen of the lesbian/gay rights movement, Schlafly's Eagle Forum stimulated opposition to women's equality by appealing to homophobia: "Militant homosexuals from all over America have made the ERA issue a hot priority. Why? To be able finally to get homosexual marriage licenses, to adopt children and raise them to emulate their homosexual 'parents,' and to obtain pension and medical benefits for odd-couple 'spouses.' . . . Vote NO on 6! The Pro-Gay E.R.A."[58] In its rise to power, the New Right successfully manipulated homophobia to increase opposition to gender equality and explicitly condemned all attempts to accord lesbians and gay men the equal protection of the law.

That 1970s Argument: The Anxiety of Right-Wing Women

Right-wing groups hope that the strategies they used against feminism in the 1970s can also be utilized against the gay marriage movement. For example, the Right tries to build support for its antihomosexual politics among mainstream Americans by claiming that the lesbian/gay rights movement, like the feminist movement, threatens the status of women. This strategy worked well in the 1970s with the first generation of New Right women who mobilized in opposition to the ERA and *Roe v. Wade*. Status was a key concern for those women. "At the beginning of the contemporary women's movement, in 1968, women of all classes found themselves in something like the same boat." Most were homemakers and/or low-level employees. However, over the course of the next two decades "homemakers suffered a tremendous loss in social prestige" as "high-status women" began choosing careers over homemaking. Consequently, conservative homemakers—who, after all, had done what society said they were supposed to do—found themselves facing "status degradation," and they understandably resented it.[59]

Twenty-five years later, many Christian Right women see lesbians and gays as threatening the special status of heterosexual marriage, and again they feel diminished. For example, the Christian Right group Concerned Women for America (CWA), which claims to be the largest women's group in the country, wants heterosexual marriage to maintain its privileged status in American society and continue to function as the justification for special rights available only to heterosexual Americans. The group consistently asserts that the struggle of lesbians and gay men for the right to marry is not an attempt to participate in the institution of marriage but rather an attempt to "undermine marriage" and destroy the family.[60] In strictly logical terms this makes no sense. Aren't lesbians and gays actually *reinforcing* the legitimacy of marriage as an institution through their struggle for the right to marry? Indeed many within the LGBT community have criticized this struggle for doing precisely that and not much more.[61] While same-sex marriage would not undermine the institution of marriage in general, it would undermine the *traditional patriarchal heterosexual vision of marriage* in particular, which is precisely what the Christian Right desperately wants to reinforce.

The Christian Right consistently blames a wide array of complicated societal problems on feminism and the lesbian/gay rights movement—even the military abuse of Iraqi prisoners at Abu Ghraib prison during 2003 and 2004.[62] Vehemently opposed to government-sponsored social programs, Christian Right women favor laws that force *individual men* to take responsibility for the children they father and for the mothers who bear those children. The 1970s generation feared that the changes inaugurated by feminism—legal equality for women, reproductive freedom, no-fault divorce, and the loosening of sexual mores—would make it easier for men to get out of their familial commitments. As opposed to feminists who wanted the right to compete equally with men, antifeminist women, for the most part, did not have the educational level or job skills that would allow them to pursue satisfying careers, if forced to work outside the home.[63]

Many traditional women feared that the ERA would eliminate the legal requirement for husbands to support their wives financially in exchange for domestic labor.[64] (In the early 1970s, family law "often made important distinctions between family members based solely on their sex," but "by the late 1970s, these laws had almost all been changed, struck down as unconstitutional . . . or become unenforceable because they were presumptively unconstitutional."[65]) Phyllis Schlafly told homemakers that the ERA would say,

"Boys, supporting your wives isn't your responsibility anymore."[66] At the same time, the rise of "no-fault" divorce laws during this period further threatened the economic security of traditional "housewives." As Schlafly put it, "even though love may go out the window, the obligation should remain. ERA would eliminate that obligation."[67]

To this day, many Christian Right women condemn no-fault divorce, which permits the dissolution of marriage without having to demonstrate a legitimate reason before a judge—such as infidelity, desertion, or extreme cruelty—because it "allows one person to decide when a relationship can be severed,"[68] and it does not automatically reward the wronged party with extra economic benefits. They fail to mention that women file the majority of divorce suits. While it's true that women often suffer a decline in their standard of living upon divorce, would forcing people to stay married against their will really help the position of women? Wouldn't addressing the disparity in men's and women's wages help more?

While pay equity, safe and affordable childcare, and universal health insurance constitute a progressive solution to the problems caused by the fragility of marriage (over half of which now end in divorce) and callousness of deadbeat dads, many right-wing women demand the return of a traditional patriarchal vision of marriage, ignoring the reality of social change.[69] Moreover, their policy solutions suggest they are more interested in reconsolidating patriarchy than in solving social problems. For example, while fathers should certainly take economic responsibility for their children, it's important to note that the fathers of poor children are often quite poor themselves, and so cannot adequately support a family. Consequently, insisting that *only* they, and not the government, have a responsibility to support their children will not actually ameliorate the problem of childhood poverty.

Many conservative women also worry about the effects of sexual freedom on their position in society. In the 1970s, traditional women feared that the loosening of sexual mores would make it more difficult for them to keep their marriages intact and thus maintain their economic security. Kristen Luker's interviews with the first generation of "pro-life" women revealed the following insight:

If women plan to find their primary role in marriage and the family, then they face a need to create a "moral cartel" when it comes to sex. . . . If many women are willing to sleep with men outside of marriage, then the regular sexual activity that comes with marriage is much less valuable an incentive to marry. . . . [For] traditional women, their primary resource for marriage is the promise of a stable home, with everything it implies: children, regular sex, a "haven in a heartless world." Thus, a social ethic that promotes more freely available sex . . . limits their abilities to get into a marriage in the first place, and it undermines the social value placed on their presence once within a marriage.[70]

As the saying goes, "Why buy the cow, when you can get the milk for free?" For the first generation of Christian Right women, the ostensive sexual liberation of many feminist women threatened to destabilize the marital bargain that many traditional women relied upon and thus to undermine their position in society.[71] They feared that, given the option, their husbands might abandon them for younger, more interesting women.

Do today's Christian Right women fear that if given the choice their husbands might prefer other men? Perhaps. After all, antigay activist Paul Cameron tells them that "the evidence is that men do a better job on men, and women on women, if all you are looking for is orgasm." If you want "the most satisfying orgasm you can get," he explains, "then homosexuality seems too powerful to resist. . . . It's pure sexuality. It's almost like pure heroin. It's such a rush." In opposition, he tells us, "marital sex tends toward the boring" and generally "doesn't deliver the kind of sheer sexual pleasure that homosexual sex does."[72] Although the American Psychological Association expelled Cameron for ethics violations in 1983, he still serves as an oft-quoted right-wing "expert" on homosexuality.[73] In light of his comments, it would be understandable for Christian Right women to feel anxious about their ability to keep their husbands interested in monogamous, heterosexual marriage.

Some on the Right insist that with the important role played by women in the traditional family already undermined by feminism, the specter of same-sex marriage threatens to render women completely useless. For example, William Mattox, a *USA Today* columnist and Alliance for Marriage supporter, argues that "in the same way that polygamy teaches that women are inferior to men, 'gay marriage' implicitly teaches that women are superfluous to men, that women make no unique and irreplaceable contribution to family life. Indeed, 'gay marriage' teaches that the most basic unit of human society—marriage—does not need a woman to be complete."[74]

Despite this interesting rhetorical strategy, however, same-sex marriage does not actually undermine the position of women. In fact, the majority of same-sex couples seeking marriage are women—57 percent of the 3,395 same-sex couples who wed in San Francisco between February 12 and March 11, 71 percent of those who wed in Portland between March 3 and April 20, and 66 percent of first-day applicants in Massachusetts were women, as are two-thirds of Vermont civil unions.[75] Since access to the civil benefits of marriage will help these women take care of each other as they age, gay marriage clearly helps rather than hurts women by making it easier for them to survive outside the bounds of patriarchal marriage—which is exactly what that Right opposes.

The Christian Right wants to continue portraying lesbians and gay men as inordinately driven by sexual desire and so unable to form long-term relationships. The visibility of committed same-sex couples illustrates the ordinariness of most lesbian and gay people's lives and demonstrates an alternative to the Christian Right's rigid view of proper gender roles and narrow definition of what constitutes a family. Because of their particular theological beliefs (discussed in chapter 4), many conservative Christians insist that men and women are fundamentally different beings that come together to reproduce and must remain coupled in order to rear their children. Because homosexuality disconnects sex from reproduction, they reason, homosexual relationships must be fleeting, driven by sexual gratification alone. As Beverly LaHaye puts it, "it is the compulsive desire for sexual gratification without lasting commitment, the high rate of promiscuity, and the self-defined morality among homosexuals that sap the vitality of the family structure, making it something less than it was, is, and should be." Consequently, "homosexual relationships are not only the antithesis to family, but also threaten its very core."[76]

Clearly the desire of many same-sex couples to marry and to raise children demonstrates that lesbians and gay men are not primarily seeking hedonistic gratification. In fact, the first same-sex couple to receive a marriage license in San Francisco has been together for over fifty years, whereas half of all heterosexual marriages end in divorce. Most lesbians and gay men want the same types of relationships that straight people do. In fact, an estimated "64 to 80 percent of lesbians and 46 to 60 percent of gay men report that they are in committed partner relationships," and "studies show that gay and lesbian relationships are comparable to opposite-sex relationships in terms of quality of the relationship and satisfaction in the relationship."[77] Furthermore, according to 2000 census data, "lesbian couples . . . parent at about three quarters of the rate of married straight couples, and gay male couples parent at about half the rate as married straight couples"—and this only includes couples with at least one child living with them.[78] Nevertheless, despite empirical evidence, Christian Right groups purposely disseminate misinformation in an attempt to bolster their political agenda of marginalizing lesbians and gay men and reconsolidating the tradition of male dominance.

Phony Populism on the Right

Right-wing opponents of gay marriage claim that they stand for the interests of ordinary people when they oppose legal equality for all. This rhetorical strategy worked well during the 1970s when opponents of the ERA portrayed feminism as advancing the interests of elite career women at the expense of ordinary housewives and working-class women.[79] That is to say, because the ERA would require laws to treat men and women the same, it would not only prohibit discrimination against women but would also eliminate "special protections" for women workers. Consequently, Schlafly opposed it with arguments such as the following: "It comes with exceedingly poor grace for a woman who sits at a comfortable desk to demand legislation which will deprive a woman who stands on her feet all day of the right to have a chair."[80] Yet although Schlafly claimed to speak for working-class women, it was "middle-class women [who] performed the day-to-day activist tasks that defeated ERA."[81] Furthermore, a recent study of the origins of the New Right reveals its mass base to comprise not the farmers and blue-collar working folks of George Wallace's segregationist South or even the lower-middle-class white ethnics who became "Reagan Democrats," but rather the educated, affluent, upwardly mobile white suburbanites, who reap material benefits from tax cuts and reduced government spending, from real estate development and the military-industrial complex, and from the traditional entitlements of white Christian America.[82]

In its attack on same-sex marriage, the Right continues its pseudopopulist pose, claiming to speak for the interests of ordinary people who are supposedly being attacked by an elite "homosexual lobby." As Chip Berlet and Matthew Lyons have argued, Christian Right "movement propaganda often portray[s] gay men, like feminists, as a wealthy, privileged elite misusing their power to impose their immoral agenda on society."[83] For example, Ken Connor, a Family Research Council fundraiser, says, "the Human Rights Campaign [HRC] and the other groups in the homosexual lobby have very deep pockets. Big corporations, elite foundations, and Hollywood celebrities underwrite the homosexual lobby with tens of millions of dollars every year."[84] Similarly, Andrea Sheldon, the executive director of the Traditional Values Coalition, calls HRC "the wealthiest extremists of the Left."[85] In reality, however, antigay groups outspend lesbian/gay groups "by at least a four-to-one ratio."[86] Moreover, contrary to myth, gay men actually earn 20 to 25 percent less income than do heterosexual men. "Lesbians appear to earn about the same as heterosexual women, but lesbian couples earn less than straight couples because women, on average, earn less than men."[87] Finally, many state and local antigay marriage groups that promote themselves as "grassroots" are actually funded by wealthy national organizations.[88]

Neopatriarchy: The Religious Version

Joining the opposition to same-sex marriage are advocates of the fatherhood movement, who seek to restore traditional gender roles and reestablish the patriarchal family as the dominant and privileged family form in America, even though it has been shown to undermine the status of women in society.[89] Because no evidence exists that lesbian and gay couples are less functional than heterosexual ones, or that their children are more likely to suffer negative effects, allowing same-sex couples to marry and have children would clearly undermine the myth that the patriarchal heterosexual family is the superior family form.[90] Consequently, the fatherhood activists repeatedly assert that children need not just two parents, but both a *masculine father* and a *feminine mother* in order to develop properly.

The fatherhood movement blames feminism and single mothers for the social problems caused by men and teenaged boys. While the packaging of their arguments varies slightly, advocates of this school of thought generally make a similar claim: Refusing to respect natural gender differences, feminists have pathologized masculinity and futilely attempted to change the behavior of men and boys. They have undermined the rightful authority of men as the head of the household, attempted to change the natural division of labor that exists between mothers and fathers, and propagated the idea that a woman can fulfill the role traditionally played by a man, thus rendering fathers superfluous to family life. Consequently, men have lost interest in fulfilling their traditional family responsibilities, and boys have no one to teach them how to become responsible men. Detached from the civilizing influence of the traditional patriarchal family, males increasingly cause a wide array of social problems, and everybody suffers.[91]

Focus on the Family president James Dobson makes this argument from a Christian Right perspective. In *Bringing Up Boys* (2000), he insists that traditional gender roles are natural and cannot be changed. He points to the continued power of men in society as evidence of their natural dominance: "After thirty years of feminist influence and affirmative-action programs," only seven CEOs of Fortune 500 companies and eleven U.S. senators are women. Moreover, "there have been forty-three presidents of the United States, all of them male. The National Organization for Women has pointed to these discrepancies to 'prove' that patriarchy and discrimination prevail in the culture. The more likely explanation, however, is biochemical and anatomical."[92]

Dobson strongly opposes attempts to change the gender socialization of children and explicitly links this "unisex" idea to "the powerful gay and lesbian agenda," whose

> propagandists are teaching a revolutionary view of sexuality called "gender feminism," which insists that sex assignment is irrelevant. . . . Taking that concept to its illogical conclusion, the feminists and homosexual activists want to dissolve the traditional roles of mothers and fathers, and, in time, eliminate such terms as *wife, husband, son, daughter, sister, brother, manhood, womanhood, boy, girl, masculine,* and *feminine*. These references to sexual identity are being replaced with gender-neutral terms, such as *significant other, spouse, parent, child,* and *sibling*.[93]

While Dobson sees this as dangerous for both sexes, it is particularly harmful for boys: "I urge you to protect your boys from those who are espousing these postmodern views. . . . Protect the masculinity of your boys, who will be under increasing political pressure in years to come."[94]

Because gender differences were "carefully designed by the Creator," so that men and women would complement each other in heterosexual marriage, men should not "be feminized, emasculated, and 'wimpified.' "[95] Because women have the "privilege and blessing" of bearing children, "they are inclined toward predictability, stability, security, caution, and steadiness." Men, on the other hand, "are designed to provide for their families physically and to protect them from harm and danger. . . . Men are also ordained by Scripture for leadership in their homes."[96] When a family lacks both a male and a female, children suffer, especially boys. Whether due to no-fault divorce, irresponsible childbearing by single women, or male dysfunction, not having an involved father is "catastrophic for males."[97] Also problematic are fathers who have "surrendered their authority at home and are either altogether uninvolved or they are trying to nurture their children in ways that are more characteristic of mothers." When gender differences are not clearly delineated at home, this is "terribly confusing to boys."[98]

Dobson believes that a breakdown of traditional gender roles within the family fosters homosexuality in children. The prevention of homosexuality among boys requires the involvement of a properly masculine heterosexual father, especially during the early years. Dobson relies on the work of Joseph Nicolosi, a leading proponent of the Christian Right's "ex-gay" movement,[99] who urges parents to scrutinize their children for signs of "prehomosexuality," so professionals can step in before it is too late. While "feminine behavior in boyhood" is clearly a sign, so is "nonmasculinity," defined as not fitting in with male peers.[100] "The father," Nicolosi asserts, "plays an essential role in a boy's normal development as a man. The truth is, Dad is more important than Mom." In order to ensure heterosexuality, the father "needs to mirror and affirm his son's maleness. He can play rough-and-tumble games with his son, in ways that are decidedly different from the games he would play with a little girl. He can help his son learn to throw and catch a ball. . . . . He can even take his son with him into the shower, where the boy cannot help but notice that Dad has a penis, just like his, only bigger."[101]

Based solely on the work of Nicolosi, Dobson concludes, "If you as a parent have an effeminate boy or a masculinized girl, I urge you to get a copy [of Nicolosi's book] and then seek immediate professional help." Beware, however, of "secular" mental health professionals who will most certainly "take the wrong approach—telling your child that he is homosexual and needs to accept that fact." Instead, Dobson recommends a referral to either Exodus International, the leading organization of the ex-gay ministries, or the National Association for Research and Therapy of Homosexuality, "formed to oppose the 1973 decision by the American Psychological Association to no longer classify homosexuality as an emotional or mental disorder."[102]

Dobson's emphasis on the important role played by fathers bolsters the arguments of the "fatherhood movement," which emerged during the 1990s. One of the first organizations to spearhead this movement was the Promise Keepers (PK), founded by Bill McCartney, who is known to be antigay,[103] in 1990 as a "Christ-centered ministry dedicated to uniting men through vital relationships to become godly influences in their world."[104] This organization wants to restore fathers to their rightful place at the head of the patriarchal family.[105] PK member Tony Evans advises husbands: "Sit down with your wife and say something like this: 'Honey, I've made a terrible mistake. I've given you my role. I gave up leading this family, and I forced you to take my place. Now I must reclaim that role.'" Although phrased in a supportive way, the Promise Keeper's claim is nonnegotiable: "Don't misunderstand what I'm saying here," Evans continues, "I'm not suggesting that you *ask* for your role back, I'm urging you to *take it back*. . . . Your wife's concerns may be justified. Unfortunately there can be no compromise here. If you're going to lead you must lead. Be sensitive. Listen. Treat the lady gently and lovingly. But *lead!*"[106] Dobson's group Focus on the Family published the Promise Keepers' manifesto, *Seven Promises of a Promise Keeper.*[107]

Neopatriarchy: The Secular Version

Institute for American Values president David Blankenhorn advances a similar agenda using secular arguments. His book *Fatherless America* (1995)[108] and the follow-up volume *The Fatherhood Movement* (1999)[109]—coedited with Wade Horn (George W. Bush's Assistant Secretary of Health and Human Services) and Mitchell Pearlstein—blames the "declining child well-being in our society" not on growing levels of poverty, deteriorating public services, lack of safe and affordable childcare, the lower income of women, child abuse, racism, or misogyny, but rather on fatherlessness. Despite empirical evidence to the contrary,[110] Blankenhorn insists that fatherlessness is "the engine driving our most urgent social problems, from crime to adolescent pregnancy to child sexual abuse to domestic violence against women."[111] While some conservatives argue that "the best antipoverty program for children is a stable, intact family," Blankenhorn demands more: "a married father on the premises."[112]

Like those on the explicitly Christian Right, Blankenhorn insists that children need not just two involved parents but more specifically *a male father and a female mother enacting traditional gender roles.* Blankenhorn claims that "gendered parental roles derive precisely from children's needs." During childhood "the needs of the child compel mothers and fathers to specialize in their labor and to adopt gender-based parental roles." Consequently, men and women should stick with traditional roles, Blankenhorn insists, even if this conflicts with their "narcissistic claims" to personal autonomy.[113]

Like Dobson, Blankenhorn condemns attempts to equalize the roles of mothers and fathers in child rearing, and derides what he calls the new "like-a-mother father" who changes diapers and does other traditionally female tasks.[114] While Blankenhorn barely mentions lesbians and gay men in his analysis, his argument clearly justifies opposition to same-sex marriage. Obviously, his insistence that proper childhood development requires heterosexual parents who enact traditional gender roles indicates that, in his view, homosexual couples cannot raise healthy children, a belief supported by no empirical evidence. In addition, however, Blankenhorn specifically advocates laws to prohibit unmarried women from accessing sperm banks,[115] which lesbians have been increasingly doing, generating the so-called "gaby boom." Perhaps he shares the fear of CWA that gender equality would mean that "lesbian women would be considered no different from men," especially once they get access to male seed.[116] If that were to happen, where would that leave men?

In addition, the lack of explicit references to homosexuality should not be interpreted as a lack of homophobia. As Jean Hardisty has discovered, since the mid-1980s, antigay organizations have tended to "highlight the religious principles undergirding their anti-homosexual politics only when they are targeting other Christians. When organizing in the wider political arena, they frame their anti-gay organizing as a struggle for secular ends, such as 'defense of the family.'"[117] Thus in Christian Right circles you get James Dobson, in secular political circles David Blankenhorn, and in academic circles communitarian scholars (discussed in the next chapter). Despite variations on the theme, one thing remains constant: the normative vision presented by these activists gives lesbians and gay men absolutely no place in family life and, by extension, no place in democratic society.

Blankenhorn and other "family values ideologists," like Barbara Defoe Whitehead and David Popenoe, claim to focus on the well-being of children when they make their arguments for restoring fathers to their rightful place at the head of the neopatriarchal family. As political scientists Jyl J. Josephson and Cynthia Burack have demonstrated, however, their repeated misreadings of empirical studies of child well-being and their lack of advocacy for policies to help children beyond calling for the return of the traditional family render their motives suspect. At the same time, their emphasis on reestablishing traditional gender roles within families, despite "extensive feminist analysis and empirical evidence" documenting the ways in which "gender role differentiation in families is connected to stratification in economic, political and social life" in a way that harms women, leads Josephson and Burack to conclude that the real agenda of the fatherhood movement is the reconsolidation of male authority over women in both private and public[118]—what I call neopatriarchy. No wonder ostensibly secular "family values ideologist" Whitehead is admired by prominent Christian Right leaders, such as Pat Robertson, Bevery LaHaye, and her husband Timothy, a coauthor of the popular evangelical "Left Behind" series.[119]

Conclusion

The extension of the traditionally heterosexual institution of marriage to encompass lesbian and gay couples challenges the heartfelt beliefs of many conservative Americans. Right-wing supporters of neopatriarchy are using a variety of discursive strategies to appeal to those Americans—using rhetoric that not only plays on their fears but also resonates with cherished cultural myths about the traditional family. Yet many of those same Americans also embrace a deep commitment to the values of American democracy, which is why antigay activists often frame their fundamentally antidemocratic positions in democratic terms.

What this chapter has argued, however, is that despite the superficial appeal to commonsense notions about families and fathers and tradition, the antigay agenda of the neopatriarchal Right actually undermines many of America's most precious democratic values, including personal liberty, gender equality, and equal treatment before the law. The debate about gay marriage brings two sets of traditions into conflict—the tradition of heterosexual-only marriage with the democratic tradition of legal equality, individual choice, equal rights, and fair treatment. Lesbian and gay advocates of marriage do not seek to destroy tradition completely. Instead, they dream of a time when they and their families will be respected members of American society.

Notes

1. MSNBC NEWS, "Calif. judge strikes down gay marriage ban: Ruling says there is 'no rational purpose' for limiting unions," March 14, 2005, http://msnbc.msn.com/id/7182628/ [accessed 14 March 2005].

2. Sara Diamond, Roads to Dominion (New York: Guilford Publications, 1995), 5–11.

3. John Egerton, Speak Now against the Day: The Generation before the Civil Rights Movement in the South (Chapel Hill, NC: University of North Carolina Press, 1994), 455.

4. Maurice Isserman and Michael Kazin, American Divided: The Civil War of the 1960s, 2nd ed. (Oxford: Oxford University Press, 2000), 27.

5. Egerton, Speak Now, 456.

6. Jean V. Hardisty, Mobilizing Resentment: Conservative Resurgence from the John Birch Society to the Promise Keepers (Boston: Beacon Press, 1999), 38. For an interesting case study, see Lisa McGirr, Suburban Warriors: The Origins of the New American Right (Princeton, NJ: Princeton University Press, 2001).

7. Norberto Bobbio, Left & Right: The Significance of a Political Distinction (Chicago: University of Chicago Press, 1996).

8. Earl Black and Merle Black, The Rise of Southern Republicans (Cambridge, MA and London: Belknap Press of Harvard University Press, 2002), 3; Mary C. Brennan, Turning Right in the Sixties: The Conservative Capture of the GOP (Chapel Hill & London: University of North Carolina Press, 1995), 49–50.

9. For an in-depth study of the segregationist South, see Egerton, Speak Now.

10. Sean Cahill, Same-Sex Marriage in the United States: Focus on the Facts (Lanham, MD: Lexington Books, 2004), 19.

11. Carolyn Lochhead, "Pivotal day for gay marriage in U.S. nears Massachusetts move to legalize weddings may intensify backlash in other States," *San Francisco Chronicle*, May 2, 2004, www.sfgate.com/cgi-bin/article.cgi?file=/chronicle/archive/2004/05/02/MNGM26EHU81.DTL [accessed 3 May 2004].

12. Steve Sailer, "Is love colorblind?—public opinion about interracial marriage," *National Review*, July 14, 1997, www.findarticles.com/p/articles/mi_m1282/is_n13_v49/ai_19617224 [accessed 1 April 2005].

13. *Loving v. Virginia*, 388 U.S. 1 (1967).

14. For a fuller discussion of the movement, see Terry H. Anderson, *The Movement and the Sixties: Protest in America from Greensboro to Wounded Knee* (Oxford: Oxford University Press, 1995), chapter 1, and Isserman and Kazin, *America Divided*, chapter 2.

15. *Brown v. Board of Education of Topeka*, 347 U.S. 483 (1954).

16. *Brown v. Board of Education II*, 349 U.S. 294 (1955).

17. Martin Luther King, Jr., "Letter from the Birmingham City Jail (16 April 1963)," in *American Political Thought*, 5th ed., ed. Kenneth M. Dolbeare and Michael S. Cummings (Washington, DC: CQ Press, 2004), 433–40, 436.

18. King, "Letter from Birmingham Jail," 436.

19. King, "Letter from Birmingham Jail," 436.

20. King, "Letter from Birmingham Jail," 436–37.

21. Diamond, *Roads to Dominion*, 70.

22. Diamond, *Roads to Dominion*, 75.

23. Isserman and Kazin, *America Divided*, 32.

24. Diamond, *Roads to Dominion*, 78–79, 81.

25. Egerton, *Speak Now*, 617.

26. Diamond, *Roads to Dominion*, 71.

27. Diamond, *Roads to Dominion*, 72.

28. Diamond, *Roads to Dominion*, 81.

29. Black and Black, *Rise of Southern Republicans*.

30. Black and Black, *Rise of Southern Republicans*, 4.

31. Diamond, *Roads to Dominion*, 63.

32. Diamond, *Roads to Dominion*, 65, 110.

33. Brennan, *Turning Right in the Sixties*, 124.

34. Eric Planin and Thomas B. Edsall, "Divides Accompanied Tenure and Ensuing Years," *Washington Post*, June 9, 2004.

35. Egerton, *Speak Now*, 618.

36. Cited in Diamond, *Roads to Dominion*, 73.

37. Cited in Diamond, *Roads to Dominion*, 74, her emphases removed.

38. George Wallace, "Gubernatorial Inaugural Speech" (1963), www.archives.state.al.us/govs_list/inauguralspeech.html [accessed 29 June 2004].

39. Diamond, *Roads to Dominion*, 82.

40. Carolyn Lochhead, "Pivotal day for gay marriage in U.S. nears Massachusetts move to legalize weddings may intensify backlash in other States," *San Francisco Chroni-*

cle, May 2, 2004, www.sfgate.com/cgi-bin/article.cgi?file = /chronicle/archive/2004/05/ 02/MNGM26EHU81.DTL [accessed 3 May 2004].

41. Mary Ann Glendon, "For Better or for Worse? The federal marriage amendment would strike a blow for freedom," *Wall Street Journal*, February 25, 2004, www.opinion journal.com/editorial/feature.html?id = 110004735 [accessed 19 March 2004], emphasis added.

42. Glendon, "For Better or for Worse?", emphasis mine.

43. Robert Bork, "Stop Courts from Imposing Gay Marriage: Why We Need a Constitutional Amendment," *Wall Street Journal*, August 7, 2001, www.wsj.com [accessed 8 August 2001], emphasis mine.

44. Robert H. Bork, *The Tempting of America: The Political Seduction of the Law* (New York: Simon & Schuster, 1990).

45. Quote from Robert Knight, Peter LaBarbera, and Kenneth Ervin, II, "The Bush Administration's Republican Homosexual Agenda: The First 100 Days," May 31, 2001, http://cultureandfamily.org/library/papers/22pb000.shtml [accessed 16 July 2002]. See also *C&F Report* Staff, "Ashcroft's Second in Command Speaks at Justice Dept. Gay Pride Celebration," *Culture & Family Report*, June 19, 2002, http://cultureandfamily.org/report/ 2002–06–19/n_doj.shtml?print [accessed 18 July 2002].

46. Hanna Rosin, "A Family Business: For the Rev. Lou Sheldon and His Daughter, Marriage Means Only One Thing," *Washington Post*, May 20, 2004, C1.

47. Keith Boykin, "Whose Dream? Why the Black Church Opposes Gay Marriage," *Village Voice*, May 24, 2004.

48. Hardisty, *Mobilizing Resentment*, 38.

49. Diamond, *Roads to Dominion*, 91.

50. Sara M. Evans, *Born for Liberty: A History of Women in America* (New York: Free Press, 1997), 275.

51. Evans, *Born for Liberty*, 276.

52. Mansbridge, *Why We Lost the ERA*, 1.

53. Mansbridge, *Why We Lost the ERA*, 109–10.

54. Diamond, *Roads to Dominion*, 161.

55. Mansbridge, *Why We Lost the ERA*, 5–6.

56. Kristin Luker, *Abortion and the Politics of Motherhood* (Berkeley, CA: University of California Press, 1984).

57. Hardisty, *Mobilizing Resentment*, 72.

58. Mansbridge, *Why We Lost the ERA*, 137.

59. Mansbridge, *Why We Lost the ERA*, 105–7.

60. Concerned Women of America, "History: 1978–2001," http://cwfa.org/about/his [accessed 2 April 2002].

61. See Michael Warner, *The Trouble with Normal: Sex, Politics, and the Ethics of Queer Life* (New York: Free Press, 1999), and Valerie Lehr, *Queer Family Values: Debunking the Myth of the Nuclear Family* (Philadelphia: Temple University Press, 1999).

62. Robert Knight, "Iraq Scandal Is 'Perfect Storm' of American Culture," www.cwfa

.org/articledisplay.asp?id = 5663&department = CWA&categoryid = misc [accessed 21 June 2004].

63. Mansbridge, *Why We Lost the ERA*, 105–7.

64. Mansbridge, *Why We Lost the ERA*, 108.

65. Mansbridge, *Why We Lost the ERA*, 91. See her chapter 9 for a full discussion of costs and benefits of the ERA versus tradition for the status of women.

66. Quoted in Mansbridge, *Why We Lost the ERA*, 109.

67. Mansbridge, *Why We Lost the ERA*, 108.

68. Trudy Hutchens, "Marriage: The State of the Union," 1996, 4, http://cwfa.org/library/family/1996–10_fv_marriage.s [accessed 2 April 2002].

69. See Stephanie Coontz, *The Way We Never Were: American Families and the Nostalgia Trap*, 2nd ed. (New York: Basic Books, 2000).

70. Luker, *Abortion and the Politics of Motherhood*, 208–9.

71. See also David Popenoe, "Challenging the Culture of Fatherlessness," in *The Fatherhood Movement: A Call to Action*, ed. Wade F. Horn, David Blankenhorn, and Mitchell B. Pearlstein (Lanham, MD: Lexington Books, 1999), 21.

72. Quoted in Robert Dreyfuss, "The Holy War on Gays," *Rolling Stone*, March 18, 1999, 41.

73. Hardisty, *Mobilizing Resentment*, 102.

74. William Mattox, Jr., "Gay Marriage Devalues Women," *USA Today*, August 21, 2001, www.allianceformarriage.org/reports/fma/usatoday.htm [accessed 15 July 2002].

75. Evelyn Nieves, "The Women's Marriage March: Majority of Same-Sex Couples Who Took Vows Are Female," *Washington Post*, May 25, 2004, and Associated Press, "Women In Vermont Form More Civil Unions," April 7, 2002, www.telegram.com/news/inside/vtlesbians.html [accessed 7 April 2002].

76. Beverly LaHaye, "The Homosexual Agenda" (Concerned Women for America, 1991), 8.

77. Cahill, *Same-Sex Marriage*, 55.

78. Cahill, *Same-Sex Marriage*, 57.

79. Phyllis Schlafly, *The Power of the Positive Woman* (New York: Crown Publishing Group, 1977).

80. Quoted in Diamond, *Roads to Dominion*, 169.

81. Diamond, *Roads to Dominion*, 169.

82. McGirr, *Suburban Warriors*.

83. Chip Berlet and Matthew N. Lyons, *Right-wing Populism in America: Too Close for Comfort* (New York: Guilford Press, 2000), 237.

84. Quoted in Cahill, *Same-Sex Marriage*, 26.

85. Quoted in Cahill, *Same-Sex Marriage*, 26.

86. Cahill, *Same-Sex Marriage*, 26.

87. Cahill, *Same-Sex Marriage*, 59.

88. Cahill, *Same-Sex Marriage*, 27.

89. Jyl J. Josephson and Cynthia Burack, "The Political Ideology of the Neo-Traditional Family," *Journal of Political Ideologies* 3, no. 2 (1998), 213–31.

90. See Judith Stacey and Timothy J. Biblarz, "(How) Does the Sexual Orientation of Parents Matter?" *American Sociological Review* 66, no. 2 (April 2001): 159–83.

91. For examples of this argument see Lionel Tiger, *The Decline of Males: The First Look At an Unexpected New World for Men and Women* (New York: St. Martin's Griffin, 2000); Christina Hoff Sommers, *The War against Boys: How Misguided Feminism Is Harming Our Young Men* (New York: Simon & Schuster, 2000); and James Dobson, *Bringing Up Boys: Practical Advice and Encouragement for Those Shaping the Next Generation of Men* (Wheaton, IL: Tyndale House Publishers, Inc., 2000).

92. Dobson, *Bringing Up Boys*, 23.

93. Dobson, *Bringing Up Boys*, 16–17.

94. Dobson, *Bringing Up Boys*, 17.

95. Dobson, *Bringing Up Boys*, 26, 27.

96. Dobson, *Bringing Up Boys*, 27.

97. Dobson, *Bringing Up Boys*, 56.

98. Dobson, *Bringing Up Boys*, 72.

99. Hardisty, *Mobilizing Resentment*, 117.

100. Dobson, *Bringing Up Boys*, 119.

101. Dobson, *Bringing Up Boys*, 122.

102. Dobson, *Bringing Up Boys*, 123. Quotation from Hardisty, 117.

103. McCartney is explicitly antigay. In 1992 he "said at a press conference that homosexuality was a 'sin' that is 'an abomination of almighty God.'" See Hardisty, *Mobilizing Resentment*, 115.

104. Bill McCartney, *Seven Promises of a Promise Keeper* (Nashville, TN: Word Publishing, 1999), 235.

105. Cited in Linda Kintz, *Between Jesus and the Market: The Emotions That Matter in Right-wing America* (Durham, NC: Duke University Press, 1997), 129.

106. Cited in Kintz, *Between Jesus and the Market*, 129, emphasis in the original.

107. Russ Bellant, "Promise Keepers: Christian Soldiers for Theocracy," in *Eyes Right! Challenging the Right Wing Backlash*, ed. Chip Berlet (Boston: South End Press, 1995, 82.

108. David Blankenhorn, *Fatherless America: Confronting Our Most Urgent Social Problem* (New York: Basic Books, 1995).

109. Horn, Blankenhorn, and Pearlstein, eds. *The Fatherhood Movement*.

110. Josephson and Burack, "Neo-Traditional Family," 213–31.

111. Blankenhorn, *Fatherless America*, 1.

112. Blankenhorn, *Fatherless America*, 43.

113. Blankenhorn, *Fatherless America*, 101.

114. Blankenhorn, *Fatherless America*, 99.

115. Blankenhorn, *Fatherless America*, 223.

116. Concerned Women for America, "'Second Wave's' Last Hurrah: Equal Rights

Amendment Resurrected," November 3, 1999, http://cwfa.org/library/family/1999-11-03_era.shtml [accessed 3 April 2002].

117. Hardisty, *Mobilizing Resentment*, 38.

118. Josephson and Burack, "Neo-Traditional Family," 224–25.

119. Josephson and Burack, "Neo-Traditional Family," 229f. For more information about the series, see www.leftbehind.com/.

CHAPTER SIX

~

Are Lesbian and Gay Americans Actually Citizens? The Homophobic Myopia of Communitarianism

What therefore is a majority taken collectively, if not an individual who has opinions and most often interests contrary to another individual that one names the minority? Now, if you accept that one man vested with omnipotence can abuse it against his adversaries, why not accept the same thing for a majority? Have men changed in character by being united?

—Alexis de Tocqueville, *Democracy in America*[1]

If the United States is a democracy, then shouldn't the people decide whether or not they want to legalize gay marriage? Many advocates of communitarianism say "yes" because they emphasize the importance of the public will as the basis of democratic governance. Communitarianism forms one strand in an academic school of thought called "democratic theory," which argues that American democracy is not working as well as it should. Elections present limited options; they do not ensure that the issues that most concern citizens are on the agenda or that they will be addressed in the way citizens want. Democratic theorists generally see our current system—run by career politicians, partisan zealots, and powerful interest groups, and consequently detached from ordinary people and their concerns—as a very limited vision of democracy that does not adequately enact the will of the people. They want to give citizens a greater role in setting the normative direction for public policy, a level of participation that goes well beyond simply voting in elections every few years.

137

Communitarianism stresses that democratic self-government requires popular sovereignty: the people have the right to govern themselves, and public policy should reflect the will of the citizenry. But if democracy means popular sovereignty, then how can same-sex marriage be justified democratically, since the majority of American citizens apparently do not embrace it? Aren't opponents of gay marriage correct in arguing that the will of the people has been trampled by the series of recent court decisions, especially the Massachusetts case, in which the state's Supreme Court ordered the legalization of same-sex marriage, that have bolstered the gay marriage cause? Shouldn't citizens have the opportunity to decide for themselves whether gay marriage is acceptable? Shouldn't different states be allowed to address the controversial issue in different ways?

Communitarians often emphasize the importance of shared values as the foundation for democratic self-government and hope to reintroduce moral reasoning into political discussions. For example, critical of what they see as an overemphasis on individual rights, some stress the need for responsible and virtuous citizens, willing to fulfill their civic duties for the good of the community. In addressing social problems, "communitarians seek to rely neither on costly government programs nor on the market alone, but on the powerful 'third force' of the community. By reawakening communities and empowering communities to assert their moral standards, communitarians seek to hold individuals accountable for their conduct."[2] For many communitarians, gay marriage undermines the traditional values of communities, and so it weakens rather than strengthens democratic self-government.

This chapter responds to a variety of communitarian concerns surrounding same-sex marriage. First, I contest the claims of some communitarian critics by exposing their assertions as based on "commonsense" biases, rather than empirical data or historical evidence. Second, I argue that because communitarianism is a theory of democracy, it must include a commitment to legal equality that precludes systematic discrimination against a minority group of citizens. Moreover, the communitarian vision of self-government calls for the inclusion of all citizens as equal participants in democratic society and for laws that serve the common good, rather than just particular interests—both of which preclude the marginalization of lesbian and gay citizens. Finally, I examine the logic of communitarian arguments, showing how the problems they note can be addressed without resorting to antidemocratic solutions.

Communitarian Theory: The Importance
of Popular Sovereignty

Communitarian theorist Michael Sandel discusses the ways in which the privileging of liberal values, like individualism and the notion of "rights as trumps," undermines the possibility of civic life by denying that Americans owe anything to each other *as citizens* and consequently undermining the possibility that citizens can work together to solve shared problems. Arguing primarily against the theoretical vision of John Rawls (discussed in chapter 3), Sandel summarizes contemporary liberalism as follows: "Its central idea is that government should be neutral toward the moral and religious views its citizens espouse. Since people disagree about the best way to live, government should not affirm in law any particular vision of the good life. Instead, it should provide a framework of rights that respects persons as free and independent selves, capable of choosing their own values and ends."[3] While liberalism strives to maintain peace in a pluralistic society by mandating a neutral state that allows each individual the freedom to pursue his or her own individual conception of the good life, Sandel considers this vision inadequate. His approach criticizes liberal political theory for valorizing the idea that political decisions can be made without taking a stand on moral controversies ("the bracketing of moral claims"), for allowing individual rights claims to override every other political consideration ("rights as trumps"), and for overstressing abstract individualism without recognizing the particularities that make people's lives meaningful or the ways in which our lives are interrelated and interdependent ("the unencumbered self").

In his attempt to dislodge the philosophical dominance of liberalism, Sandel contests liberalism's claim that it presents us with a neutral framework within which each person has the right to pursue his or her own good. Instead, he argues, liberalism actually institutionalizes a particular vision of the good, in which the values of toleration, freedom, and social cooperation always trump other moral values. While recognizing the benefits of such a system, Sandel also suggests "it is not always reasonable to set aside competing values that may arise from substantive moral and religious doctrines. At least where grave moral questions are concerned, whether it is reasonable to bracket moral and religious controversies for the sake of political agreement partly depends on which of the contending moral or religious doctrines is true."[4] For example, the liberal solution to the debate over abortion—"the right to choose"—makes sense only if liberals are correct in arguing that abortion is not murder; if the Catholic Church is correct and abortion is indeed murder, then it cannot be allowed under the guise of individual choice.

Sandel's communitarian approach maintains that democracy requires popular sovereignty—the will of the people should form the basis of law and public policy—not just the protection of individual rights. What if the citizens of a particular community believe that God condemns homosexuality as morally wrong? What if those citizens consider their moral beliefs not simply a personal choice but rather a commandment from God? What if they understand themselves as fundamentally constituted by their religious worldview? What if they want to pass their vision of the world along to their children? Shouldn't they be able to govern themselves in accordance with their own fundamental beliefs about right and wrong? Why should they have to capitulate to what they consider immoral practices, just because some individuals claim they have a right to choose their own lifestyles? Sandel wants citizens to deliberate about moral issues and make substantive decisions about what kind of society they want to live in.

In his discussion of homosexuality, Sandel rejects the liberal approach to the issue, which "holds that people should be free to choose their intimate associations for themselves, regardless of virtue or popularity of the practices they choose, so long as they do not harm others."[5] Personally, Sandel does not condemn homosexuality as immoral. In fact, he criticizes liberalism because it "leaves wholly unchallenged the adverse views of homosexuality itself," producing only a "thin and fragile toleration" of gays and lesbians.[6] ("I don't like gays but we have to tolerate them, just like we have to tolerate all degenerates.") Sandel suggests that lesbian/gay relationships should be defended on moral grounds rather than simply tolerated on the basis of equal rights. One could argue, he explains, that "much that is valuable in conventional marriage is also present in homosexual unions. On this view, the connection between heterosexual and homosexual relations is not that both are the products of individual choice but that both realize important human goods."[7] Sandel prefers the communitarian defense because it does not play into what he sees as the problematic "motifs of contemporary liberalism— rights as trumps, the neutral state [with its bracketing of moral claims], and the unencumbered self—[that] figure with increasing prominence in our moral and political culture" and that are directly undermining the possibility of creating a rich civic culture in which we can all share.[8]

Communitarian scholar Robin West agrees with Sandel that gay marriage should be defended in moral terms, but not because it offers the same thing as heterosexual marriage. Instead, she suggests, gay marriage may in fact be morally superior to straight marriage in certain respects. For example, as opposed to traditional marriage, same-sex marriage "has never been predicated on the presumed desirability of subordinating the female sex. There is no history, in the history of same-sex marriage, of a 'marital rape exemption,' according to which one of the partners is entitled to sex on demand, regardless of the consent or desire of the other." Nor, one might add, does it entail the gendered division of labor—and the so-called double shift—that often overburdens women in heterosexual marriages. Consequently, West believes that gay marriage has the potential to make the institution of marriage more egalitarian. "Should same-sex marriage ever become a reality in this culture," she argues, "it whould [sic] 'normalize' the ideal of a for-life union between sexual equals."[9]

Convinced of the limitations of liberalism, progressive political theorist Valerie Lehr shares the communitarian position that conflicts over gay marriage should be resolved via public deliberation rather than adjudicated as rights claims. "Central to my critique," she writes, "is the argument that the extension of rights depoliticizes issues that need to be subject to public debate and discussion. To foreclose such controversies through the extension of rights is not to resolve them; it is to deny the full significance of such questions for society by containing debate."[10] Lehr hopes that such discussions will yield progressive results: "The extension of marriage and family rights to gays and lesbians would serve to foreclose serious questioning of the values embedded within current understandings of marriage and family. Such foreclosure would mean that the extension of rights will have taken away the possibility of enhancing freedom," by establishing more progressive approaches to family policy besides bolstering the monogamous dyad.[11]

While Sandel, West, and Lehr clearly sympathize with the desire of lesbians and gays to be respected, the problem remains that the communitarian approach they proffer empowers *communities* to make moral determinations about homosexual relationships, and so it leaves open the possibility that communities might criminalize such relationships rather than respect them. While democratic self-government does entail popular sovereignty, by definition it also includes equality among citizens; in fact, that is the starting assumption of democracy. (And this is true whether you consider the United States a liberal democracy or a republic.) Consequently, if a majority violates the principle of civic equality and votes to take away the rights of a minority group, it turns itself into a nondemocratic community. Would anyone argue that the segregationist South was a democratic community because the majority who wanted to subordinate African Americans were able to put their will into law?

Communitarian Practice: Why Popular Sovereignty Alone Is Not Enough

Despite the wish of progressive communitarians that citizens might construct a shared moral vision that fully includes lesbians and gay men, a 1998 report by the Council on Civil Society, *A Call to Civil Society: Why Democracy Needs Moral Truth*, presents the more likely outcome of the communitarian model. The council's plan for strengthening American democracy emphasizes the importance of supporting families with two *married* parents[12] and the need to *increase* the "influence of religion in public life."[13] Granted, neither of these conservative agenda items is wholly problematic from a democratic perspective when properly contextualized. Certainly, our society should support the efforts of married couples with children to "raise healthy, caring, productive, and morally grounded children," and certainly, we should respect religious values that lead to "neighbor-love" and "help to drive progressive change."[14] Additionally, to be fair, the report also includes a large number of progressive recommendations as well, like better family leave and improved public education.

These caveats notwithstanding, the council's primary emphasis on marriage and religion as providing the necessary moral foundation for democracy leaves little room for lesbians and gay men, who are denied the civil right of marriage and whose sexual practices are condemned by most organized religions as sinful and immoral. While the council seems to studiously avoid directly addressing the specter of gay marriage, council chair Jean Bethke Elshtain, a prominent "democratic theorist" at the University of Chicago, has made clear elsewhere that she opposes such a possibility.[15] She explicitly embraces "a normative vision of the family—mothers, fathers, and children," insisting that her preferred family form "is not only *not* at odds with democratic civil society but is in fact, now more than ever, a prerequisite for that society to function."[16] While she fails to explain why she believes the heterosexual-only family constitutes a necessary prerequisite for a fully functioning democracy—a strong claim to make with no argumentation—her vision clearly leaves no place for lesbians or gay men within democratic society.[17]

While Elshtain's vision may very well resonate with the commonsense assumptions of many Americans, she provides no evidence to support her empirical claims; she *simply asserts* the connection between traditional families and democratic self-government—and the causal relationship between "the breakdown of the family" and the decline of civil society—*without actually arguing it*. As social scientist Judith Stacey puts it, "Elshtain unapologetically" privileges the heterosexual family and opposes equal marriage and family rights for same-sex couples, "despite consistent research findings that lesbians and gays parent at least as successfully as heterosexuals."[18] Elshtain seems to let her academic credentials stand in for actual argumentation.

While there is nothing wrong with scholars taking stands on controversial political issues, it's important to recognize that Elshtain offers not a well-substantiated scholarly argument but simply a personal opinion. The ideological nature of her opinion becomes evident when we look at the council's links to the neopatriarchalists discussed (or footnoted) previously. The Council for Civil Society was cosponsored by the Institute for American Values, headed by David Blankenhorn, a leader of the Fatherhood Movement. Antigay activists Maggie Gallagher and William Mattox are affiliate scholars of the institute, and antifeminist writer Christina Hoff Sommers, the author of *The War against Boys*, serves as an advisor. Mary Ann Glendon signed the council's report.

The council also has ties to the Bush administration's White House Office for Faith-Based and Community Initiatives (OFBCI).[19] The office was part of Bush's plan to eliminate any remaining barriers to religious organizations receiving federal funds for providing social services, which many believe violates the separation of church and state. In a report titled "Leaving Our Children Behind: Welfare Reform and the Gay, Lesbian, Bisexual and Transgender Community," the National Gay and Lesbian Task Force argues that the Bush administration's program of "charitable choice" actually constitutes a "massive transfer of tax dollars to religious institutions . . . [that] often would come with no demand for fiscal accountability, no requirement that religious institutions not discriminate, and no safeguard against recipients of social services being subjected to proselytizing and other forms of coercive activity."[20] Council on Civil Society members include John DiIulio, Jr., who formerly ran the OFBCI, which came under fire for allowing the Salvation Army to discriminate against lesbians and gay men in hiring and still receive federal funds, and Don Eberly—the former director of the National Fatherhood Initiative—also employed at the OFCBI.

Eberly explicitly links the neopatriarchal and communitarian emphases on the "traditional" family and conservative religion to the neoliberal agenda of free markets and minimal government. Diagnosing the central problem for American democracy as "moral decline," rather than "civic disengagement," Eberly recommends religious piety as the solution to public problems—an approach to religion that emphasizes inward devotion and moral purity. According to Eberly, religion needs to play a key role in civil society as "both a legitimate wellspring of personal values and as perhaps the richest source of renewed social capital [social trust] in communities."[21] While some people blame "governmental malfeasance and feckless politicians" for the decline of trust, Eberly believes that "a more likely source of our cynicism is the rupture of our primary relationships within the family, or our marriages, and our fellowship with our fathers."[22]

Appealing to the narrow stereotypes about gender frequently invoked by Christian conservatives and providing absolutely no empirical evidence to document his claims, Eberly insists that "it is fathers who cultivate a spirit of reasonableness and compromise, a capacity to trust and be trustworthy, a willingness to be helpful and empathetic, and a capacity to act with self-restraint and respect toward others."[23] Mothers merely play a "biologically determined role."[24] According to his view, "fathering, unlike mothering . . . is heavily influenced by the wider culture."[25] Therefore, Eberly insists, "there can be no healthy democracy without dads."[26] While Eberly's argument may seem absurd to many, it articulates major themes in the burgeoning "fatherhood movement" that politically opposes both feminism and equality for lesbian and gay citizens, as discussed in the previous chapter.

In light of the antihomosexual politics of the council and its affiliates, it should come as no surprise that communitarianism has been criticized for illustrating the problems of majoritarianism. In response, the influential communitarian guru Amitai Etzioni stresses that "American society has both constitutional and moral safeguards against majoritarianism that communitarians should very much respect. These safeguards basically work by *differentiation*, by defining some areas in which the majority has not had and ought not have a say and those in which it does and should. We are not a simple democracy but a constitutional one. That is, some choices, defined by the Constitution, are declared out of bounds for the majority."[27] Etzioni reminds us that any democratic version of communitarianism must include protection for basic rights for all—including lesbian and gay citizens. With this caution, he reiterates a central concern of Alexis de Tocqueville about the danger of the tyranny of the majority.

It is the argument of this book that the civil rights of lesbians and gay men, including the right to marry, constitute precisely the type of issue that should not require community approval. Public deliberation would be an appropriate way to address a range of issues: Where do we draw the line on thorny issues of church and state? What role should the family play in a democratic society? How can we best socialize children to become active citizens? What types of policies would best help families flourish? Communitarians do and should address these questions, but, in a democratic society, the solutions cannot include discrimination against lesbian and gay citizens.

Communitarian Misreadings of the Civic Republican Tradition

Communitarian scholars sometimes ground their calls for change with appeals to the American Founding. For example, a diverse group of communitarian theorists now stress that the American Founders believed that democracy requires virtuous citizens in order to function effectively. While virtue was a concern at the Founding, the moralistic and individualistic notion of virtue most often invoked by conservative communitarians differs markedly from the ideal of *civic virtue* espoused by our republican founders, such as the "antifederalists." That is to say, when the republican Founders invoked "virtue," they generally referred to "the idea of what we would now call 'public spirit,' a disposition to do things and make sacrifices for the good of the community of which one is a member, and not to set one's own narrow notion of private interests before everything else."[28]

It is important to note that the concept of civic virtue did not come from the Protestant religious beliefs embraced by some of the Founders but rather arose from the civic republican tradition, which provides a democratic theory of government that historically stood opposed to the political sovereignty of Christianity.[29] Moreover, civic virtue—what Machiavelli called *virtu*—derives from the Latin word for *man* and connotes virility.[30] Thus, in the civic republican tradition it relates to manly citizenship, not to Christian notions of women's chastity. As Stephanie Coontz has noted, the idea that "private values and family affections form the heart of public life . . . represents a sharp break with . . . the early republican tradition."[31]

While the American Founders did want virtuous citizens, many communitarians invoke the concept of "virtue" in a historically and theoretically inaccurate way. For example, socially conservative historian Gertrude Himmelfarb—wife of neoconservative founding father Irving Kristol and mother of William Kristol, founder and editor of the *Weekly Standard*, an influential neoconservative publication—begins her discussion of the decline of American democracy by commenting, "Long before the founding of the American republic, Montesquieu explained that 'virtue' is the distinctive characteristic of a republic."[32] Immediately thereafter, she segues into a discussion of the "moral decline" of American democracy, pinpointing a number of trends, including "out-of-wedlock births, teenage pregnancy, . . . promiscuity," divorce, and abortion.[33] While she doesn't explicitly mention homosexuality, she would no doubt put it on her list of immoral sexual behavior. Thus, by the way she lays out her argument, Himmelfarb implies that an increasing level of sexual freedom, particularly among women, undermines the virtue necessary for republican self-government. But what connection do the personal sexual activities of women and other citizens have to do with their public-spiritedness (civic virtue)?

Harvard law professor and antigay activist Mary Ann Glendon also misrepresents the ideas of the Founders when she asserts that American democracy "requires (as the authors of *The Federalist Papers* put it) a higher degree of virtue in its citizens than any other form of government."[34] This is not actually true; *The Federalist Papers* barely mention virtue.[35] Moreover, the Federalists are best known for creating a system of government that does not rely on virtue but rather fuels its opposite, self-interest, in a way that controls faction (Federalist Paper #10). Moreover, while the Federalists did use the rhetoric of republicanism, James Madison's famous definition of a "republic" as representative government (in Federalist Paper #10) actually redefines the term in a way contrary to the larger tradition, as explained in chapter 1 of this book.[36]

Civic republican political theorists ground their belief in popular sovereignty on the Roman law that "what affects all must be decided by all."[37] Logically, the principle "what affects all must be decided by all" also implies that what does not affect all is not decided by all. This is especially true in light of the fact that liberty for both the republic and its citizens forms a foundational value for civic republicanism. In other words, popular sovereignty is not totalitarianism;[38] it does not give the government power to control the most personal decisions a person makes in his or her life, including those decisions related to intimate relationships and sexuality. Moreover, decisions that do affect all must be articulated in law, which by definition treats everyone the same—as articulated in the slogan, "the rule of law not the rule of men."

"Seedbeds of Virtue": Restoring the Patriarchal Family

Communitarians who emphasize individual moral virtue also espouse the idea that the family functions as a necessary "seedbed of virtue," instilling in children the virtues necessary for democratic citizenship. Citing Alexis de Tocqueville's depiction of American democracy from the 1830s, Glendon argues that "the American version of the democratic experiment leaves it primarily up to families, local governments, schools, religious and workplace associations, and a host of other voluntary groups to teach and transmit republican virtues and skills from one generation to the next." She specifically mentions virtues such as "deliberation, compromise, consensus-building, civility, reason-giving and tolerance."[39] Glendon explains that "Tocqueville took for granted that, in America, many of the requisite habits and beliefs would be taught and transmitted with families—chiefly by women, who were the main teachers of children and the 'keepers of orderly peaceful homes,'" and she uses this to justify her assertion that the family is "first and foremost among these 'seedbeds of virtue.'"[40]

On the surface Glendon's argument makes sense and sounds democratic: Children need to be socialized to become democratic citizens, and the family can play an important role in that process. Yet Glendon actually makes a much more conservative and controversial claim: She believes that only the patriarchal, heterosexual family can function as the seedbed of virtue necessary for the American democracy to flourish. First, by citing Tocqueville, she invokes his patriarchal view of the family, which he describes as follows: "In America the independence of woman is irretrievably lost within the bonds of marriage."[41] Writing just a decade before the beginning of the "first wave feminism" in 1848—the political struggle of women for the right to vote and own property—Tocqueville argues that Americans have never

> imagined that democratic principles should have the consequence of overturning marital power and introducing confusion of authorities in the family. They have thought that every association, to be efficacious, must have a head, and that the natural head of the conjugal association is the man. They therefore do not deny him the right to direct his mate; and they believe that in the little society of husband and wife, as well as in the great political society, the object of democracy is to regulate and legitimate necessary powers, not to destroy all power.[42]

Tocqueville insists that "in the United States the woman scarcely leaves the domestic circle and is in certain respects very dependent within it."[43]

While Tocqueville's description reinforces the ideological vision of contemporary conservatives, a large body of scholarship on women's history demonstrates that his description was inaccurate. Throughout the nineteenth century, women all across the country, in the Northeast, Midwest, and West, actually did leave their homes to form voluntary organizations in order to do important public work.[44] In other words, "women did not stay home and focus on the family during the nineteenth century but instead entered civil society to address the problems created by industrialization, formed social reform movements, built institutions to build a social justice agenda, and demanded that government take an active role in solving public problems."[45] While they had not yet reached their zenith, these activities were well underway at the time Tocqueville wrote *Democracy in America*. Thus, his view of marriage and family was as ideological then as it is today.

Second, while Glendon's conservative agenda is not apparent in some of her writings, the fact is that she actively advocates against lesbians and gays in her political work. While she does not mention the issue in *Seedbeds of Virtue*, Glendon so strongly opposes same-sex marriage that she has taken an active role in drafting both the Federal Marriage Amendment and the Massachusetts amendment designed to re-outlaw same-sex marriage. In fact, according to a Coalition for Marriage spokesperson, Glendon "has been kind of an on-call [person], someone to give us legal opinions on various language proposals, and she has been helping us to understand various proposals offered by legislators." This has been particularly helpful, the man notes, because "when someone like Professor Glendon speaks, she speaks with authority and is well-respected." In fact, she is currently considered "the leading legal expert for gay-marriage opponents on Beacon Hill." Moreover, because of her conservative views on homosexuality and abortion, in 2004 Pope John Paul II appointed Glendon "to lead the Pontifical Academy of Social Sciences, which produces research to help the church establish its social policy."[46] How can Glendon, who emphasizes the importance of virtues like "deliberation, compromise, consensus-building, civility, reason-giving and tolerance" in her academic work, justify such a politics of discrimination?[47]

The Conservative Politics of Liberal Communitarianism

In direct response to the rise of communitarianism, particularly the work of Michael Sandel, a "revisionist" school of liberal political theory now emphasizes the important role of virtue in liberal democracies.[48] This liberal communitarianism is an innovative approach because historically liberalism developed as an alternative to a politics of virtue and in fact begins with the assumption of self-interested individuals, the antithesis of virtuous republican citizens. Liberal communitarianism argues that even though political liberalism constitutes a theory in which government must remain neutral toward conceptions of the good life, a properly functioning liberal democracy nevertheless requires citizens who have the virtues necessary for life in a free society. In making this argument liberal communitarians essentially agree with traditional communitarians, like Glendon and Elshtain, about the important role of the family in democratic society.[49]

George Mason law professor and Hoover Institute scholar Peter Berkowitz explains liberal communitarianism as follows: "Liberal theorists have increasingly come to appreciate the capacity of a liberal framework to respect the role of moral virtue, civic association, and even religious faith in the preservation of a political society based on free and democratic institutions."[50] That is, the traditional liberal "concern for the dignity and well-being of individuals has been complemented by consideration of the role of communities in forming individuals who are capable not only of caring for themselves and cooperating for mutual advantage but also of developing enduring friendships, sustaining marriages, and rearing children."[51] Liberal communitarians often suggest that in the nineteenth-century age of free markets and small government, religion and traditional gender roles created a context in which the moral virtues necessary for self-government in a liberal democracy could develop.

Citing Tocqueville, Berkowitz lauds the "formation of character" through "the family and the discipline of religion" in early America.[52] He roots the alleged demise of American democracy in divorce, unwed motherhood, and fatherless families and cites the traditional family and organized religion as "seedbeds of virtue" necessary to the proper functioning of a free society. For Berkowitz, "intact, two-parent families" are a vitally important source of the moral virtue upon which liberal democracy depends.[53] But "with more than half of all new marriages expected to end in divorce," he argues, "with unwed mothers accounting for 30 percent of all births, and with single-parent families becoming increasingly common, the family . . . cannot readily serve . . . as a steady reservoir of the necessary virtues."[54]

In making the case for the importance of virtue in liberal society, however, Berkowitz, like others, inserts a conservative political agenda into his argument, an agenda that he neither explains nor supports with evidence. First, like Himmelfarb and Glendon, he shifts from a discussion of the virtues needed by a democratic society to an argument for *moral* virtue, a term that implies a connection with a larger metaphysical belief system, usually religion. Arguing "that the public good in a liberal state depends upon moral virtue," he suddenly announces "that *the sources of moral virtue in such a state are intact, two-parent families,* a vibrant civil society, and active citizen participation."[55] Berkowitz does not actually demonstrate that "intact, two-parent families," as opposed to other types of functional families, are the source of moral virtue but rather simply asserts it.

Communitarian theorists of virtue, like Glendon, Berkowitz, and others, provide the intellectual underpinnings for the Republican Party's platform position: "We rely on the home, as did the founders of the American Republic, to instill the virtues that sustain democracy itself. That belief led Congress to enact the Defense of Marriage Act, which a Republican Department of Justice will energetically defend in the courts. For the same reason, we do not believe sexual preference should be given special legal protection or standing in law."[56] Here again, an emphasis on the home as the primary "seedbed of virtue" somehow gets associated with an antigay political agenda, when it's not clear why it has to be.

What Lessons Does the Traditional Family Teach?

Surprisingly, William Galston, the University of Maryland political philosopher who worked in the Clinton White House, makes the same conservative argument about the family as do Glendon and Berkowitz. Galston argues that "the operation of liberal institutions is affected in important ways by the character of citizens (and leaders), and that at some point, the attenuation of individual virtue will create pathologies with which liberal political contrivances, however technically perfect their design, simply cannot cope."[57] As opposed to Berkowitz, however, Galston at least tries to demonstrate the alleged connection between the traditional family and democratic virtues. His approach distinguishes between "intrinsic traditionalism," which sees traditional morality as superior, and "functional traditionalism," which sees a link between "certain moral principles and public virtues or institutions needed for the successful functioning of a liberal community."[58]

Galston insists that "if a plausible (not necessarily conclusive) link can be forged between some aspect of traditional morality (e.g., intact two-parent family) and some feature of liberal public purposes, institutions, or conduct, then a rational basis exists for liberal public policy that endorses and helps sustain that aspect of tradition."[59] For example, because households headed by single mothers are more likely to be impoverished than households in which there is a man's salary and because poor children are more likely to experience a variety of social problems, Galston concludes that "the best anti-poverty program for America's children is a stable, intact family"[60]—an argument that disrespects families headed by single parents and same-sex couples. He does not consider other arguably more effective solutions to poverty, such as high-quality public schools in all neighborhoods, a livable minimum wage, or safe, affordable childcare.

Galston also makes a more specific argument about how the family instills virtue in children. It's important to note at the get-go that while his defense of the family does not explicitly specify the patriarchal heterosexual family form in particular, it is clear that he endorses that ideological vision for several reasons. First, he makes arguments similar to those of the antihomosexual communitarians and neopatriarchalists *without any caveats*. Second, he explicitly praises Mary Ann Glendon and Jean Bethke Elshtain for having "already said nearly every thing that needs saying on [the subject of the family]."[61] Third, Galston signed *A Call to Civil Society: Why Democracy Needs Moral Truths*, which says the number one priority for American democracy should be "to increase the likelihood that more children will grow up with their two married parents"[62]—and since lesbians and gays cannot legally marry that includes only heterosexual families. While one would expect his discussion to clarify exactly why only a traditional heterosexual family can properly prepare children for democratic citizenship, it does not. To the contrary, his argument seems to suggest the opposite.

Galston catalogues a wide array of virtues necessary for liberal democracy. An examination of how the particular virtues cited by Galston relate to the traditional family produces three different arguments. First, many of the virtues Galston emphasizes, while originally acquired in a family, do not require a patriarchal heterosexual family form in particular. For example, important virtues like civility, the work ethic, delayed gratification, adaptability, discernment, and "the ability to work within constraints on action imposed by social diversity and constitutional institutions" could certainly be instilled in children by any functional family, including one headed by same-sex parents. Galston makes no argument for the superiority of heterosexuals in fostering these characteristics in children, and such an argument does not make sense nor is it supported by empirical evidence.[63]

Second, the traditional patriarchal family could actually undermine a number of important virtues extolled by Galston. For example, he argues that independent individualism and diversity characterize a liberal society.[64] While children certainly need to learn independence, how does the traditional patriarchal family, in which wives are dependent upon their husbands' leadership and economic support, teach the virtue of independence to future female citizens? Galston must be focusing on boys only. He also fails to explain how legalized discrimination against nontraditional families fosters a respect for diversity.

Additionally, Galston argues that children must learn "to understand, to accept, and to act on the core principles of one's society." This "is particularly important in liberal communities," he argues, because they "tend to be organized around abstract principles rather than shared ethnicity, nationality, or history."[65] But if one of the fundamental principles of liberal democracy is legal equality for all citizens, again we must ask: what lessons does a child learn about equality growing up in a patriarchal nuclear family in which men lead and women submit? While the traditional family may provide certain benefits to children, it is unclear how it teaches them the universal principle of equality for all citizens, especially since this family form models gender inequality, a point political theorist Susan Okin made well over a decade ago.[66]

Third, a number of the democratic virtues Galston emphasizes could be undermined by the normative vision of the Christian Right. For example, Galston emphasizes "the willingness to *listen seriously to a range of views*" and the "willingness to set forth one's own views intelligibly and candidly as the basis of *a politics of persuasion rather than manipulation or coercion*."[67] This directly relates to the virtue of *tolerance*. While Galston stresses that the virtue of tolerance does not require a belief that all lifestyles are "equally good," it does mean that "the pursuit of the better course should be (and in some cases can only be) the consequence of *education or persuasion rather than coercion*."[68] While open-mindedness, tolerance, and noncoercion certainly constitute important virtues for any democratic society, they are not hallmarks of those supporting the antigay agenda espoused by the Christian Right.

So why do communitarians and their Christian Right supporters insist that the *traditional* family plays such an important role in socializing children? Is it the message of *conformity* communicated in a society that allows no diversity of family forms? Is it the lesson in female *subordination* taught by the wife's gracious submission to her husband's authority as the head of the household? Wade Horn, president of the National Fatherhood Initiative (and Bush administration appointee), emphasizes the importance of *obedience*: "Well socialized children have learned to listen to and obey the directions of legitimate authority figures, such as parents and teachers; under-socialized children have not."[69] While parents and teachers may understandably desire obedience in children, that "virtue," like conformity and subordination, is not usually considered a central virtue of democratic citizenship, which requires active participation in self-government and the use of one's own reason, not obedience to authority, conformity, and subordination, as in a dictatorship.

Christian Right leader James Dobson would agree wholeheartedly with Horn's praise of obedience. In *The New Dare to Discipline* Dobson stresses that respect for authority must be instilled in young children in order to avoid teenage rebellion and ensure respect for traditional religious values. This message is best communicated, he believes, by spanking children with a switch or a paddle any time they show defiance or willfully disobey their parents. As he puts it, "a controlling but patient hand will eventually succeed in settling the little anarchist, but probably not until he is between three and four."[70] Dobson stresses a spanking must be severe enough to make the child cry genuinely from pain rather than simply from anger or humiliation. While ostensibly condemning child abuse, Dobson praises the child-rearing practices of his wife, who once "stung" their *fifteen-month-old* daughter's "little legs" with a "switch" for disobeying an "order."[71] He also notes "there are those in the Western world who will not rest until the government interferes with parent-child relationships with all the force of law. It has already happened in Sweden."[72]

While people of good will may differ on the question of spanking children, one has to wonder why Dobson makes corporal punishment a central plank in his right-wing *political* platform.[73] Does physical punishment in childhood help produce conservative adults? According to a study by social scientists Michael Milburn and Sheree Conrad, subjection to frequent harsh corporal punishment during childhood directly correlates with punitive and authoritarian political attitudes. People with such backgrounds are "more likely to identify themselves as politically conservative and to hold conservative attitudes toward abortion, the use of military force, and the death penalty" and to express "prejudice and intolerance toward particular minority groups," including gays and lesbians.[74] Indeed, many Protestant fundamentalists strongly endorse the harsh physical punishment of children.[75] Perhaps these findings help explain the motivation behind Dobson's ostensibly nonpolitical views on child rearing, as well as the real agenda behind the traditional "family values" campaign.[76]

Teaching Democratic Virtues

If democratic self-government actually requires citizens who possess certain civic virtues, we should not, as a society, count on the family to inculcate those virtues in children. Relying on the family as the primary seedbed of virtue has three problems. First, many families are dysfunctional and consequently may not be reliable producers of democratic virtues. For example, a home plagued by domestic violence or child physical or sexual abuse or headed by alcoholics or drug addicts cannot be counted on to teach children democratic virtues. And even families without such glaring problems often have their own pathologies.

Second, parents have a variety of approaches to child rearing, from the very permissive to the very strict. In general, parents want to make sure that their children learn the basic moral and religious values they endorse, which may or may not line up squarely with democratic principles. People differ in their views of child rearing, and conservative parents certainly have the right to run strict authoritarian households (as long as they do not cross the line into child abuse). However, there is no reason to think that such households will instill in children the types of virtues required by a pluralistic democracy. Many conservative parents will more likely focus on instilling moral absolutism, obedience, and respect for authority in their children, rather than teaching them tolerance, critical thinking, and independent decision making. Moreover, the patriarchal family models male dominance and thus does not teach children of either sex gender equality, a fundamental principle of contemporary democracy.

Third, if liberal democracy needs particular virtues, wouldn't society be better served by deliberately instilling those virtues in children via institutions like the public schools, rather than hoping that families will produce the necessary virtues? Indeed, as Glendon herself points out, Tocqueville argued that "the American version of the democratic experiment leaves it primarily up to families, local governments, schools, religious and workplace associations, and a host of other voluntary groups to teach and transmit republican virtues and skills from one generation to the next."[77] He did not portray the family as the only or even the primary "seedbed of virtue." Moreover, civic virtue, defined as public-spiritedness, develops not necessarily through "the family and the discipline of religion," as communitarians like Berkowitz would have it, but also through engagement with other citizens in civil society.[78] People can acquire public-spiritedness as they work with other citizens to help solve shared problems, even if they originally acted on the basis of self-interest. Thus, fortunately, we do not have to rely on the often-dysfunctional family as the primary "seedbed of virtue."

Conclusion

Lesbian and gay Americans are citizens and as such they are entitled to the same equality and respect as heterosexual Americans. While many may view the traditional heterosexual family as the most desirable family form, there is no evidence that it does a better job of producing democratic citizens. And even if there were, lesbian and gay citizens would still have the right to form families and raise children, just like anyone else. While democratic self-government requires popular sovereignty, it also requires legal equality for all citizens.

The conservative communitarian thinkers discussed in this chapter profess the desire to strengthen American democracy, yet they advocate legal discrimination against lesbian and gay citizens. While claiming the mantle of "democratic theory," they seek to exclude lesbians and gays from participation in marriage and family, which they see as the foundation of American democracy. They portray marriage as a virtual panacea for a whole host of social ills, yet they refuse to allow same-sex couples access to that civil institution through which they can protect themselves and their families. Anti-gay democratic theory is a contradiction in terms. In fact, I would go so far as to assert that anyone who calls him or herself a democratic theorist must support legal equality for all, since legal equality is the necessary foundation for all forms of democracy. You simply cannot advocate discrimination against a minority group and also portray yourself as a supporter of democracy.

Notes

1. Alexis de Tocqueville, *Democracy in America*, trans. and eds. Harvey C. Mansfield and Delba Winthrop (Chicago: University of Chicago Press, 2000), 240.

2. Institute for Communitarian Policy Studies, "The Communitarian Vision," www.gwu.edu/~icps/vision.html [accessed 19 April 2004].

3. Michael J. Sandel, *Democracy's Discontent: America in Search of a Public Philosophy* (Cambridge, MA: Belknap Press of Harvard University Press, 1996), 4.

4. Sandel, *Democracy's Discontent*, 19.

5. Sandel, *Democracy's Discontent*, 104.

6. Michael Sandel, "Moral Argument and Liberal Toleration," in *New Communitarian Thinking: Persons, Virtues, Institutions, and Communities*, ed. Amitai Etzioni (Charlottesville and London: University of Virginia Press, 1995), 86.

7. Sandel, *Democracy's Discontent*, 104.

8. Sandel, *Democracy's Discontents*, 108.

9. Robin West, "Gay Marriage and Liberal Constitutionalism: Two Mistakes," in *Debating Democracy's Discontent: Essays on American Politics, Law, and Public Philosophy*, eds. Anita L. Allen and Milton C. Regan, Jr. (Oxford: Oxford University Press, 1998), 262.

10. Valerie Lehr, *Queer Family Values: Debunking the Myth of the Nuclear Family* (Philadelphia: Temple University Press, 1999), 14.

11. Lehr, *Queer Family Values*, 14–15.

12. The Council on Civil Society, *A Call to Civil Society: Why Democracy Needs Moral Truth*, A Report to the Nation from the Council on Civil Society (1998), 18. Available at www.americanvalues.org/html/r-call_to_civil_society.html [accessed 24 June 2004].

13. *Call to Civil Society*, 26.

14. *Call to Civil Society*, 8.

15. Jean Bethke Elshtain, "Against Gay Marriage—II: Accepting Limits," *Commonweal* CXVIII:22 (1991), 685–86.

16. Jean Bethke Elshtain, "The Family and Civic Life," in *Rebuilding the Nest: A New Commitment to the American Family*, ed. David Blankenthorn, Steven Bayme, and Jean Bethke Elshtain (Milwaukee, WI: Family Service America, 1990), 122, emphasis hers.

17. Elshtain, "Against Gay Marriage."

18. Judith Stacey, *In the Name of the Family: Rethinking Family Values in the Postmodern Age* (Boston: Beacon Press, 1996), 70. For a discussion of empirical studies of lesbian and gay parenting, see her chapter 5.

19. The full list of council members is: Enola Aird, John Atlas, Dan Coats, John DiIulio, Jr., Don Eberly, Jean Bethke Elshtain, Francis Fukuyama, William A. Galston, Robert George, Claire Gaudiani, Mary Ann Glendon, Ray Hammond, Sylvia Ann Hewlett, Thomas C. Kohler, Joseph Lieberman, Glenn C. Loury, Richard J. Mouw, Margaret Steinfels, Cornel West, Roger E. Williams, James Q. Wilson, and Daniel Yankelovich.

20. Bill Berkowitz, "Tilting at Faith-Based Windmills: Over a Year in the Life of President Bush's Faith-Based Initiative," *The Public Eye*, Summer 2002, 22–26, 22.

21. Don Eberly, "Civic Renewal or Moral Renewal," *Policy Review*, September–October 1998, 5, his brackets, www.policyreview.com/sept98/renewal.html [accessed 30 June 2004].

22. Eberly, "Restoring Civil Society through Fatherhood," in *The Faith Factor in Fatherhood*, ed. Don Eberly (Lanham, MD: Lexington Books, 1999), 251–63, 256.

23. Eberly, "Restoring Civil Society," 255.

24. Eberly, "Restoring Civil Society," 260.

25. Eberly, *America's Promise: Civil Society and the Renewal of American Culture* (Lanham, MD: Rowman & Littlefield, 1998), 55.

26. Eberly, "Restoring Civil Society," 253.

27. Amitai Etzioni, "Old Chestnuts and New Spurs," in *New Communitarian Thinking*, 23.

28. Pole, *American Constitution*, 12–13.

29. R. Claire Snyder, "A Strange Drift to the Right: The Civic Historiography of Michael Sandel," *New Political Science: A Journal of Politics and Culture* 25, no. 3 (September 2003): 307–26.

30. Hannah Fenichel Pitkin, *Fortune Is a Woman: Gender and Politics in the Thought of Niccolo Machiavelli* (Berkeley, Los Angeles, and London: University of California Press, 1984), 25.

31. Stephanie Coontz, *The Way We Never Were: American Families and the Nostalgia Trap* (New York: Basic Books, 2000), 96.

32. Gertrude Himmelfarb, *One Nation, Two Cultures* (New York: Vintage Books, 1999), 19.

33. Himmelfarb, *One Nation*, 20–22.

34. Mary Ann Glendon, "Introduction," in *Seedbeds of Virtue: Sources of Competence, Character, and Citizenship in American Society*, ed. Mary Ann Glendon and David Blankenhorn, (Lanham, MD: Madison Books, 1995), 1–2.

35. Pole, *American Constitution*.

36. Robert A. Dahl, *On Democracy* (New Haven, CT: Yale University Press, 1998), 16–17.

37. Maurizio Viroli, *Republicanism* (New York: Hill & Wang, 2002), 4.

38. J. L. Talmon accuses the republican political theory of Jean-Jacques Rousseau of laying the groundwork for totalitarianism in *The Origins of Totalitarian Democracy* (London: Secker & Warburg, 1952). For a refutation of that claim, see Snyder, *Citizen-Soldiers and Manly Warriors*, chapter 3.

39. Glendon, "Introduction," *Seedbeds of Virtue*, 4.

40. Glendon, "Introduction," 2.

41. Alexis de Tocqueville, *Democracy in America*, ed. Harvey C. Mansfield and Delba Winthrop (Chicago and London: University of Chicago Press, 2000), 565.

42. Tocqueville, *Democracy in America*, 574.

43. Tocqueville, *Democracy in America*, 576.

44. See Mary Ryan, *Women in Public: Between Banners and Ballots, 1825–1880* (Baltimore: Johns Hopkins University Press, 1990); Anne Firor Scott, *Natural Allies: Women's Associations in American History* (Urbana and Chicago: University of Illinois Press, 1991); Sara M. Evans, *Born for Liberty: A History of Women in America* (New York: Free Press Paperbacks, 1997); Sandra Haarsager, *Organized Womanhood: Cultural Politics in the Pacific Northwest, 1840–1920* (Norman and London: University of Oklahoma Press, 1997); Wanda A. Hendricks, "Agents of Social Welfare," in *Gender, Race, and Politics in the Midwest: Black Club Women in Illinois* (Bloomington, IN: University of Indiana Press, 1998); Cynthia A. Kierner, *Beyond the Household: Women's Place in the Early South, 1700–1835* (Ithaca, NY: Cornell University Press, 1998); and Gayle Gullett, *Becoming Citizens: The Emergence and Development of the California Women's Movement, 1880–1911* (Urbana and Chicago: University of Illinois Press, 2000), among others.

45. For an overview of women's activities and a longer discussion of my argument,

see R. Claire Snyder, "Radical Virtue: Women in Nineteenth-Century Civil Society," *New Political Science: A Journal of Politics and Culture* 26, no. 1 (March 2004): 51–69, 51.

46. Scott S. Greenberger, "Harvard law professor named to Vatican post," *Boston Globe*, March 10, 2004.

47. Glendon, "Introduction," *Seedbeds of Virtue*, 4.

48. Stephen Macedo, *Liberal Virtues: Citizenship, Virtue, and Community in Liberal Constitutionalism* (New York: Oxford University Press, 1990); William A. Galston, *Liberal Purpose: Goods, Virtues, and Diversity in the Liberal State* (Cambridge: Cambridge University Press, 1991); and Peter Berkowitz, *Virtue and the Making of Modern Liberalism* (Princeton, NJ: Princeton University Press, 1999).

49. For a discussion of the ways in which these different approaches to communitarianism are coming together, see Etzioni, *New Communitarian Thinking*.

50. Berkowitz, *Virtue*, 23.

51. Berkowitz, *Virtue*, 24.

52. Berkowitz, *Virtue*, 188.

53. Berkowitz, *Virtue*, 26.

54. Berkowitz, *Virtue*, 173–74.

55. Berkowitz, *Virtue*, 26.

56. Republican National Committee, "Party Platform," www.rnc.org/About/Party Platform/default.aspx?Section = 4 [accessed 5 Aug. 2004].

57. William Galston, "Liberal Virtues and the Formation of Civic Character," in *Seedbeds of Virtue*, 38.

58. William Galston, "The Reinstitutionalization of Marriage: Political Theory and Public Policy," in *Promises To Keep: Decline and Renewal of Marriage in America*, ed. David Popenoe, Jean Bethke Elshtain, and David Blankenhorn (Lanham, MD: Rowman & Littlefield, 1996), 280–81. For a discussion of the flaws in this type of argument, see Coontz, *Way We Never Were*; Jyl J. Josephson and Cynthia Burack, "The Political Ideology of the Neo-Traditional Family," *Journal of Political Ideologies* 3, no. 2 (1998): 213–31; and Stacey, *In the Name of the Family*.

59. Galston, "Reinstitutionalization of Marriage," 280–281.

60. Galston, "Reinstitutionalization of Marriage," 274–75.

61. Galston, "Reinstitutionalization of Marriage," 271.

62. *Call to Civil Society*, 18.

63. Judith Stacey and Timothy J. Biblarz, "(How) Does the Sexual Orientation of Parents Matter?", *American Sociological Review* 66, no. 2 (April 2001): 159–83.

64. Galston, "Liberal Virtues," 43, emphasis mine.

65. Galston, "Liberal Virtues," 43.

66. Susan Moller Okin, *Justice, Gender, and the Family* (New York: Basic Books, 1989).

67. Galston, "Liberal Virtues," 48, emphasis mine.

68. Galston, "Liberal Virtues," 44, emphasis mine.

69. Cited in Eberly, *America's Promise*, 54. Eberly praises Horn's recognition that "the

differences between the parenting styles of fathers and mothers indicate that fathers are essential to developing impulse control in the young" (55).

70. James Dobson, *The New Dare to Discipline* (Wheaton, IL: Tyndale House Publishers, Inc., 1992), 27.

71. Dobson, *Dare to Discipline*, 35–36.

72. Dobson, *Dare to Discipline*, 63.

73. Many studies have documented the detrimental impact of corporal punishment on children. See Phillip Greven, *Spare the Child: The Religious Roots of Punishment and the Psychological Impact of Physical Abuse* (New York: Vintage Books, 1992), and Murray Strauss with Denise A. Donnelly, *Beating the Devil Out of Them: Corporal Punishment in American Families* (New York: Lexington Books, 1994).

74. Michael A. Milburn and Sheree D. Conrad, *The Politics of Denial* (Cambridge, MA: MIT Press, 1996), 223, 227. Philip Greven concurs that "authoritarianism has always been one of the most pervasive and enduring consequences of physical punishment." See *Spare the Child*, 198.

75. See Greven, *Spare the Child*, and Milburn and Conrad, *The Politics of Denial*.

76. For an interesting and insightful discussion of the political work done by the ostensibly nonpolitical activities of Dobson, see Paul Apostolidis, *Stations of the Cross: Adorno and Christian Right Radio* (Durham, NC: Duke University Press, 2000).

77. Glendon, "Introduction," 2.

78. Snyder, "Radical Virtue."

CHAPTER SEVEN

~

Marriage Equality and Sexual Freedom: Toward a More Progressive Union

So far I have argued, hopefully persuasively, that the fundamental principles of liberal democracy—legal equality, individual liberty, civil rights, personal autonomy, human dignity, and the state of fairness—require the legalization of same-sex marriage, as a matter of principle, regardless of whether or not a majority approves. In making this argument, I have addressed a number of mainstream conservative arguments against same-sex marriage. Conservatives are not the only critics of gay marriage, however. A number of progressive scholars, many operating within the academic field of "queer theory," also oppose gay marriage, but for different reasons. First, they think the LGBT movement's recent emphasis on the right to marry has pushed the movement in a conservative direction and narrowed the field of political possibilities. Second, they argue that gay marriage may actually result in the stifling of sexual freedom by reinforcing the traditional idea that sexual relations should occur only within the bounds of monogamous marriage.

While not at the center of American political debates, these arguments frequently arise in academic discussions. Indeed, I have presented the research for this book in a variety of academic venues and have given a number of public talks sponsored by universities. In every instance, the most common line of criticism I have received comes from the progressive or queer perspective. This chapter responds to some of the main points made by left-wing critics, arguing that the liberal democratic approach utilized in this book *not only* requires the legalization of same-sex marriage (legal equality,

161

civil rights) *but also* protects the right of consenting adults to engage sexually with other consenting adults without state interference (individual liberty, personal autonomy). It also argues that because gay marriage is a civil rights issue, it should be supported as a matter of principle. Finally, fighting for the right to marry does not preclude working for more progressive policies designed to help people in general, not just married couples, take care of themselves and each other.

Will Gay Marriage Decrease Sexual Freedom?

English professor and "queer" activist Michael Warner is one of the key critics of the same-sex marriage effort. In *The Trouble with Normal: Sex, Politics, and the Ethics of Queer Life*, he argues that achieving the goal of gay marriage will result in a curtailment of sexual freedom. That is to say, he strongly opposes what he sees as the normalizing push toward gay marriage within the LGBT community, and he particularly condemns the correlative tendency among some gay marriage advocates to valorize the "Good Gay" (like the character Will on the hit TV show "Will and Grace"), who simply wants to marry and live like straight people, at the expense of the "Bad Queer" (like the Jack character), who insists on openly embracing a "deviant" lifestyle that most people don't understand[1]—like drag kings and drag queens, leather Daddies and leather dykes, the transgendered and the polyamorous. Warner fears that the legalization of gay marriage will further marginalize nonconforming sex and gender radicals and revive a 1950s mentality that stigmatizes the nonmarried and the nonmonogamous, refusing to respect their relationships as valid or include them in social life.

While the legalization of gay marriage certainly won't usher in an age of nonjudgmental open-mindedness toward all sexual practices, it seems very unlikely that it will catapult American society back to the period before the sexual revolution. While the pressure on heterosexual couples to marry has not gone away, unmarried straight couples do not face the kind of stigma and discrimination they did in the 1950s, when people were denied promotions, excluded from social events, and openly pitied by married folks. There is no sensible reason to believe that gay marriage will reverse decades of change in social mores. (Indeed, if that were the case, many conservatives would support it!) Certainly, it will not diminish the constant stream of sexually titillating images generated by the corporate-owned media—a major accelerant to the loosening of sexual mores, especially among the young. While some people will no doubt continue to stand in judgment of those who have non-normative gender identities or sexual desires or who express themselves in unorthodox ways, that intolerance needs to be addressed via education; it certainly does not constitute a valid reason to deny same-sex couples legal equality and the civil right to marry.

Warner argues that because gay marriage has the potential to integrate lesbian and gay couples into the mainstream of American society, it threatens to destroy the distinctive "queer culture" that has developed over the years in places like San Francisco and New York City. Warner portrays this subculture as sexually liberationist, nonjudgmentally inclusive, and fundamentally egalitarian: "Everyone's a bottom, everyone's a slut, anyone who denies it is sure to meet justice at the hands of a bitter, shady queen, and if it's possible to be more exposed and abject then it's sure to be only a matter of time before someone gets there, probably on stage and with style."[2] While people may differ in terms of how they would characterize queer culture or evaluate the scene Warner describes, the question he raises about assimilation and its corrosive effect on the distinctiveness of subcultures is an important one. Indeed assimilation forms a quintessential challenge to many immigrant communities, and the same would be the case for the queer community. Yet many minority groups have been able to maintain their distinctive cultural traditions while also participating in mainstream American society.

Warner believes that LGBT people will only be accepted into mainstream society if they downplay or hide their sexuality. He tells an anecdote about a gay man who had an article published in a gay magazine but was afraid to show his mother the publication because of all the sexually explicit sex ads contained within. So he founded a new gay magazine called *Hero*, which boasted "no sexy underwear ads, no personals, no ads for phone sex or adult web sites, no stories on sex, no ads for HIV medication."[3] It claimed to be "'the magazine for the rest of us.'"[4] Warner sees this as a renunciation of gay sex: "To gain respect, to erase the barrier of stigma that shames him before his mother, he must purify the group. And the way to do that, for a gay man, is to redeem gay identity by repudiating sex."[5] Warner sees gay marriage as another way of downplaying gay sexuality.

Contrary to what Warner implies, however, gay marriage does not render homosexuality invisible but rather makes lesbians and gays more visible. With state validation and protection, lesbians and gay men will feel more comfortable coming out in public, having their weddings announced in local newspapers, placing pictures of their spouses on their desks at work, and acting like straight married couples do in public. This in turn will make it easier and safer for nonmarried lesbians and gays to come out as well.

Moreover, same-sex marriage actually foregrounds lesbian/gay sexuality, rather than hides it. Everybody knows married people have sex (or are supposed to). If people view a pair of men or women as just friends, they might not think of them as lovers. If people know that a same-sex couple is married, however, they will assume they are sexually involved. Thus, contrary to what Warner asserts, gay marriage actually publicizes homosexuality rather than conceals it.

At the same time, gay marriage does do what Warner says, but in a good way: It takes what is seen as "deviant" and makes it acceptable. People who used to imagine that homosexuals must be inordinately driven by sexuality—otherwise why would they choose such a stigmatized life?—might come to see that same-sex relationships are about a lot more than just sex; they are also about all the mundane things that heterosexual marriage is about—having someone to come home to, eating together, doing dishes, keeping house, paying bills, watching TV. Gay marriage *is* about sex. but not *only* about sex—just like heterosexual marriage.

Does Gay Marriage Empower the State to Regulate Sexuality?

Warner also condemns the push toward gay marriage because he believes that civil marriage necessarily entails governmental regulation of sexuality. This claim has two parts—that marriage regulates the sexual lives of the married and that it requires the policing of extramarital sex. But does civil marriage really constitute state regulation of sexuality? The phrase *regulation of marital sex* implies an active policing of what goes on between partners in the privacy of their own home. While state-recognized marriage does require the state to determine who can and cannot get married (prohibiting relatives and minors for example), it does not necessarily mean that the state is regulating the internal workings of the relationship. While it's true that the state has in the past enacted laws regulating marital sex, and some of these laws are still on the books—for example, the state of Maryland has a law making all sexual positions except missionary illegal—the *Lawrence v. Texas* case is generally viewed as rendering all such laws unconstitutional.[6] In fact, because of *Lawrence*, in January 2005 the Virginia Supreme Court struck down a centuries-old state law against fornication. As Joanna Grossman notes, although the law "dated back nearly 200 years, [it] had not been enforced criminally against a consenting adult since the middle of the nineteenth century. As this long history and lack of enforcement indicates, fornication laws are a relic of a past in which most non-marital sexual conduct was considered criminal behavior."[7] In any case, the political theory of liberalism presented in this book to justify same-sex marriage precludes governmental meddling in the private sexual relations of individuals, married or not, so it supports Warner's call for sexual autonomy rather than undercuts it.

Warner also insists, however, that state-recognized marriage necessarily entails government persecution of sexual relations outside of marriage. Pulling together a large number of issues that need to be disentangled, Warner makes the following (very strong) claim:

> As long as people marry, the state will continue to regulate the sexual lives of those who do not marry. It will continue to refuse to recognize our intimate relations—including cohabiting partnership—as having the same rights or validity as a married couple. It will criminalize our consensual sex. It will stipulate at what age and in what kind of space we can have sex. It will send the police to harass sex workers and cruisers. It will restrict our access to sexually explicit materials. All this and more the state will justify because these sexual relations take place outside of marriage. In the modern era, marriage . . . is the zone of privacy outside of which sex is unprotected.[8]

While it is historically true that the state has done those things, the criminalization of extramarital sex does not *necessarily* go hand in hand with the existence of state-recognized marriage.

In fact, the political theory of liberalism prohibits the state from policing the sexual relations of consenting adults. The same political philosophy that prevents the state from prohibiting same-sex marriage on the basis of religious morality also demands that the state leave individuals free to pursue their own vision of the sexual good life, even if this means extramarital relations. In fact, Warner actually concedes this at one point in his essay: "The ability to imagine and cultivate forms of the good life that do not conform to the dominant pattern would seem to be at least as fundamental as any putative 'right to marry.'"[9] And here he is right: The principles of America's dominant public philosophy justify both same-sex marriage (legal equality and civil rights) and sexual freedom (right to privacy and personal autonomy). If state action contradicts this, it's a problem of application, not a problem of philosophy. Marriage equality and sexual freedom are not mutually exclusive.

Warner's claims in the long paragraph quoted above are overly sweeping, and he conflates too many issues. One has to make a distinction, for example, between what the liberal democratic state cannot legitimately do and what it can. It cannot criminalize the consensual sexual practices of adults, for example, but it can restrict sex in public places and erect age of consent laws designed to protect children from exploitation by adults, although such laws must be the same for gays and straights to be just.

Warner's rant also invokes the following question: If a cohabiting couple wants the "same rights" as a married couple, why wouldn't they simply get married? Right now, cohabitation without marriage exists as a different type of relationship than marriage. Indeed, one of the virtues of cohabitation is that it's not as legally binding as marriage. For example, some people choose not to marry in order to protect their finances in the event that the relationship ends. Those people would not want cohabitation to automatically entail the "same rights" as marriage. If they wanted to be married, they would get married. As it currently stands, however, only heterosexual couples get to make a choice between marriage and cohabitation. Cohabitation outside of wedlock is currently the only option for same-sex couples, even if they want the rights and responsibilities of marriage. If gay marriage were legally recognized, some same-sex couples might choose not to marry or not to marry right away, and that would be their choice.

Warner fears that the legalization of same-sex marriage will mean that no other type of relationship will be respected as legally valid. Interestingly, empirical evidence from other countries actually contradicts Warner's argument. As legal scholar William Eskridge reveals, "State recognition of same-sex unions in the West is part of a larger trend whereby the modern state is now offering a menu of government-sanctioned regulatory options from which romantic couples can choose, based in part on the level of commitment they have for or would like to present to each other"[10]—although this is not yet the case in the United States. Eskridge argues that the emergence of a variety of legal options for couples "argues strongly against the suggestion that state recognition of same-sex marriage means that the state will normalize all of its regulations around marriage and marriage alone."[11] This empirical evidence contradicts Warner's contention that the legalization of gay marriage will foreclose the possibility of the state recognizing other types of relationships. The creation of a menu of options might be a positive development, as long as all options are available to both same- and opposite-sex couples.[12] Marriage for straights and civil unions for gays should not be an acceptable alternative because it violates the principle of legal equality—"separate but equal" is "inherently unequal."[13]

Of course, as long as benefits accrue to marriage, the choice to marry cannot be fully free. Warner illustrates this point by quoting feminist philosopher Claudia Card:

> My partner of the past decade is not a domestic partner. She and I form some kind of fairly common social unit which, so far as I know, remains nameless. Along with such namelessness goes a certain invisibility. . . . We do not share a domicile (she has her house; I have mine). Nor do we form an economic unit (she pays her bills; I pay mine). Although we certainly have fun together, our relationship is not based simply on fun. We share the sorts of mundane details of daily living that [Richard] Mohr finds constitutive of marriage (often in her house, often in mine). We know a whole lot about each other's lives that the neighbors and our other friends will never know. In times of trouble, we are each other's main support. Still, we are not married. Nor do we yearn to marry. Yet if marrying became an option that would legitimate behavior otherwise illegitimate and make available to us social securities that will no doubt become even more important to us as we age, we and many others like us might be pushed into marriage. Marrying under such conditions is not a totally free choice.[14]

Card and Warner make an important point here: As long as American citizens want the government to provide married people with benefits that help them take care of each other and their children, people's choices will not be completely unconstrained. But allowing same-sex couples, like Card and her partner, the option of legal marriage does not take anything away from them. They could choose to remain as they are. Card seems critical of gay marriage, yet she admits that if she had the option of receiving state benefits, she would probably take it. This is a peculiar position to take. She seems to be implying that she wants the state to protect her from making choices against her beliefs by not allowing her the option of marriage. While it's true that the fact that marriage accrues benefits does influence people to marry, it still remains a choice, even if not a completely free one—as if there ever is such a thing.

At academic conferences, I often hear similar arguments from progressive heterosexuals. They say they "do not believe in marriage" because historically marriage played a key role in the subjugation of women, because it's a central prop in the "heteronormative" social order, because it distributes benefits in an unequal way, because it infringes on individual freedom, and/ or because it is a conservative institution. Despite their beliefs, however, many of these folks have chosen to exercise their option to marry because they want the benefits or because they don't want to be subjected to societal judgment for raising children outside of wedlock. That is certainly their choice. It is curious, however, that they then stand as critics of the *gay* marriage movement, arguing that lesbians and gays shouldn't be pursuing marriage because the institution is so conservative and problematic. Yet as far as I know, none of them is lobbying to take benefits away from heterosexual couples.

There are many criticisms to be made of the quest for gay marriage, but as I have argued throughout this book, marriage is a civil right that must be extended to all people, regardless of gender or sexuality. Arguing against gay marriage because you are ambivalent about marriage in general, or your own marriage in particular, is like arguing that women should not have struggled for the right to vote because voting is such an anemic form of participation, and we should really be working for a more participatory version of democracy. If giving special benefits to married couples is unfair, then work to reverse that long-standing tradition. But if special benefits are going to be available only to married couples, then the opportunity to marry must be available to all citizens.

Should Married Couples Get Special Benefits?

In *Queer Family Values: Debunking the Myth of the Nuclear Family*, political theorist Valerie Lehr also argues that the recent emphasis on marriage within the LGBT movement constricts its political vision and undermines the possibility of pursuing a more progressive political agenda. Lehr favors social policies that help people in all types of relationships flourish, rather than gay marriage, which reinforces the traditional bias toward households organized around a monogamous dyad. Policies like universal health care, higher wages, and safe, affordable childcare would do a better job helping families take care of each other, she argues, than would the right to marry. Lehr also believes that the LGBT community should not be focusing so much political energy on securing marriage rights, when other issues are arguably more important and would have a positive impact on a larger number of people. For example, an employment nondiscrimination policy or well-funded programs for LGBT youth would arguably do more good for more people than extending the right to marry.

The movement for gay marriage is to a large extent, but not exclusively, the fight of lesbians and gays to have access to a wide array of benefits currently available only to heterosexuals. Lehr questions whether it is just for married people to receive special benefits not available to single people or those in other types of relationships. First, she argues, the distribution of benefits through marriage is unfair because it advantages some people more than others. Not only does it provide benefits only to the married, but it reinforces class hierarchy. For example, "a couple can enjoy economic benefits only in cases where at least one partner has a job that provides benefits. . . . Since family benefits are benefits provided largely by private business and the state, . . . they are most available to those with either unionized or professional jobs." Consequently, same-sex marriage further benefits the already advantaged.[15] While it will help some lesbian and gay people get access to insurance, it will not solve the health insurance crisis or the general shrinking of worker benefits.

Second, same-sex marriage does nothing for people who organize their familial lives in nontraditional ways—people who share households with nonsexual partners or extended family, who have more than one life partner (e.g., polygamous relationships and long-term threesomes), or who coparent with friends or engage in "othermothering," that is "caring for a child who happens to need care at a particular moment."[16] Why should a person be able to add a spouse or child to an insurance policy but not an elderly parent? Why should a husband or wife receive Social Security survivorship benefits and not a best friend? Why should a spouse be allowed hospital visitation rights but not a roommate? These are good questions and certainly appropriate topics for public deliberation, but they do not constitute a valid justification for discrimination.

It is also important to realize that the relationship of marriage differs in important ways from the relationships just mentioned. First, a husband or wife is not the same as a roommate, a best friend, a temporary foster child, or an elderly parent. For example, you might not want your roommate to make end-of-life decisions on your behalf. You might not want your best friend to file joint taxes with you. You might not want a temporary foster child to inherit all your property when you die. You probably do not want your elderly parent to be your primary social companion. In contrast, a married person would probably want his or her spouse to do all those things, which is why civil marriage provides a default set of legal entanglements that makes it easy for two people to sign on for a package of rights and responsibilities.

Second, while you may very well want to be able to put a roommate, a best friend, a temporary foster child, or an elderly parent on your health insurance, universal health coverage would be a more effective way to provide for all citizens, even those who are unconnected and unloved. Finally, equating a committed same-sex intimate relationship with the kind of relationship a person has with a roommate, a friend, or a blood relative denigrates the nature of the relationship by refusing to give it the same kind of special status accorded heterosexual marriages.

While I personally support a broad progressive agenda aimed at helping all Americans and their families, again, I view the legalization of same-sex marriage as a matter of principle. Just as heterosexual marriage is not the panacea many social conservatives say it is, gay marriage will not eliminate homophobia or remedy all social injustices. At the same time, support for gay marriage does not preclude working toward more progressive public policies—or even rethinking the connection between benefits and marriage. We do not always get to pick and choose our political battles; choices are never completely free and unconstrained. In the case of same-sex marriage, it was the American court system, following the logic inherent in liberal political theory, that pushed the issue to the front of the political agenda. But now gay marriage is an idea whose time has come.

Despite the forcefulness of my argument, many Americans will continue to believe that homosexuality is morally wrong because of their deeply held religious beliefs. The great advantage of liberal democracy, however, is that it provides a way for people to live peacefully and respectfully together despite their different moral perspectives. While the American people will no doubt remain personally divided over the issue of gay marriage, those who love American democracy should support the right to civil marriage for lesbian and gay couples as a matter of principle—because legal equality is too important to undermine. The fundamental principles of American democracy require that lesbian and gay citizens be accorded the same rights and responsibilities as any other American citizen, and this includes the right to marry and be treated with respect. We do not have to all like each other or approve of each other's choices, but we do have to make sure that everyone is treated fairly and equally before the law, because that is what it means to be an American.

Notes

1. Michael Warner, *The Trouble with Normal: Sex, Politics, and the Ethics of Queer Life* (New York: Free Press, 1999), 114.

2. Warner, *The Trouble with Normal*, 34.

3. Warner, *The Trouble with Normal*, 41.

4. Warner, *The Trouble with Normal*, 42.

5. Warner, *The Trouble with Normal*, 42.

6. Brian Alexander, "Legislating your sex life: A search of sex laws turns up some surprises," MSNBC, December 14, 2004, www.msnbc.msn.com/id/6620768/ [accessed 30 March 2005].

7. Joanna Grossman, "The Virginia Supreme Court Strikes Down the State's Fornication Law, Indicating That Other States' Antiquated Laws Will Fall If Challenged," Find Law.com, January 25, 2005, writ.news.findlaw.com/grossman/20050125.html [accessed 29 January 2005].

8. Warner, *The Trouble with Normal*, 96.

9. Warner, *The Trouble with Normal*, 112.

10. William N. Eskridge, Jr., *Equality Practice: Civil Unions and the Future of Gay Rights* (New York: Routledge, 2002), ix.

11. Eskridge, *Equality Practice*, 211.

12. Yuval Merin, *Equality for Same-Sex Couples: The Legal Recognition of Gay Partnerships in Europe and the United States* (Chicago and London: University of Chicago Press, 2002).

13. *Brown v. Board of Education of Topeka*, 347 U.S. 483 (1954).

14. Claudia Card, "Against Marriage and Motherhood," *Hypatia* 11.3 (Summer 1996), 1–23, 7. Cited in Warner, *Trouble with Normal*, 106–7.

15. Valerie Lehr, *Queer Family Values: Debunking the Myth of the Nuclear Family* (Philadelphia: Temple University Press, 1999), 32.

16. The phrase "othermothering" comes from Patricia Hill Collins, *Black Feminist Thought: Knowledge, Consciousness, and the Politics of Empowerment* (Boston: Unwin Hyman, 1990); also see Lehr, *Queer Family Values*, 34.

Index

~

About the Author

R. Claire Snyder is associate professor of government and politics in political theory at George Mason University . She also serves as a faculty fellow at the Women and Politics Institute at American University. Snyder's undergraduate and graduate teaching interests include the history of political thought, normative political theory, feminist theory, and women and politics. Overall, her research engages the conversation of democratic theory from a progressive feminist perspective. Her previous publications include *Citizen-Soldiers and Manly Warriors: Military Service and Gender in the Civic Republican Tradition* (Rowman & Littlefield, 1999), as well as numerous articles and essays on topics related to democratic theory, women's civic engagement, and the Christian Right. Her current research agenda includes a study of civic republicanism in historical perspective, a genealogy of Third Wave feminism, and a volume on democratic theory. Snyder has a Ph.D. in political science from Rutgers University and a B.A. cum laude from Smith College.